The Raccolta:
Or
Collection of
Indulgenced Prayers
&
Good Works

Ambrose St John

Must Have Books
503 Deerfield Place
Victoria, BC
V9B 6G5
Canada
trava2911@gmail.com

ISBN: 9781774642177

Copyright 2021 – Must Have Books

THE RACCOLTA

OR COLLECTION OF INDULGENCED PRAYERS

Translated by Fr. Ambrose St. John

The Raccolta: or Collection of Indulgenced Prayers.

Translated by Ambrose St. John, of the Oratory of St. Philip Neri, Birmingham.

Authorized Translation

APPROVAL OF THIS TRANSLATION

(TRANSLATION.)

MOST BLESSED FATHER.

In order to promote thereby the piety of the faithful in England, Ambrose St.
John, Priest of the Oratory of St. Philip Neri, in the Diocese of Birmingham,
humbly prays for permission to print in English a translation of the book
entitled *Raccolta di Orazioni &c. alle quali sono annesse le SS.
Indulgenze,* having first obtained the approbation of his Eminence the Cardinal
Archbishop of Westminster; and also that the faithful who make use of this
translation may gain all the Indulgences annexed to the original.

After an audience of the Holy Father, granted February 3, 1856, our most Holy Lord Pius IX., by Divine Providence Pope, on an application made by me, the undersigned Secretary of the Sacred Congregation for the Propagation of the Faith, has of his goodness answered by Rescript in favour of the grace, according to the terms of the petition, provided the translation be made from the last Roman edition, and it being understood that the Decree printed at the end of this edition remains in full force.

Given at Rome from the House of the same Sacred Congregation, on the day and year aforesaid.

Gratis, without any payment on any plea whatever.

AL. BARNABÒ, *Secretary.*

In the place of + the seal.

We approve of this Translation by virtue of the above Rescript of His Holiness.

N. CARDINAL ARCHBISHOP.

Westminster, Oct. 23, 1857.

TO THE HOLY SOULS IN PURGATORY, THE CONTINUATOR OF THE "RACCOLTA."

Whilst I endeavour to satisfy the devotion of a large number of the faithful by a thirteenth Roman reprint of the *Raccolta* of Indulgenced Prayers, containing the additional grants of our present reigning Sovereign Pontiff Pius IX., I feel myself bound to adhere religiously to the pious mind of its compiler, who, out of his special devotion to you, my beloved souls, many times dedicated it to you. This he did, partly that he might in this way make a public attestation of his debt of gratitude to you, as he was wont to declare that he had received many graces and blessings from the Giver of all good through your intercession, and partly because this work of his has a special reference to you, and in a manner belongs to you. True it is, that it is of great benefit to the living, since it teaches them that, in order to gain the Indulgences, they must approach the Sacraments with due dispositions, and so keep themselves in the grace of God. Its special benefit, however, belongs to you, since it is *you* who reap the fruit of the suffrage of so many Indulgences gained by the faithful and made applicable to you: and this is why I also dedicate this work to you.

Accept, then, beloved souls, this offering, slender though it be; have respect to the end I set before myself, and the loving heart with which I offer it to you. Forget not, ye chosen ones of God, to manifest in my behalf your mighty aid, and obtain for me from God the remission of my guilt, and the gift of holy perseverance, that hereafter I may come with you to love and enjoy Him for all eternity: all this I trust you will obtain for me; and in humbleness of heart I pray God that this work may ever produce in the faithful who are yet in the flesh the fruits of eternal life, and aid you to enter into that kingdom of glory whither your hearts are already gone before.

NOTE ON THE COMPILER OF THE RACCOLTA

The compiler of the *Raccolta* was a Roman priest by name Telesphorus Galli, canon of this celebrated Basilica of St. Mary in Cosmedin, Consulter of the Holy Congregation of Indulgences and Holy Relics. Thus much we know of him from the decree of the said Holy Congregation, printed at the end of this *Raccolta*. He was a man of great piety, ardently seeking the good of souls, not only by exercising his sacred ministry, but also by promulgating different devotional works which he printed and published. He was open-handed to the poor, most devout to the Most Holy Sacrament of the Altar, which he used to visit every day wherever it was exposed for the Forty Hours. Nor was he less devoted to the holy souls in purgatory, by whose intersession he had often obtained great graces from God throughout the whole course of a life of seventy-seven years and twenty-nine days; for to them and in their behalf he had with heroical charity ceded and given over during his life all the suffrages which should he made for him after his death, which took place February 17, 1845. Moreover, in his last will he expressed a wish that a memorial should be engraved on his tombstone, how that it was his desire that this faithful on earth should continue in his place to offer up their suffrages for those holy souls. Thus epitaph may be read in the public cemetery of S. Spirito in Sassia, the place his chose for his burial.

ON HOLY INDULGENCES, AND THE CONDITIONS REQUISITE FOR GAINING THEM

TO THE DEVOUT READER.

Two bitter fruits are produced in the soul by sin; first, *Guilt,* which deprives us of grace and the friendship of God; and second, *Its Penalty,* which forbids us the enjoyment of God in Paradise. The penalty of sin is twofold, being partly eternal, partly temporal. Guilt, together with the eternal penalty of sin, is entirely remitted to us by means of the infinite merits of Jesus Christ in the Sacrament of Penance, provided only that we approach that Sacrament with fitting dispositions. On the other hand, as regards the temporal penalty of sin, inasmuch as it is not commonly wholly remitted to us by this Sacrament, very much remains to be discharged, either in this life by means of good works or penance, or else in the next life by means of the fire of Purgatory. But what man is he that can penetrate into the deepest and most hidden judgments of God? Who can tell how much in this present life the Divine Justice may exact in payment of the debt he owes to God, or whether his penances have gained for him the entire, or only the partial remittance from God of that temporal penalty which he has to undergo; and who will not think it a fearful mode of payment, to satisfy in the fire of Purgatory in the life to come? Blessed for ever, then, and praised be the most merciful and tender heart of our Divine Redeemer, Jesus Christ, who imparted to his Holy Catholic Church, from its very origin, the power to apportion, and to us the capability to participate in this treasure of Holy Indulgences, by means of which we are enabled with lightest burden to ourselves to pay to the justice of God all we owe Him for our sins after their eternal penalty and guilt have been remitted.

For, indeed, these Indulgences form a treasury which abides continually before the face of God, - a treasury, that is, of the merits and satisfaction of Jesus Christ, of the most Blessed Virgin Mary, and of the Saints - a treasury which might technically be called the valuation price of the superabundant and infinite satisfactions of our Divine Redeemer, of the Blessed Virgin Mary, and of the Martyrs amid other Saints, being all that portion of their works of penance not necessary for the expiation of their own sins. For this reason it is that Holy Indulgences are called by the Holy Council of Trent *heavenly treasures.* This is the doctrine inculcated by the Sovereign Pontiff Clement VI. of blessed memory, in the following words: "Jesus Christ did by his superabundant holy Passion bequeath to His Church militant here on earth an infinite treasure, not laid up in a napkin, nor hidden in a field, but committed by if Him to be dispensed for the welfare of the faithful by the hands of blessed Peter, who has the keys of heaven, and by his successors here on earth, the vicars of Jesus Christ. To the mass of this treasure are added also all the merits of the Blessed Mother of God, and of all the elect, from the first just man even to the last." These riches, being infinite, have never diminished, and never will diminish; but, like a mighty ocean, suffer no loss, draw from it what you will.

True it is, however, that Christians are not at liberty to take and to use this treasure as they please; but only as determined by the Holy Church and this Sovereign Pontiff, *when*, and *how*, and in what measure. Hence Indulgences are distinguished into two classes. Some are called Partial; and these are given for days, or periods of forty days, called "Quarantines," or for a year or years. Others are called Plenary, or *in forma Jubilaei*.

By Partial Indulgences, of days that is, or quarantines, or years, so much temporal penalty is remitted to the recipient of them as he would have had imposed upon him of old by the penitential canons of the Church, which penances were given in days, quarantines, or years. Plenary Indulgences, or Indulgences *in forma Jubilaei,* are in their effect one and the same thing; the only difference being, that where the Indulgences are granted *in forma Jubilaei*, confessors have powers of jurisdiction conferred on them to absolve from reserved cases, to dispense from or commute all simple vows, &c. By all such Indulgences, *all* the temporal penalty is remitted to us which we owe to God for all those sins in regard of which, though pardoned, we were still debtors, so that theologians teach us, that were we to die immediately after gaining worthily a Plenary Indulgence, we should go straight to heaven. The same may be said of the holy souls in purgatory, whenever in suffrage for them we gain a Plenary Indulgence applicable to them, provided the Divine justice deign to accept it in their behalf.

From all this we may easily gather, devout readers, how highly we ought to prize these Indulgences, how great their value is, and how mighty their efficacy; and lastly, how great a benefit they are spiritually to all faithful Christians. Hence the Holy Council says, "that the usage of Indulgences is most wholesome to Christian people, *Indulgentiarum usum Christiano populo maxime salutarem esse*;" wherefore it ought to be a holy duty in every Christian to endeavour to gain them, as far as he is able, as well for his own spiritual good, as by way of suffrage in behalf of the faithful departed.

To gain an Indulgence, several conditions are requisite.

i. First, it is requisite that we should be in a state of grace, that is, living in favour with God; for whosoever before God is in his guilt of unremitted sin, and liable to its eternal penalty, is not, and cannot be, whilst continuing in that state, in a capacity to receive the remission of the temporal penalty. The best advice, then, that can be given is, to make an act of perfect contrition, when confession is impossible, before doing the works enjoined for gaining an Indulgence, accompanying this with a firm resolution to go to Confession, in order that by so doing we may gain the grace of God, should it happen to have been lost.

ii. Secondly, since the Church, in opening the Treasury of Holy Indulgences, has ever obliged faithful Christians to do some good work under specified circumstances of time, place, &c., so it is to be remembered that she requires their *personal and devotional* fulfilment of *all* the works enjoined, both as to time, manner, and object, according to the precise letter of the grant by which the Indulgence has been conceded: as, for instance, when in the grant it is said that the work ought to be done kneeling, or standing, or at the sound of the bell, or at such an hour, such a day, or contrite, or having Confessed and Communicated, &c: so that, should any of the works enjoined be omitted, either wholly or in some notable portion of them, be it through ignorance, or negligence, or inability; or should any one of the conditions of time, place, &c. prescribed, fail to have been observed for any reason whatsoever, - then the Indulgence in question is not gained.

Here it will not be amiss to call attention to certain general decrees of the Holy Congregation of Indulgences relative to Confession, Communion, and Prayers, as these are works always enjoined in the grants of Indulgences.

First, then, as to Confession:- for all persons who have the praiseworthy custom of going to Confession at least once a week when not lawfully hindered, it is admitted that such a weekly Confession is sufficient for gaining all the Indulgences which occur day after day, provided they do the other works which are enjoined them; nor is it necessary to make another fresh Confession on purpose. This, however, would of course be absolutely indispensable, were a person to be conscious that he had fallen into a mortal sin since his last Confession. Indulgences, however, of the Jubilee, whether ordinary or extraordinary - granted, that is, in the form of a Jubilee, - are excepted from this general rule, inasmuch as in order to gain such Indulgences, besides the works enjoined, the Confession ought to be made within the time appointed in the grant of such Indulgences: this is evident from the decree of time Holy Congregation of Indulgences dated December 9, 176 h, approved by

Pope Clement XIII.

Secondly, as regards the Communion which has to be received, especially for gaining Plenary Indulgences, although the days for making it are specified, yet on high festivals, when the Indulgence time begins with First Vespers of the Feast, the Communions may be anticipated on the Vigil or day preceding the festival, according to the declaration of the said Holy Congregation in their decree of June 12, 1892, confirmed by Pope Pius VII.; and Pope Gregory XVI. of holy memory, by another decree of the same Holy Congregation of March 19, 1841, declared, that by a Confession and Communion made on Holy Saturday, a Plenary indulgence might be gained by assisting devoutly at the Papal Benediction*, and that at the same time the Paschal precept might be fulfilled.

* On Easter Day

And thirdly, as regards the Prayers which are directed to be said for gaining Indulgences:- these may be recited by two or more persons alternately in prayers such as time Rosary, Litanies, the *Angelus*, the *De profundis*, and other such-like prayers. This is expressly declared by the above-named holy Pontiff, Pius VII., in a decree of the S. Congregation under date Feb. 29, 1820. Note here, that poor deaf and dumb people who cannot say the prayers prescribed for gaining the holy Indulgences annexed to such prayers, ought to visit the church (should such a condition be prescribed in the grant), raising up their souls and thee affections of their hearts to God. Should it happens that the prayers are to be said publicly, then they can gain such Indulgences by lifting up their souls and hearts to God, provided they are there present in body with the rest of the faithful; should, however, the prayers be prescribed to be said privately, then they may obtain from their own Confessors a commutation of such prayers into some other external good work. This is clear from time Resolution of the S. Congr. of Indulgences, Feb. 16, 1852, confirmed by Pope Pius IX., in an audience of March 15, the same year.

iii. As a third and last condition of gaining a Plenary Indulgence and remission of all sins, venial included, it is required that we detest these said venial sins, and moreover lay aside every affection to all such sins in general, as well as to each in particular. God grant us of His holy grace that such dispositions be found in all those Christians who are desirous of gaining these Indulgences; and grant us likewise to remember, that whilst we do our utmost to gain them, we ought always, notwithstanding, to endeavour at the same time to bring forth worthy fruits of penance, and by means of other wholesome penal works, as well as works of mercy and devotion, to pay to the Divine justice some satisfaction for the misdeeds we have done.

This, devout reader, I have thought it right to say to you by way of preface, in presenting to you this collection of prayers and pious exercises, to which Sovereign Pontiffs have granted holy Indulgences, Plenary and Partial. It is a treasure neglected by many of the faithful, partly because its existence, and partly because its value, is not known, and so men take not that account of it which they ought. I have given it the name of "A Collection of Prayers," &c., because I should indeed have taken on myself too arduous a task had I endeavoured to gather unite one volume all the prayers and pious works to which Indulgences are annexed. Accordingly I have restricted myself to those alone which can be practised for the most part by all faithful Christians; and I have specified the Indulgence annexed to each such prayer or work, by quoting distinctly the constitutions, briefs, or rescripts of the Sovereign Pontiffs by whom they were conceded, after having verified them with the greatest exactness. Marvel not, dear reader, that in this last edition you find not, as you have heretofore found in other editions of this collection, the historical account of the origin of certain devotions to which afterwards Indulgences were annexed, since, as I have to add for your benefit the last grants made by time and care of our present holy Pontiff Pius IX., I was afraid lest, by making the *Raccolta* too bulky, I should prevent some from using it so frequently as they otherwise would, as very often occurs with books intended for daily use. This is the reason also why you will find that in mentioning the grant, brief, or rescript, I have left out the words "for ever," since, in order to obviate the necessity of this constant repetition, it is enough for you to be told once for all, that all Indulgences in the present *Raccolta* were granted by the goodness of Sovereign Pontiffs *for ever* and I have therefore contented myself with inserting these words only where such grants were once made for a certain term. Moreover, without repeating the words, "these Indulgences are applicable to the Holy Souls in Purgatory," or "these prayers may be said in any language, provided the version be correct, and approved by the S. C. of Indulgences," I think it enough to say, once for all, that our holy Father Pius IX. made these two concessions in favour of all Indulgences in this book, by a decree of the said S. C. of Indulgences, dated Sept. 30, 1852.

And now I will beg you, dear reader, to select out of this *Raccolta* for your own use those prayers and pious works which God moves you to adopt, or which your own devotion points out to you as most adapted to your own state; and I entreat you also to use them with perseverance for your own spiritual welfare, and in suffrage for holy souls in purgatory, renewing every morning the intention of gaining those Indulgences to which you may be entitled by time prayers or good works which you do that day, according to the advice of Blessed Leonard in his Sacred Manual, § xxii. Thus cleansing more and more your soul from sin, you may hope with confidence after death that you will soon arrive at the enjoyment and love of God for ever in Paradise. May that blessing be to thee, reader, and to me also!

THE MOST HOLY TRINITY

1. ANGELIC TRISAGION.

In order that the faithful might have a constant inducement to make renewed acts of adoration, praise, and blessing to God, by means of the following *Trisagion*; Pope Clement XIV., by a decree of the Sacred Congregation of Indulgences dated June 26, 1770, confirmed afresh *for ever* this grant of his predecessor, Pope Clement XIII., viz.-
i. An indulgence of 100 days, once a day, to all thus faithful who, with contrite hearts adoring the Most Holy Trinity, shall devoutly recite this Trisagion, *Sanctus*, &c.
ii. The same indulgence three times on every Sunday, as well as on the Festival and during the Octave of this Most holy Trinity;
iii. A plenary indulgence for ever, once in a month, to all these who throughout the same month shall have said daily this Angelic Trisagion as above; to be gained on any one day when, after Confession and Communion, they shall visit some church, and pray according to the intention of the Sovereign Pontiff.

Sanctus, Sanctus, Sanctus, Dominus Deus exercituum: Plena est terra gloria tua: Gloria Patri, Gloria Filio, Gloria Spiritui Sancto.

Holy, Holy, Holy, Lord God of Hosts, earth is full of Thy Glory. Glory be to the Father, Glory be to the Son, Glory be to the Holy Ghost.

2. SEVEN GLORIA PATRI'S, ETC., SAID BY THREE PERSONS CONJOINTLY.

Pope Pius VI., in order to sanction the devout exercise begun in France with the approbation and under the auspices of Monsignor Beaumont, Archbishop of Paris, of happy memory, granted, by a decree of the S. Congr. of Indulgences, dated May 15, 1784 -

13

i. An indulgence of 100 days, daily, and an indulgence of seven years and seven quarantines every Sunday, to all the faithful who, with contrite hearts, shall recite three several times a day (that is, morning, noon, and evening) seven *Gloria Patri's* and one *Ave Maria,* in honour of the Mystery of the Most Holy Trinity, of the Incarnation of the Divine Word, and His most holy Mother Mary;

ii. A plenary indulgence to those who shall recite every day, three times a day as above, seven *Gloria Patri's* and one *Ave Maria* to be gained twice a month, that is, on any two Sundays in the month, when, after Confession and Communion, they shall visit some church, and pray according to the intention of the Sovereign Pontiff.

It is, however, requisite, in order to gain these Indulgences, that there should be a pious union of three persons, who civilly agree amongst themselves to recite, either together or by themselves, the said seven *Gloria Patri's* and one *Ave Maria;* and that, should any one of the three die, or in some other way fail to say these prayers, then the other two should find a substitute, so that the pious union of three persons may be always maintained.

3. THREE GLORIA PATRI'S IN THANKSGIVING, ETC.

Pius VIII., of holy memory, granted by a rescript of the S. Congr. of Indulgences, dated July 11, 1815, to all the faithful -

i. An indulgence of 300 days for reciting every morning, noon, and evening, three *Gloria Patri's* in thanksgiving to the Most Holy Trinity for the graces and special privileges granted to most holy Mary in her glorious Assumption into heaven;

ii. An indulgence of 100 days for each several time they are said;

iii. A plenary indulgence once a month, on any one day, to those who, after Confession and Communion, should, during the said month, have said without any intermission the three *Gloria Patri's* three times a day as aforesaid.

4. MASS, AND THANKSGIVING PRAYERS, ETC.

At the prayer of the priests of the Pious Union of St. Paul, erected in Rome, Pius VII., by a decree of the S. Congr. of Indulgences, dated April 28, 1815, grants to all the faithful who, with contrite hearts and with devotion, assist at the Mass and accompanying Thanksgiving-Prayers to the Most holy Trinity for the high gifts and privileges bestowed on most Holy Mary, and pray according to the intention of the Sovereign Pontiff -

i. An indulgence of 300 days every time they assist at the said exercise;

ii. A plenary indulgence twice a month, should they assist at it every day for a month, on any two days when, truly penitent for their sins, they shall, after Confession and Communion, pray as aforesaid.

As regards the said Mass, one only Votive Mass of the Most Holy Trinity is permitted to be celebrated each day, and this in one church alone in each several city, or village, &c., which church shall be designated by the ordinary; and the Mass may he said on days when the office is of an ordinary double festival. On days when the rite is a major double, or double of the second class, the Mass of the day must be said with a Commemoration of the Most Holy Trinity; this permission, however, does not extend to Sundays of the first class, or other days which are doubles of the first class. The above-named permission rests on two decrees of the S. Congr. of Rites, April 15 and July 13, 1815, which contain also the approval of the following prayers to be recited after the said Mass. To render this devotion easier to be accomplished, the said Mass may be applied according to the intention of benefactors, or for any other pious object whatever; it may likewise be applied in suffrage for the faithful departed, even on those days when, according to the rubrics, the Mass of Requiem ought to be said: this is clear from this Papal rescript of January 10, 1807, given through the *Segretaria* of Memorials, and preserved in the Archivium of the said Pious Union of St. Paul.

THE THANKSGIVING-PRAYERS TO BE SAID BY PRIEST AND PEOPLE AFTER THE MASS AS ABOVE.

In nomine Patris, &c.

i. Most Holy Trinity, Father, Son, and Holy Ghost, Three Persons and One God, we profoundly adore Thee, and with all the love of our whole heart we give Thee thanks for the high gifts and privileges granted to Mary most holy in her glorious and Immaculate Conception.

Three Gloria Patri's *and one* Ave.

ii. Most holy Trinity, Father, Son, and Holy Ghost, we profoundly adore Thee, and with all the love of our whole heart we give Thee thanks for the high gifts and privileges granted to Mary most holy in her glorious Nativity.

Three Gloria Patri's *and one* Ave.

iii. Most Holy Trinity, Father, Son, and Holy Ghost, we profoundly adore Thee, and with all the love of our whole heart we give Thee thanks for the high gifts and privileges granted to Mary most holy in her glorious Presentation in the Temple.

Three Gloria Patri's *and one* Ave.

iv. Most Holy Trinity, Father, Son, and Holy Ghost, we profoundly adore Thee, and with all the love of our whole heart we give Thee thanks for the high gifts and privileges granted to Mary most holy in her glorious Annunciation.

Three Gloria Patri's *and one* Ave.

v. Most Holy Trinity, Father, Son, and Holy Ghost, we profoundly adore Thee, and with all the love of our whole heart we give Thee thanks for the high gifts and privileges granted to Mary most holy in her glorious Visitation.

Three Gloria Patri's *and one* Ave.

vi. Most Holy Trinity, Father, Son, and Holy Ghost, we profoundly adore Thee, and with all the love of our whole heart we give Thee thanks for the high gifts and privileges granted to Mary most holy in her glorious Purification.

Three Gloria Patri's *and one* Ave.

vii. Most Holy Trinity, Father, Son, and Holy Ghost, we profoundly adore Thee, and with all the love of our whole heart we give Thee thanks for the high gifts and privileges granted to Mary most holy in her most glorious Assumption.

Three Gloria Patri's *and one* Ave.

Lastly, we give Thee most hearty thanks for that Thou hast exalted and glorified the most Holy and most sweet name of Mary throughout the whole world.

PRAYER TO THE MOST HOLY VIRGIN.

Mary, dear mother! mother most amiable! tender mother! mother full of love and sweetness for thy clients and children! we pray thee, by this our loving act of thanksgiving to the Most Holy Trinity, obtain for all of us grace ever to employ the powers of our soul, and our five senses, to the honour and glory o

God, One in Three Persons, directing all our actions to Him, and loving Him with pure Heart, even as thou didst love Him here on earth; that thus we may be able to attain to the enjoyment of Him in the bliss of heaven with thee for ever and ever.
Bless us in the name of the Father, and of the Son, and of the Holy Ghost.

All say Salve Regina, *and then* -

V. Benedicamus Patrem, et Filium cum Sancto Spiritu.
R. Laudemus et superexaltemus eum in saecula

Oremus.
Omnipotens sempiterne Deus, qui dedisti famulis tuis in confessione verae Fidei aeternam Trinitatis gloriam agnoscere, et in potentia Majestatis adorare Unitatem; quaesumus ut ejusdem Fidei firmitate ab omnibus semper muniamur adversis. Per Christum Dominum nostrum. R. Amen.

V. Let us bless the Father, Son, and Holy Ghost.
R. Let us praise and exalt Him above all for ever.

Let us pray.
Almighty and eternal God, who hast given to us Thy servants grace by the Confession of the true faith to acknowledge the glory of the eternal Trinity, and in the power of Thy Majesty to worship the Unity; grant, we beseech Thee, that by the firmness of this our faith we may ever be defended from all adversities. Through Christ our Lor. R. Amen.

5. OTHER THANKSGIVING-PRAYERS.

By a rescript of the *Segretaria* of the Office of Memorials dated July 19, 1822 (the original of which is preserved in this *Segretaria* of the S. Congr. of Indulgences), Pope Pius VII. granted to all this faithful of both sexes who shall recite the following prayers to the Most Holy Trinity, in thanksgiving for the privileges bestowed upon the most holy Virgin Mary on her Assumption into heaven -
i. An indulgence of 300 days once a day;
ii. A plenary indulgence to those who shall have recited them every day for an entire month; provided that, after Confession and Communion, they pray to God for our holy Mother the Church, &c.
He commanded, moreover, that printed copies of these prayers should be distributed *gratis*; and forbade their being sold, notwithstanding any permission previously given to this contrary.

THE PRAYERS.

Adore the Eternal Father, saying a Pater, Ave, a*nd* Gloria, *and then say,*

I adore Thee, Eternal Father, in union with all the heavenly host, my Lord and my God; rendering Thee infinite thanks on the part of Mary, most holy Virgin, Thy well-beloved daughter, for every grace and favour Thou hast granted her, and, above all, for the great power with which Thou didst honour her in her Assumption into heaven.

Adore the Eternal Son, saying a Pater, Ave, *and* Gloria, *and then say,*

I adore Thee too, Eternal Son, in union with all the heavenly host, my God, may Lord, and my Redeemer, rendering Thee infinite thanks on the part of Mary, Virgin most blessed, Thy well-beloved mother, for every grace and favour Thou hast granted her, and, above all, for the gift of highest wisdom with which Thou didst glorify her in her Assumption into heaven.

Adore the Holy Ghost, saying a Pater, Ave, *and* Gloria, *and then say,*

I adore Thee also, O holy Ghost the Paraclete, my God and my Lord, and in union with all the heavenly host I render Thee infinite thanks in the name of the most blessed Virgin, Thy most loving Spouse, for every grace and favour Thou hast granted her, and above all for that most perfect and divine charity with which Thou didst inflame her most holy and most pure heart in the act of her most glorious Assumption into heaven. In the name of Thy most chaste Spouse, I humbly beg of Thee to grant me the grace of remission of all my most grievous sins which I have committed from the first moment when I was able to sin until this day, for all of which I grieve exceedingly, firmly purposing rather to die than ever again offend Thy Divine Majesty; and relying on the high merits and most powerful protection of this Thy most loving Spouse, I beg of Thee to grant to me and to N. time most precious gift of Thy Divine grace and love, vouchsafing me those lights and special helps whereby Thy eternal providence has predetermined to will my salvation, and to bring me to Thyself.

Then say three times,

Sancta Maria, et omnes Sancti et Sanctae Dei, intercedite pro nobis ad Dominum, ut nos mereamur ab eo adjuvari et salvari. Amen.

Holy Mary, all ye holy men and women, saints of God, intercede for us to our Lord, that we may merit to receive help and salvation at his hands. Amen.

TO THE MOST BLESSED VIRGIN.

I acknowledge thee and I venerate thee, most holy Virgin, Queen of Heaven, Lady and Mistress of the Universe, as Daughter of the Eternal Father, as Mother of His well-beloved Son, and most loving Spouse of the Holy Spirit. Kneeling at the feet of thy great majesty, with all humility I pray thee in thy divine charity, the gift with which thou wert so bounteously enriched on thy assumption into heaven, to vouchsafe to grant in thy favour and thy pity, so far as to place me under thy most safe and faithful protection, and to receive me into the number of those thy happy and highly favoured servants whose names thou dost carry graven on thy virgin breast. Deign, Mother and Lady most tender, to accept this poor heart, my memory, my will, and all my other powers and senses, internal and external; accept my eyes, my ears, my mouth, my hands, my feet; govern them all in conformity to the good pleasure of thy Son, as I intend by every movement of them to give thee infinite glory. And by that wisdom with which thy well-beloved Son glorified thee, I pray and beseech thee to obtain for me light and vision clearly to know myself and my own nothingness, and in particular to know my sins, that so I may hate and loathe them; I pray thee also to obtain for me light to discern the snares of the infernal enemy, and all his modes of attack, whether open or hidden. Above all, most tender mother, I beg of thee the grace of N.

Say three times,

Virgo singularis,
Inter omnes mitis,
Nos culpis solutos
Mites fac et castos.

Virgin of all virgins
To thy shelter take us;
Gentlest of the gentle!
Chaste and gentle make us.

Oremus.
Famulorum tuorum, quaesumus Domimie, delictis ignosce; ut qui tibi placere de actibus nostris non valemus, Genitricis Filii tui Domini nostri intercessione

salvemur. Per eumdem Dominum nostrum Jesum Christum, &c.
Benedicat et custodiat nos omnipotens et misericors Dominus, Pater, et Filius, et Spiritus Sanctus. Amen.

Let us pray.
Pardon, O Lord, we beseech Thee, the sins of Thy servants; that we, who know not how to please Thee by our own actions, may be saved by the intercession of the Mother of Thy Son our Lord. Through the same our Lord, Jesus Christ. May the almighty and merciful Lord, Father, Son, and Holy Ghost, bless and preserve us. Amen.

6. THREE OFFERINGS, WITH THREE PATER NOSTER'S, ETC.

Pope Leo XII. of holy memory, by an autograph rescript, dated Oct. 21, 1823, granted to all faithful Christians -
i. The indulgence of 300 days, for every time that they shall devoutly recite the following three offerings to the Most Holy Trinity to obtain a good death;
ii. The plenary indulgence, to those who shall recite them every day for a month; to be gained at the end of the said month, on any one day when, having Confessed and Communicated, they shall pray according to the intentions of the Sovereign Pontiff.

The above-named original rescript is preserved in the Archivium of the RR. FF. Minor Observant at the Convent of Ara Coeli in Rome.

THE OFFERINGS.

i. We offer to the Most Holy Trinity the merits of Jesus Christ, in thanksgiving for the most Precious Blood which He shed in the garden for us; and by his merits we beseech the Divine Majesty for pardon of our sins.

Pater. Ave. Gloria.

ii. We offer to the Most Holy Trinity the merits of Jesus Christ, in thanksgiving for His most precious death endured on the cross for us; and by His merits we beseech the Divine Majesty for the remission of the pains due to our sins.

Pater. Ave. Gloria.

iii. We offer to the Most Holy Trinity the merits of Jesus Christ, in thanksgiving for His unspeakable charity, by which He descended from heaven to earth to take human flesh, and to suffer and die for us upon the cross; and by His merits we beseech the Divine Majesty to bring our souls to the glory of heaven after our death.

Pater. Ave. Gloria.

7. TRIDUO, OR NOVENA, ETC.

At the prayer of time Procurator-General of Discalced Trinitarian Fathers, his Holiness Pope Pius IX., in a decree of the Holy Congregation of Indulgences, dated August 8, 1847, grants to all the faithful -

i. An indulgence of seven years and seven quarantines, for every day of the Triduo or Novena they shall keep in honour of the Most Holy Trinity, either in public or private, previous to the Feast, the first Sunday after Pentecost, or at any other time of the year.

ii. A plenary indulgence to those who shall keep such Novena or Triduo completely: to be gained by any one on the day when, after Confession and Communion, he shall visit some public church, and pray there for some time according to the intention of His Holiness.

APPENDIX

162. INVOCATION OF THE THREE HOLY NAMES (TRISAGIO) IN THE ACT OF MAKING THE SIGN OF THE HOLY CROSS.

By a Brief of July 28, 1863, the Sovereign Pontiff Pius IX. granted -
The indulgence of fifty days, to all the faithful every time that, with contrite hearts, they sign themselves with the form of the Cross, pronouncing at the same time, in honour of the Most Holy Trinity, the words:
In the name of the Father, of the Son, and of the holy Ghost.

8. ACTS OF FAITH, HOPE, AND CHARITY.

Pope Benedict XIV., considering how useful, or rather how indispensably necessary, it is for the eternal salvation of Christians that they should make frequent use of the acts of Faith, Hope, and Charity, in order to excite them to a more frequent exercise of the said acts, whilst he confirmed the grant of indulgences already made to this effect by Pope Benedict XII., Jan. 15, 1728, granted afresh by a decree of the S. Congr. of Indulgences, dated Jan. 28, 1756 -

i. A plenary indulgence once a month to all those who shall every day devoutly recite the said acts, and at the same time make them with their hearts. This Indulgence may be gained on any day when, truly penitent for their sins, they shall, after Confession and Communion, pray for our holy mother the Church, &c.

He granted likewise *in articulo mortis* -

ii. A plenary indulgence and an indulgence of seven years and seven quarantines every time they shall make these acts devoutly in their hearts, and say them with their lips. A common form of these acts is subjoined. However, Benedict XIV., in the above-named decree, declares that no particular form of words or expressions is necessary for gaining these Indulgences ; but that any one may use any form he pleases, provided "that it expresses and explains the particular motives of each one of the three theological virtues."

ACTS OF THE THEOLOGICAL VIRTUES.

Act of Faith.

I most firmly believe, because God, who is the infallible Truth, hath so revealed to the Holy Catholic Church, and through the Church reveals to us, that there is one only God in three divine Persons, equal and distinct, Father, Son, and Holy Ghost; that the Son became man by taking to Himself flesh and a human soul through the operation of the Holy Ghost in the womb of the most pure Virgin Mary that He died for us upon the cross, rose again, ascended into heaven, and from thence shall come again at the end of the world to judge all the living and the dead, to give Paradise for ever to the good, and hell to the wicked; moreover, upon the same motive I believe all that the same holy Church believes and teaches.

Act of Hope.

O my God, because Thou art almighty, infinitely good and merciful, I hope that by the merits of the Passion and Death of Jesus Christ our Saviour Thou wilt grant me eternal life, which Thou, who art the most faithful, hast promised to all those who shall do the works of a good Christian, as I purpose to do by Thy holy help.

Act of Charity.

O my God, because Thou art the highest and most perfect good, I love Thee with my whole heart, and above all things; and rather than offend Thee, I am ready to lose all things else; and moreover for Thy love I love and desire to love my neighbour as myself.

9. PRAISES TO THE HOLY NAME OF GOD.

For the love we owe to God, and for the honour of His most Holy Name, the following devout act of praise is to be said by way of reparation for the grievous offences which are committed against that Holy Name by blasphemies; and in order that all the faithful may he incited to say them with devotion, for every time that they are said with a contrite heart Pope Pius VII. granted -
i. One year's indulgence, by a rescript of July 23, 1801 through his Eminence the Cardinal Vicar, which document is kept in the *Segretaria* of his court.
By a decree of the S. Congr. of Indulgences, dated August 8, 1847, our holy Lord Pius IX. grants likewise in addition to the above -
ii. A plenary indulgence once a month to all those who at least once a day recite this said act of praise, provided that, being truly contrite, they Confess and Communicate, and visit some church or public oratory and pray there according to the intention of His Holiness.

THE ACT OF PRAISE.

Blessed he God.
Blessed be His Holy name.
Blessed be Jesus Christ, true God and true man.
Blessed be the name of Jesus.
Blessed be Jesus in the most Holy Sacrament of time Altar.
Blessed be the great Mother of God, the most holy Mary.
Blessed he her holy and Immaculate Conception.

Blessed be the name of Mary, Virgin and Mother.
Blessed be God in His holy angels and in His saints.

10. CHAPLET OF ACTS OF THE LOVE OF GOD, ETC.

By a decree of the S. Congr. of Indulgences, dated August 11, 1818, Pope Pius VII. granted to all faithful Christians who, with a contrite heart, shall recite time following Chaplet of acts of the love of God, with five *Gloria Patri's* -
i. An indulgence of 300 days, daily.
Moreover, to those who shall recite it frequently in the month, i.e. at least ten times, he granted besides the said Partial Indulgence -
ii. A plenary indulgence once a year, on any one day when, after Confession and Communion, they shall visit some church and pray to God according to the intention of this Sovereign Pontiff.

THE CHAPLET OF ACTS OF LOVE.

1. O my God, and Sovereign Good, would that I had always loved Thee
2. My God, I detest the time when I loved Thee not.
3. How could I ever live so long without Thy holy love?
4. And Thou too, my God, how couldst Thou bear with me?
5. My God, I give Thee thanks for Thy great patience.
6. But now I desire to love Thee for over.
7. I am content rather to die than love Thee not.
8. Take from me my life, O my God, if I am not to love Thee.
9. The grace I beg of Thee is ever to love Thee.
10. With Thy love I shall be blessed.
Glory be to this Father, &c.

1. My God, I would see Thee loved by all.
2. Happy should I be, could I but shed my blood that all might love Thee.
3. They who love Thee not are blind indeed.
4. My God, give them Thy light.
5. Miserable indeed are they who love not Thee, the Sovereign Good.
6. My God, let me never be one of these wretched ones who love Thee not.
7. My God, be Thou my joy, and all my good.
8. I would be wholly Thine for ever.
9. Who shall separate me from Thy love?
10. Come, all ye creatures, love ye my God.
Glory be to the Father, &c.

1. My God, I would I had a thousand hearts wherewith to love Thee.

2. I would that I had all hearts of all men wherewith to love Thee.

3. I would there were more worlds, that all might love Thee.

4. How blessed would he be who could love Thee with the hearts of all possible creatures!

5. Thou meritest, my God, to be so loved.

6. My heart is too poor, too cold, to love Thee.

7. Alas for the dead coldness of men in loving their sovereign Good

8. Alas for the miserable blindness of the world, which knows not Thee, who art true love.

0. O blessed inhabitants of heaven, who know and love Him!

10. O blessed necessity of loving God!

Glory be to the Father, &c.

1. My God, when will the time come that I shall burn with love for Thee?

2. How happy then will be my lot!

3. But since I know not how to love Thee, I will at least rejoice that there are others who love Thee with their whole hearts.

4. In particular I rejoice that Thou art loved by all angels and all saints in heaven.

5. With the hearts of all these I unite the love of my poor heart.

6. In a special manner I intend to love Thee with the love with which those Saints who loved Thee best have loved Thee.

7. Wherefore I intend to love Thee with the love wherewith St. Mary Magdalene, St. Catherine, and St. Teresa loved Thee.

8. With the love wherewith St. Augustine, St. Dominic, St. Francis Xavier, St. Philip Neri, and St. Louis Gonzaga loved Thee.

9. With that same love wherewith Thy Holy Apostles, especially St. Peter, St. Paul, and the beloved Disciple, loved Thee.

10. With that same love wherewith St. Joseph the great Patriarch loved Thee.

Glory be to the Father, &c.

1. Moreover I intend to love Thee with that love wherewith Mary most holy loved Thee when on earth.

2. In particular with that love wherewith she loved Thee when she conceived Thy Divine Son in her virgin womb, when she brought Him forth, when she suckled Him, and when she saw him die.

3. Yet more, I intend to love Thee with that love wherewith she loves Thee, and will love Thee for ever in heaven.

4. But to love Thee worthily, O my God of infinite goodness, not even this love suffices.

5. Wherefore I would love Thee as Thy Son, the Divine Word made Man, did love Thee.

8. As He loved Thee when He was born.

7. As He loved Thee when He died upon the cross.
8. As He loves Thee ever in those sacred tabernacles where He lies hid.
9. And with that love with which He loves Thee, and will love Thee in heaven for all eternity.
10. Lastly, I intend to love Thee with that love with which Thou lovest Thyself; and since that is impossible, grant me, O my God, of Thy tender pity, that I may love Thee as far as I know how and am able, and as much as Thou art pleased that I should love Thee. Amen and amen.
Glory be to the Father, &c.

Oremus.
Deus, qui diligentibus Te bona invisibilia praeparasti, infussde cordibus nostris tui amoris affectum; ut Te in omnibus et super omnia diligentes, promissiones tuas, quae omne desiderium superant, consquamur. Per Dominum nostrum Jesum Christum, etc.

Let us pray.
O God, who hast prepared invisible good things for them that love Thee; pour Thy love into our hearts, that we, loving Thee in all things and above all things, may attain Thy heavenly promises, which exceed all that we can desire.
Through our Lord Jesus Christ, &c.

11. PRAYERS AND PETITIONS.

By a rescript of the S. Congr. of Indulgences, dated March 3, 1827, Pope Leo XII. granted to all the faithful who, with a contrite heart and with devotion, should recite the following prayers and petitions once a day -
i. An indulgence of 300 days;
ii. A plenary indulgence to such as shall recite them every day for a month, on any one of the three last days of the month, and who, after Confession and Communion, shall visit some church or public oratory, and pray according to the intention of the Sovereign Pontiff.
It was moreover his will that copies of the said prayers and petitions should be printed and distributed gratis.

THE PRAYERS AND PETITIONS.

O Father! O Son! O Holy Ghost!
O Holy Trinity! O Jesus! O Mary!
O ye blessed angels of God, all ye Saints of Paradise, men and women, obtain

for me these graces, which I ask through the Precious Blood of Jesus Christ:
1. Ever to do the holy will of God.
2. Ever to live in union with God.
3. Not to think of anything but God.
4. To love God alone.
5. To do all for God.
6. To seek only the glory of God.
7. To sanctify myself solely for God.
8. To know well my own utter nothingness.
9. Ever to know more and more the will of my God.
*10. ...

Mary most holy, offer to the Eternal Father the most Precious Blood of Jesus Christ for my soul, for the holy souls in purgatory, for the needs of Holy Church, for the conversion of sinners, and for all the world.

Then say three Gloria Patri's *to the most holy Blood of Jesus Christ; one* Hail Mary, *to the sorrows of most holy Mary; and one* Requiem aeternam, &c. *for the holy souls in purgatory.*

* The Indulgence is lost if this special petition is not supplied.

12. PRAYER – "PIETATE TUA."

Pope Leo XII., of holy memory, granted -
i. Forty days indulgence to all faithful Christians every time they devoutly recite the following prayer; and
ii. An indulgence of 100 years and as many quarantines, provided it be said every Saturday for a month; as appears by a rescript in his own hand, dated July 9, 1828, deposited in the Archivium of the sacred Vatican Basilica.

DICTA ORATIO.

Pietate tua, quaesumus Domine, nostrorum solve vinculis peccatorum, et intercedente Beata semperque Virgine Dei Genitrice Maria, cum Beatis Apostolis tuis Petro et Paulo, et omnibus Sanctis nos famulos tuos, et loca nostra in omni sanctitate custody: omnes consanguinitate, affinitate, ac familiaritate nobis conjunctos a vitiis purga, virtutibus illustra pacem et salutem nobis tribue; hostes visibiles et invisibiles remove; carnalia desideria repelle; aerem salubrem indulge amicis et inimicis nostris charitatem largire; Urbem tuam custodi; Pontificem nostrum N. conserva: omnes Praelatos, Principes, cunctumqne Populum Christianum ab omni adversitate defende.

Benedictio tua sit super nos semper; et omnibus fidelibus defunctis requiem aeternam concede. Per Christum Dominum nostrum. Amen.

PRAYER.

Loosen, O Lord, we pray Thee, in Thy pity, the bonds of our sins, and by the intercession of the blessed Mary, ever Virgin Mother of God, the blessed Apostles Peter and Paul, and all saints, keep us Thy servants and our abodes in all holiness; cleanse us, our relations, kinsfolk, and acquaintances, from all vices; adorn us with all virtues; grant to us peace and health; repel our enemies visible and invisible; curb our carnal desires; vouchsafe us healthful seasons; bestow Thy charity upon our friends and our enemies; guard Thy holy city; preserve our Sovereign Pontiff Pius IX., and defend all prelates, priests, and all Christian people from all adversity. Let Thy blessing be ever upon us, and grant to all the faithful departed eternal rest. Through Christ our Lord. Amen.

13. PRAYER FOR CONFESSORS.

At the prayer of the Father-General of the Theatines, Pope Pius IX. granted – an indulgence of 100 days to all confessors who, with contrite hearts and devotion, before taking their seats in the tribunal of penance to hear Confessions, shall recite the following prayer. This indulgence may be gained once every day, as appears by the decree of the S. Congr. of Indulgences, dated March 27, 1854.

ORATIO.

Da mihi, Domine, sedium tuarum assistricem sapientiam, ut sciam judicare populum tuum in justitia et pauperos tuos in judicio. Fac me ita tractare claves regni coelorum, ut nulli aperiam cui claudendum sit, nulli claudam cui aperiendum sit. Sit intentio mea pura, zelus meus sincerus, charitas mea patiens, labor meus fructuosus. Sit in me lenitas non remissa, asperitas non severa; pauperem ne despiciam, diviti ne adulor. Fac me ad alliciendos peccatores suavem, ad interrogandos prudentem, ad instruendos peritum. Tribue, quaeso, ad retrahendos a malo solertiam, ad confirmandos in bono sedulitatem, ad promovendos ad meliora industriam: in responsis maturitatem, in consiliis rectitudinem, in obscuris lumen, in implexis sagacitatem, in arduis victoriam; inutilibus colloquiis ne detinear, pravis ne contaminer; alios salvem, meipsum non perdam. Amen.

APPENDIX

163. PRAYER OF ST. FRANCIS XAVIER FOR THE CONVERSION OF THE INFIDELS, "AETERNE RERUM OMNIUM," ETC.

By a Rescript of May 24, 1847, the Sovereign Pontiff Pius IX. granted - The indulgence of 300 days, to all the faithful who shall devoutly recite the following prayer:

THE PRAYER.

Aeterne rerum omnium effector Deus, memento abs te animas infidelum procreatas, easque ad imaginem et similitudinem tuam conditas. Ecce, Do mine, in opprobrium tuum his ipsis infernus impletur. Memento, Jesum Filium tuum pro illorum salute atrocissimam subiisse necem. Noli, quaeso, Domine, ultra permittere, ut Filius tuus ab infidelibus contemnatur; sed precibus sanctorum virorum et Ecclesiae sanctissimi Filii tui Sponsae placatus, recordare misericordiae tuae, et oblitus idololatriae et infidelitatis eorum, dice ut ipsi quoque agnoseant aliquando, quem misisti Dominum Jestum Christum, qui est salus, vita, et resurretico nostra, per quem salvati et liberati sumus: cui sit gloria per infinita saecula saeculorum. Amen.

TRANSLATION.

O God, who bringest all things into existence, remember that the souls of unbelievers have been called into existence by Thee, and that they have been made after Thy own image and likeness. Behold, O Lord, to the dishonour of Thee, with these very souls hell is filled. Remember, O God, that for their salvation Thy Son Jesus Christ underwent the most cruel death. Let it not then, I entreat Thee, Lord, be any longer permitted by Thee that Thy Son should be despised by the unbelievers; but, appeased by the prayers of holy men and of the Church, the Spouse of Thy most holy Son, do Thou remember Thy own pity, and, forgetting their idolatry and their unbelief, bring it to pass that they too may some time acknowledge Thy Son Jesus Christ, who is our salvation, life, and resurrection, through whom we are saved and set free; to whom be glory from age to age without end. Amen.

164. OFFERINGS TO HE MADE AT THE BEGINNING OF THE DAY, AND AT THE TIME OF THE HOLY MASS.

By a Brief of September 30, 1859, the Sovereign Pontiff Pius IX. granted - The indulgence of 300 days to all faithful Christians, who shall with contrite hearts devoutly say in any language at the beginning of the day the following offering: *O Lord God Almighty,* &c. He granted also another indulgence of 300 days to any one who at the time of the holy Mass shall say the other offering printed below: *Eternal Father, I offer to Thee,* &c. Moreover to those who shall have said both the prayers every day for a month he granted -

The plenary indulgence, provided that, being truly penitent, having Confessed and Communicated, they visit their own parish church, or any other church, and pray according to the intention of his Holiness.

By another Brief, dated April 11, 1860, the same Sovereign Pontiff vouchsafed to extend the above-mentioned partial Indulgence of 300 days to three years.

THE OFFERING TO BE MADE AT THE BEGINNING OF THE DAY.

O Lord God Almighty, behold me prostrate be fore Thee in order to appease Thee, and to honour Thy Divine Majesty, in the name of all creatures. But how can I do this who am myself but a poor sinner? Nay, but I both can and will, knowing that Thou dost make it Thy boast to be called Father of mercies, and for love of us hast given Thy very only-begotten Son, who sacrificed Himself upon the Cross, and for our sake doth continually renew that sacrifice of Himself upon our altars. And therefore do I - sinner, but penitent; poor, but rich in Jesus Christ - present myself before Thee, and, with the ardent love of angels and of all Thy saints, and with the tender affection of the Immaculate Heart of Mary, offer to Thee in the name of all creatures the Masses which are now being celebrated, together with all those which have been celebrated, and which will be celebrated to the end of the world. Moreover, I intend to renew the offering of them every moment of this day and of all my life, that I may thereby render to Thy infinite Majesty an honour and a glory worthy of Thee, thus to appease Thy indignation, to satisfy Thy justice for so many sins of us thy children, to render Thee thanks proportioned to Thy benefits, and to implore Thy miseries upon myself and upon all sinners; upon all the faithful, living and dead, upon Thy whole Church, and principally upon its visible Head, the Sovereign Pontiff of Rome; and lastly upon all poor schismatics, heretics, and infidels, that they also may be all converted and save their souls.

THE OFFERING TO BE MADE AT THE TIME OF THE HOLY MASS.

Eternal Father, I offer to Thee the sacrifice which Thy beloved Son Jesus made of Himself upon the Cross, and now renews upon this altar; and I offer it to Thee in the name of all creatures, together with the Masses which have been celebrated, and which shall be celebrated, in the whole world, in order to adore Thee, and to give Thee the honour which Thou dost deserve; to render to Thee due thanks for Thy innumerable benefits, to appease Thy anger for our sins, and to give Thee due satisfaction for them; to entreat Thee also for myself, for the Church, for the whole world, and for the blessed souls in purgatory. Amen.

165. PRAYER IN THE FORM OF OFFERING, "ETERNAL FATHER" ETC.

By a Rescript of April 30, 1560, the Sovereign Pontiff Pius IX. granted to all the faithful, who with contrite hearts and devotion shall say the following prayer in the form of offering -
100 days' indulgence every time they shall say it. More over, the faithful are invited to say it as they say their Rosary, by repeating it 63 times a day.

THE PRAYER

Eternal Father, we offer Thee the Blood, Passion, and Death of Jesus Christ, the Sorrows of the most holy Mary and St. Joseph, in payment of our sins, in suffrage for the holy souls in purgatory, for the wants of our holy Mother the Church, and for the conversion of sinners. Amen.

THE HOLY GHOST

14. THE HYMN, "VENI CREATOR SPIRITUS," AND THE SEQUENCE, "VENI SANCTE SPIRITUS."

By a Brief dated May 26, 1796, Pope Pius VI., of blessed memory, granted to all the faithful who one or more times a day should invoke the Holy Spirit with the hymn *Veni Creator Spiritus*, &c., or the Sequence, *Veni Sancte Spiritus*, &c., with the intention of praying for peace amongst Christian princes, &c. -
i. A plenary indulgence once a month, on any one day, after Confession and Communion.
ii. Three hundred days indulgence to those who should recite the said Hymn

and Sequence as above on Whitsunday or during its octave; and
iii. One hundred days indulgence daily, for every other day in the year.
The original Brief above named is kept in the Archivium of the Congregation
called *Prima Primaria*, in the Roman College.

THE HYMN.

Veni Creator Spiritus,
Mentes tuorum visita,
Imple superna gratia,
Quae Tu creasti pectora.

Qui diceris Paraclitus,
Altissimi Donum Dei,
Fons vivus, Ignis, Charitas,
Et Spiritalis Unctio.

Tu Septiformis munere,
Digitus Paternae dexterae,
Tu rite promissum Patris,
Sermone ditans guttura.

Accende lumen sensibus,
Infunde amorem cordibus,
Infirma nostri corporis
Virtute firmans perpeti.

Hostem repellas longius,
Pacemque dones protinus;
Ductore sic Te praevio
Vitemus omne noxium.

Per Te sciamus da Patrem,
Noscamus atque Filium,
Teque utriusque Spiritum
Credamus omni tempore.

Deo Patri sit gloria,
Et Filio, qui a mortuis
Surrexit, ac Paraclito
In saeculorum saecula. Amen.

TRANSLATION.

Come, O Creator Spirit blest!
And in our souls take up Thy rest
Come, with Thy grace and heavenly aid,
To fill the hearts which Thou hast made.

Great Paraclete to Thee we cry:
O highest gift of God most high!
O fount of life! O fire of love!
And sweet Anointing from above!

Thou in Thy sevenfold gifts art known;
Thee Finger of God's hand we own;
The promise of the Father Thou!
Who dost the tongue with pow'r endow.

Kindle our senses from above,
And make our hearts o'erflow with love
With patience firm, and virtue high,
The weakness of our flesh supply.

Far from us drive the foe we dread,
And grant us Thy true peace instead
So shall we not, with Thee for guide,
Turn from the path of life aside.

O, may Thy grace on us bestow
The Father and the Son to know,
And Thee through endless times confess'd
Of Both th' eternal Spirit blest.

All glory while the ages run
Be to the Father, and the Son
Who rose from death; the same to Thee,
O Holy Ghost, eternally.

THE SEQUENCE.

Veni Sancte Spiritus, et emitte coelitus lucis tuae radium.
Veni Pater pauperum, veni dator munerum, veni lumen cordium.
Consolator optime, dulcis hospes animae, dulce refrigerium.
In labore requies, in aestu temperies, in fletu solatium.

O lux beatissima, reple cordis intima tuorum fidelium.
Sine tuo numine nihil est in homine, nihil est innoxum.
Lava quod est sordidum, riga quod est aridum, sana quod est saucium.
Flecte quod est rigidum, fove quod est frigidum, rege quod est devium.
Da tuis fidelibus in te confidentibus sacrum septenarium.
Da virtutis meritum, da salutis exitum, da perenne gaudium. Amen.

TRANSLATION.

Holy Spirit! Lord of light!
From Thy clear celestial height
Thy pure beaming radiance give:

Come, Thou Father of the poor!
Come, with treasures which endure!
Come, Thou Light of all that live!

Thou, of all consolers best,
Visiting the troubled breast,
Post refreshing peace bestow;

Thou in toil art comfort sweet
Pleasant coolness in the heat;
Solace in the midst of woe.

Light immortal! Light Divine
Visit Thou these hearts of Thine,
And our inmost being fill:

If Thou take Thy grace away,
Nothing pure ill man will stay;
All his good is turn'd to ill.

Heal our wounds - our strength renew;
On our dryness pour Thy dew;
Wash the stains of guilt away:

Bend the stubborn heart and will;
Melt the frozen, warm the chill;
Guide the steps that go astray.

Thou, on those who evermore
Thee confess and Thee adore,

In Thy sevenfold gifts, descend:

Give them comfort when they die;
Give them life with Thee on high;
Give them joys which never end.

---

15. SEVEN GLORIA PATRI'S.*

By a rescript dated March 12, 1857, the reigning Pontiff, Pius IX., granted –
An indulgence of seven days to all who shall say seven *Gloria Patri's*, in
honour of the Holy Ghost the Fountain of Light and of Infallible Truth, with
the desire of obtaining His Seven Gifts, for the diffusion of the Faith, and for
the intention of the Supreme Pontiff.

Granted since the publication of the thirteenth edition of the *Raccolta*.

JESUS.

16. INVOCATION OF THE MOST HOLY NAME.

The Sovereign Pontiff Sixtus V., of holy memory, in his desire that all faithful
Christians should have frequently during life, in their hearts and on their lips,
the most holy Name of Jesus, together with the name of Mary, and especially at
the moment of their death, granted by his Bull "*Reddituri*," July 11, 1587 -
i. An indulgence of 100 days every time any one saluting another should say -

Laudetur Jesus Christus, - Praised be Jesus Christ;

or should answer -

In saecula, amen, - Praised for evermore.

Moreover he granted –
ii. Twenty-five days' indulgence every time any one should devoutly invoke the

35

most holy Names of Jesus and Mary; and to every one who during their lifetime has had the devout practice of saluting and answering as above, or of invoking often the said most holy Names, he granted –

iii. A plenary indulgence in the hour of death, provided that they then invoke these holy Names with at least a contrite heart, if they are unable to do so with their months.

Lastly, he granted the above-named Indulgences to preachers, as well as to all those who should exhort the faithful to salute each other in this above-named way, and to invoke frequently the most holy Names of Jesus and Mary. These Indulgences were again confirmed afresh by Pope Benedict XIII., in a decree of the S. Congr. of Indulgences, dated Jan. 12, 1728.

Moreover, to all those who should invoke the same most holy Name, with the devout ejaculation,

My Jesus, mercy!

so much used by the Blessed Leonard of Port Maurice, the Sovereign Pontiff Leo XII., of happy memory, for the special benefit of the dying, who at the time of their death cannot make long prayers, granted in the year 1824, *vivae vocis oraculo* (by word of month) -

iv. The indulgence of 100 days every time they repeat the said pious ejaculation. By a decree of the S. Congr. of Indulgences, dated Sept. 23, 1846, the Sovereign Pontiff Pius IX. graciously deigned to confirm the above for ever.

17. HYMNS AND PSALMS IN HONOUR OF HIS MOST HOLY NAME.

By a rescript, dated June 13, 1815, of the S. Congr. of Indulgences, Pope Pius VII. confirmed the following Indulgences, which had been previously granted, to any one who should devoutly recite the Psalms whose initial letters compose the most holy Name of Jesus, together with the hymns and prayer: viz.-

i. An indulgence of seven years and seven quarantines every time they are recited;

ii. A plenary indulgence once a month to any one who should recite them every day for a month, on any one day when, having Confessed and Communicated, he shall pray according to the intention of the Sovereign Pontiff;

iii. To any one who should recite them frequently in the course of the year he granted a plenary indulgence on the Feast of the most holy Name of Jesus (the Second Sunday after Epiphany), provided that on that day, after having Confessed and Communicated, he pray as above.

Moreover, by a decree of the same S. Congr. of Indulgences, dated Nov. 13,

1821, the same Pope Pius VII., of holy memory, extended the plenary indulgence no. iii. to the faithful on two other days, viz. the Feast of the Circumcision of our Lord Jesus Christ, Jan. 1, and this Feast of Jesus the Nazarene, Oct. 23; provided that on those days they pray as above, after Confession and Communion.

THE HYMN AND PSALMS.

HYMN.

Jesu dulcis memoria,
Dans vera cordi gaudia:
Sed super mel, et omnia,
Ejus dulcis praesentia.

Nil canitur suavius,
Nil auditur jucundius,
Nil cogitatur dulcius,
Quam Jesus Dei Filius.

Jesu spes poenitentibus,
Quam pius es petentibus!
Quam bonus te quaerentibus!
Sed quid invenientibus?

Nec lingua valet dicere,
Nec littera exprimere:
Expertus potest credere,
Quid sit Jesum diligere.

Sis, Jesu, nostrum gaudium,
Qui es futurum praemium:
Sit nostra in te gloria,
Per cuncta semper gaudia.
Amen.

J. Ant. In Nomine Jesu.

Ps. 99

Jubilate Deo omnis terra: * servite Domino in laetitia.

Introite in conspectu ejus, * in exultatione.

Scitote, quoniam Dominus ipse est Deus: * ipse fecit nos, et non ipsi nos.

Populus ejus, et oves pascuae ejus: * introite portas ejus in confessione, atria ejus in hymnis; confitemni illi.

Laudate nomen ejus, quoniam suavis est Dominus, in aeternum misericordia ejus: * et usque in generationem et generationem veritas ejus.

Gloria Patri, et Filio, &c.

Ant. In Nomine Jesu omne genu flectatur coelestium, terrestrium, et infernorum.

E. Ant. Ego autem.

Ps. 19.

Exaudiat te Dominus in die tribulationis : * protegat te nomen Dei Jacob.

Mittat tibi auxilium de sancto: * et de Sion tueatur te.

Memor sit omnis sacrificii tui : * et holocaustum tuum pingue fiat.

Tribuat tibi secundum cor tuum: * et omne consilium tuum confirmet.

Laetabimur in salutari tuo: * et in nomine Dei nostri magnificabimur.

Impleat Dominus omnes petitiones tuas: * nunc cognovi, quoniam salvum fecit Dominum Christum suum.

Exaudiet illum de coelo sancto suo: * in potentatibus salus dexterae ejus.

Hi in curribus, et in in equis: * nos autem in nomine Domini Dei nostri invocabimus.

Ipsi obligati sunt, et ceciderunt: * nos autem surreximus, et erecti sumus.

Domine, salvum fac regem: * et exaudi nos in die, qua invocaverimus te.

Gloria Patri, &c.

Ant. Ego autem in Domino gaudebo, et exultabo in Deo Jesu meo.

S. Ant. Sanctum et terribile.

Ps. 11.

Salvum me fac, Domine, quoniam defecit sanctus, * quoniam diminutae sunt veritates a filiis hominum.

Vana locuti sunt unusquisque ad proximum suum: * labia dolosa in corde, et corde locuti sunt.

Disperdat Dominus universa labia dolosa, * et linguam magniloquam.

Qui dixerunt: linguam nostram magnificabimus, labia nostra a nobis sunt: * quis noster Dominus est?

Propter miseriam inopum, et gemitum pauperum, nunc exurgam, dicit Dominus.

Ponam in salutari: * fiducialiter agam in eo.

Eloquia Domini eloquia casta, * argentum igne examinatum, probatum terrae, purgatum septuplum.

Tu, Domine, servabis nos, et custodies nos * a generatione Isaac in aeternum.

In circuitu impii ambulant: * secundum altitudinem tuam multiplicasti filios hominum.

Gloria Patri, &c.

Ant. Sanctum, et terribile Nomini ejus: initium sapientiae timor Domini.

U. Ant. Vocabis Nomen ejus Jesum.

Ps. 12.

Usquequo, Domine, oblivisceris me in finem? * usquequo avertis faciem tuam a me?

Quamdiu ponam consilia in anima mea, * dolorem in corde meo per diem ?

Usquequo exaltabitur inimicus meus super me* respice, et exaudi me, Domine Deus meus.

Illumina oculos meos, ne unquam obdormiam in morte; * nequando dicat inimicus meus: prevalui adversus eum.

Qui tribulant me, exultabunt, si motus fuero: * ego autem in misericordia tua speravi.

Exultabit cor meum in salutari tuo: cantabo Domino, qui bona tribuit mihi, * et psallam nomini Domini altissimi.

Gloria Patri, &c.

Ant. Vocabis Nomen ejus Jesum: Ipse enim salvem faciet populum suum a peccatis eorum.

S. Ant. Sitivit anima mea.

Ps. 128.

Saepe expugnaverunt me a juventute mea: * dicat nunc Israel.

Saepe expugnaverunt me a juventute mea: * etenim non potuerunt mihi.

Supra dorsum meum fabricaverunt peccatores: * prolongaverunt iniquitatem suam.

Dominus justus concidit cervices peccatorum: * confundantur, et convertantur retrorsum omnes, qui oderunt Sion.

Fiant sicut foenum tectorum, * quod priusquam evellatur, exaruit.

De quo non implevit manum suam, qui metit, * et sinum suum, qui manipulos colligit.

Et non dixerunt, qui praeteribant: Benedictio Domini super vos: * benediximus

vobis in nomine Domini.
Gloria Patri, &c.

Ant. Sitivit anima mea ad Nomen sanctum tuum, Domine.

HYMN.

Jesu Rex admirabilis
Et triumphator nobilis,
Dulcedo ineffabilis
Totus desiderabilis.

Quando cor nostrum visitas,
Tunc lucet ei veritas
Mundi vilescit vanitas,
Et intus fervet charitas.

Jesu dulcedo cordium,
Fons vivus, lumen mentium,
Excedens omne gaudium
Et omne desiderium.

Jesum omnes agnoscite,
Amorem ejus poscite;
Jesum ardenter quaerite,
Quaerendo inardescite.

Te nostra, Jesu, vox sonet,
Nostri Te mores exprimant;
Te corde nostra diligant
Et nunc, et in perpetuum. Amen.

V. Sit nomen Domini benedictum.
R. Ex hoc nunc, et usque in saeculum.

Oremus.
Deus, qui Unigenitum Filium tuum constituisti humani generis Salvatorem, et
Jesum vocari jussisti: concede propitius; ut cujus sanctum Nomen veneramur
in terris, ejus quoque aspectu perfruamur in coelis. Per eumdem Dominum
nostrum Jesum Christum Filium tuum, &c.

TRANSLATION OF THE ABOVE HYMNS AND PRAYER.

Jesu the very thought of Thee
With sweetness fills my breast;
But sweeter far Thy face to see,
And in Thy presence rest.

Nor voice can sing, nor heart can frame,
Nor can the memory find,
A sweeter sound than Thy blest Name,
O Saviour of mankind!

O hope of every contrite heart!
O joy of all the meek!
To those who fall, how kind Thou art!
How good to those who seek!

But what to those who find? ah! this
Nor tongue nor pen can show:
The love of Jesus, what it is,
None but His lov'd ones know.

Jesu! our only joy be Thou,
As Thou our prize wilt be;
Jesu! be Thou our glory now,
And through eternity.

II.

O Jesu King most wonderful!
Thou Conqueror renown'd!
Thou Sweetness most ineffable!
In whom all joys are found!

When once Thou visitest the heart,
Then truth begins to shine;
Then earthly vanities depart;
Then kindles love divine.

O Jesus Light of all below!
Thou Fount of life and fire!
Surpassing all the joys we know,

All that we can desire:

May every heart confess Thy Name,
And ever Thee adore;
And seeking Thee, itself inflame
To seek Thee more and more.

Thee may our tongues for ever bless;
Thee may we love alone;
For ever in our lives express
The image of Thine own.

V. Blessed be the Name of the Lord.
R. From henceforth and for evermore.

Let us pray.
God, who hast appointed Thine only begotten Son the Saviour of mankind, and hast commanded that He should be called Jesus; mercifully grant that we may enjoy the vision of Him in heaven whose holy Name we venerate on earth. Through the same Jesus Christ our Lord. Amen.

18. CHAPLET OF OUR LORD.

This Chaplet, instituted through divine inspiration about the year 1516, by the blessed Michael of Florence, a Camaldolese monk, who used to say it every day until his death, Jan. 11, 1522, is called the Chaplet of our Lord, because it is said in honour of Jesus Christ, and is composed of thirty-three *Pater noster's*, in remembrance and veneration of the thirty-three years which he lived on thee earth; to these are added five times *Ave Maria* in honour of His five most holy wounds; the first three of which are said, one at the beginning of each of the three sets of ten *Pater noster's*, and of the two remaining, one is said previous to reciting the three concluding *Pater noster's,* and the other after them. The Chaplet finishes with the *Credo* in honour of the holy Apostles its composers, and which itself contains an epitome of the Birth, Life, Passion, and Death of our Divine Lord Jesus Christ. Pope Leo X., at the prayer of the above-named blessed Michael, granted by a Bull, dated February 18, 1516, several Indulgences to any one who should keep about him the said Chaplet, or say it. Gregory XIII. did as much by means of a Brief dated Feb. 14, 1573; and Sixtus V. by another Brief, dated Feb. 3, 1589. These Indulgences were all confirmed anew by Clement X., in a special Brief, *De salute Dominici gregis,* dated July 20, 1674, who also added several more Indulgences, as follows:

i. Indulgence of 200 years every time any one shall say it, being penitent and having confessed, or having at least firmly resolved to confess.

ii. Indulgence of 150 years to any one who, having Confessed and Communicated, shall carry about him one of these Chaplets, and say it every Monday, Wednesday, and Friday, and. also on au festivals of obligation.

iii. Plenary indulgence once a year on any one day, to any one who, after Confession and Communion, shall have made a practice of saying it at least four times a week.

iv. Plenary indulgence once a month to any one who shall have said it every day for a month, and shall then, bring penitent, after Confession and Communion, pray to God, for the Holy Church, &c.

v. Plenary indulgence to any one who shall die in battle against the infidels, having been previously accustomed to say the said Chaplet three times a week, and having said it on the day of his death, or the day previous to it, provided he be penitent for his sins, and ask pardon of God for them.

vi. Plenary indulgence, and remission of all sins in the article of death, to any one who, being penitent and having confessed, shall then invoke, at least with his heart if he cannot do so with his lips, the most holy Name of Jesus; provided he has said the above-named Chaplet once during his illness with the intention of gaining this Indulgence: in the event of his recovery, he may gain the 200 years indulgence.

vii. Indulgence of twenty days to any one who shall carry about him one of these Chaplets, and invoke the adorable Name of Jesus, after he has made an examination of conscience with contrition for his sins, and said three *Pater noster's* and three *Ave Maria's* for the good estate of the Church.

viii. The indulgence of twenty years to any one who, having examined his conscience and confessed, shall, after his confession, pray to God for the advancement of the Catholic Faith, the extirpation of heresy, and the exaltation of the Holy Church, &c.; and

ix. The indulgence of ten years to any one who, having about him the said Chaplet, shall say three *Pater noster's* and three *Ave Maria's,* as often as he does any spiritual or temporal good work in honour of our Lord Jesus Christ, the Blessed Virgin Mary, or some saint, or for the good of his neighbour.

x. Any one who keeps one of the said Chaplets about him, if he is wont to practise any exercise customary in any religious order, shall participate in all the good works which are done in the order in whose pious exercises in has made the intention of sharing; if he assist at Holy Mass, he shall, by saying five *Pater noster's* and five *Ave Maria's*, supply for every defect and distraction which has happened to him through inadvertence in the course of the Mass; moreover, if on days of obligation he has been legitimately hindered from hearing Mass, he shall have the same merit as if he had assisted at it, provided he say the five *Pater noster's* and five *Ave Maria's* as above.

xi. Any one out of Rome keeping one of these Chaplets about him, shall, on the days of the Stations, gain the 200 years indulgence on visiting any church he chooses; if hindered from doing so, he shall gain the same indulgence by saying this Chaplet, the seven Pestilential Psalms, with the Litanies and prayers. The same Indulgence in Rome may be gained by any one who, being legitimately hindered from visiting the Church of the Station, shall say the Chaplet and Psalms as above

Pope Benedict XIII. afterwards, by a decree of the S. Congr. of Indulgences, dated April 6, 1727, confirmed all the above Indulgences, and added another -

xii. Plenary indulgence to anyone who, after having Confessed and Communicated, should say this Chaplet on Friday. The plenary indulgence can only be gained on the Fridays in March, and that after the works enjoined above have been fulfilled; as was declared by Pope Leo XII., in a decree of the S. Congr. of Indulgences, dated Aug 11, 1824.

In order to gain the above-named Indulgences, it is necessary that -

1. The Chaplet he blessed by the Reverend Fathers of the Camoldolese order, either hermits or monks, or else by those who have apostolical authority to bless them. Once blessed, they cannot be sold, or lent to others for the purpose of communicating to them the indulgences: in which case they would afterwards be deprived of the Indulgences annexed to them according to the brief of Pope Clement X.

2. Every one saying the Chaplet must, according to his capacity, meditate on the mysteries of the life of our Lord Jesus Christ. It is not, however, necessary either to read or recite the following short reflections, which are only added for the greater devotion of any one who might wish to make use of them.

CHAPLET OF OUR LORD

Begin with an act of contrition.

First Decade.

The Archangel Gabriel makes known to the Blessed Virgin Mary the Incarnation of the Divine Word in her pure womb.
Ave Maria

1. The Son of God made man is born of Mary the Virgin in a stable.
Pater noster.

2. The Angels rejoice and sing, *Gloria in excelsis Deo.*
Pater noster.

3. The shepherds hear the Angels' tidings, and come and adore Him.

Pater noster.

4. He is circumcised the eighth day, and called by the most Holy Name of Jesus.
Pater noster.

5. Is adored by the Magi with offerings of gold, frankincense, and myrrh.
Pater noster.

6. Is presented in the Temple, and foretold to be the Saviour of the world
Pater noster.

7. Flies from the persecution of Herod, and is carried into Egypt.
Pater noster.

8. Herod finds Him not, and murders the Innocents.
Pater noster.

9. He is carried back by Joseph and His Mother into Nazareth his home.
Pater noster.

10. Disputes in the Temple with the doctors, being twelve years old.
Pater noster.

Add the Eternal rest, &c. *if said for the departed.*

Second Decade.

Jesus is most obedient to the Blessed Virgin His Mother, and to St. Joseph.
Ave Maria.

1. When thirty years old, He is baptized by John in Jordan.
Pater noster.

2. Fasts forty days us the desert, and overcomes the tempter.
Pater noster.

3. Practises and preaches His own holy law, whereby is life eternal
Pater noster.

4. Calls His disciples, who forthwith leave all and follow Him.
Pater noster.

5. Works His first miracle of changing water into wine.
Pater noster.

6. Heals the sick, makes the lame to walk, gives hearing to the deaf, sight to the blind, life to the dead.
Pater noster.

7. Converts sinful men and sinful women, and pardons their sins.
Pater noster.

8. When the Jews persecute Him even unto death, He chastises them not, but sweetly chides them.
Pater noster.

9. Is transfigured on Mount Thabor, in the presence of Peter, James, and John.
Pater noster.

10. Enters triumphant into Jerusalem sitting on an ass's colt, and drives the profaners from the Temple.
Pater noster.

Eternal rest, &c. *as above.*

Third Decade.

Jesus takes leave of His most holy Mother before He goes to die for our salvation.
Ave Maria

1. Celebrates the Last Paschal Supper, washes the Apostles' feet.
Pater noster.

2. Institutes the most holy Sacrament of the Eucharist.
Pater noster.

3. Prays in the garden, sweats blood, and is comforted by an angel.
Pater noster.

4. Is betrayed by Judas with a kiss, is taken and bound by the officers of justice as a great malefactor.
Pater noster.

5. Is falsely accused, is buffeted and spit upon, and shamefully used before four tribunals.
Pater noster.

6. Looks tenderly on Peter after he had thrice denied Him, and converts Him; whilst Judas despairs, hangs himself, and is lost.
Pater noster.

7. Is cruelly scourged at the pillar, and receives innumerable blows.
Pater noster.

8. Is crowned with thorns, shown to the people, who cry, Crucify Him! crucify Him!
Pater noster.

9. Is condemned to die, carries the heavy cross with grievous pain upon His shoulders to Mount Calvary.
Pater noster.

10. Is crucified between two thieves, dies after three hours' most painful agony, is wounded in the side with a lance, and is buried.
Pater noster.

Eternal rest, &c. *as above.*

Jesus rises the third day, and visits first of all His most holy Mother, Mary.
Ave Maria.

1. Appears to the three Marys, and bids them tell the disciples they have seen Him risen from the dead.
Pater noster.

2. Appears to the disciples, shows them His most holy Wounds, makes Thomas touch them.
Pater noster.

3. The fortieth day after his resurrection, blesses most holy Mary His Mother and all his disciples then ascends into heaven.
Pater noster.

Let us pray to the most holy Virgin to obtain for us also the blessing of her Divine Son Jesus Christ, now and at the hour of our death.
Ave Maria.

Eternal rest, &c. *as above.*

Let us say "I believe," &c. in honour of the holy Apostles.

End with the prayer said to be St. Augustine's.

Oremus.
Deus, qui pro redemptione mundi voluisti nasci, circumcidi, a Judaeis reprobari, a Juda traditore osculo tradi, vinculis alligari, sicut agnus innocens ad victimam duci, atque conspectibus Annae, Caiphae, Pilati, et Herodis indecenter offerri, a falsis testibus accusari, flagellis et opprobriis vexari, sputis conspui, spinis coronari, colaphis caedi, arundine percuti, facie velari, vestibus exui, cruci clavibus affigi, in cruce levari, inter latrones deputari, felle et aceto potari, et lancea vulnerari: tu Domine, per has sanctissimas poenas tuas, quas ego indignus recolo, et per sanctam crucem et mortem tuam libera me (*et hunc famulum tuum .N. agonizantem*) a poenis inferni, et perducere digneris, quo perduxisti latronem tecum crucifixum; qui cum Patre et Spiritu Sancto vivis et regnas Deus per omnia saecula saeculorum. Amen.

TRANSLATION.

Let us pray.
O Lord, who to redeem the world and to free us from the pains of hell, didst vouchsafe to be born amongst men, subject to pain and to death, to be circumcised, rejected, and persecuted by the Jews, betrayed by Thy disciple Judas with a sacrilegious kiss, and as a lamb, gentle and innocent, to he bound with cords, and dragged in scorn before the tribunals of Annas, Caiphas, Pilate, and Herod; who didst suffer Thyself to be accused by false witnesses, torn by scourges, crowned with thorns, smitten with blows, insulted with spittings, to have Thy divine countenance covered out of contempt, to be many ways set at naught and outraged, to be filled with reproaches and ignominies, and, last of all, to be stripped of Thy clothes, nailed to and raised high upon a cross between two notorious thieves, to be drenched with gall and vinegar, and then pierced with a lance, and so to fulfil the mighty work of our redemption: Saviour most tender, by these Thy many cruel sufferings borne by Thee out of Thy love for me, which I, unworthy as I am, yet dare to contemplate, by Thy holy cross, and by Thy bitter death, free me (and this Thy servant *) from the pains of hell and vouchsafe to bring me to Paradise, whither Thou didst lend the penitent thief who was crucified with Thee, my Jesus, who, with the Father and with the Holy Ghost, livest and reignest God for ever and ever. Amen. (Translation from the Italian version.)

* If said for a soul in its agony.

19. THREE EJACULATIONS: JESU, ETC.

In order to increase the devotion of the faithful to Jesus and Mary by invoking their most holy Names together with the name of St. Joseph, for the purpose of recommending to them the last moments of this life, on which our eternity depends, Pius VII., by a decree of the S. Congr. of Indulgences, dated April 28, 1807, granted – An indulgence of 300 days to any one, as often as he says decently, and with a contrite heart, the three following ejaculations:

Jesus, Mary, Joseph, I offer you my heart and my soul.
Jesus, Mary, Joseph, assist me in my last agony.
Jesus, Mary, Joseph, may I breath forth my soul with you in peace.

If but one of the above is recited, then the same Pope granted to the reciter 100 days indulgence.

20. ANOTHER EJACULATION.

At the prayer of the Procurator-General of the Clerks Regular called time Somaschi, the Sovereign Pontiff Pius IX., by two decrees of the S. Congr. of Indulgences; Aug. 11, 1851, and Nov. 29, 1853, granted -
i. Fifty days indulgence every time any one says the following Ejaculation of S. Jerome Emiliani.
ii. A plenary indulgence to any one who says it at least once a day for a year, to be gained once only, on the feast of the saint, July 20, or during its octave, provided that, after Confession and Communion, he visit some church, and pray there according to the intention of his Holiness.

Dulcissime Jesu, ne sis mihi Judex, sed Salvator.
My sweetest Jesus, be not to me a Judge, but a Saviour.

APPENDIX.

166. EJACULATION, "JESUS, DEUS MEUS," ETC., "JESUS, MY GOD," ETC.

By a Rescript of May 7, 1854, the Sovereign Pontiff Pius IX. granted -
The indulgence of 50 days to all those who shall say in any language the following Ejaculation, or who with a feeling of compunction and gratitude shall exhort others to say it for the good of those who have the care of souls, or who labour for the salvation and sanctification of souls.

THE EJACULATION.

Jesus, Deus meus, super omnia amo te.
Jesus, my God, I love Thee above all things.

167. THE PRAYER, "O JESU, VIVENS IN MARIA," ETC.

By a Rescript of Oct. 14, 1859, his Holiness Pope Pius IX. granted -
The indulgence of 300 days to all the faithful who with contrite heart and with devotion shall say the following prayer:

THE PRAYER.

O Jesu, vivens in Maria, veni et vive in famulis tuis, in Spiritu sanctitatis tuae, in plenitudine virtutis
tuae, in veritate virtutum tuarum, in perfectione viarum tuarum, in communione mysteriorum tuorum, dominar omni adversae potestati in Spiritu tuo ad gloriam Patris. Amen.

TRANSLATION.

O Jesus, who dost live in Mary, come and live in Thy servants, in the spirit of Thine own holiness, in the fullness of Thy power, in the reality of Thy virtues, in the perfection of Thy ways, in the communion of Thy mysteries, - have Thou dominion over every adverse power, in Thine own Spirit, to the glory of Thy Father. Amen.

168. PRAYER TO THE MOST HOLY NAME OF JESUS, O BONE JESU."

His Holiness Pope Pius IX., by a Rescript of August 14, 1860, granted -
100 days indulgence, to be gained once a day by all those who in Rome or its district say devoutly and with contrite heart the following prayer, in any language, provided the translation be a faithful one.

THE PRAYER.

O bone Jesu! O piissime Jesu! O dulcissime Jesu! O Jesu, Fili Mariae Virginis, plene misericordia et pietate! O dulcis Jesu, secundum magnam misericordiam tuam miserere mei! O clementissimne Jesu! Te deprecor per illum Sanguinem pretiosum quem pro peccatoribns effundere voluisti, ut abluas omnes iniquitates meas, et in me respicias miserum et indignum humiliter venians petentem, et hoc Nomen sanctum Jesu invocantem. O Nomen Jesu, Nomen dulce! Nomen Jesu, Nomeu delectabile! Nomen Jesu, Nomen confortans! Quid est enim Jesus, nisi Salvator? Ergo, Jesu, propter Nomen sanctum tuum esto mihi Jesus, et salva me. Ne permittas me damnari, quem tu de nihilo creasti. O bone Jesu, ne perdat me iniquitas mea, quem fecit Omnipotens bonitas tua! O dulcis Jesu, recognosce quod tuum est, et absterge quod alienum est. O benignissime Jesu, miserere mei, dum tempus est miserendi, ne damnes me in tempore judicandi. Non mortui laudabunt te, Domine Jesu, neque omnes qui descendunt in infernum. O amantissime Jesu! O desideratissime Jesu! O mitissime Jesu! O Jesu, Jesu, Jesu, admitte me intrare in numerum electorum tuorum. O Jesu, salus in te credentium; O Jesu, solatiuin ad te confugientium. O Jesu, Fili Mariae Virginis, infunde in me gratiam, sapientiam, charitatem castitatem et humilitatem, ut possim te perfecte diligere, te laudare, te perfrui, tibi servire, et in te gloriari, et Omnes qui invocant Nomen tuum, quod est Jesus. Amen.

TRANSLATION

O good Jesu! O most tender Jesu! O most sweet Jesu! O Jesus, Son of Mary the Virgin, full of mercy and kindness! O sweet Jesu, according to Thy great mercy, have pity on me! O most merciful Jesu, I entreat Thee by that precious Blood of Thine, which Thou didst will to pour forth for sinners, to wash away all my iniquities, and to look upon me, poor and unworthy as I am, asking humbly pardon of Thee, and invoking this holy Name of Jesus. O Name of Jesus, sweet Name! Name of Jesus, Name of joy! Name of Jesus, Name of strength! Nay, what meaneth the Name of Jesus but Saviour? Wherefore, O Jesu, by Thine own holy Name, be to me Jesus, and save me. Suffer me not to be lost, - me, whom Thou didst create out of nothing. O good Jesu, let not my iniquity destroy what Thy Almighty goodness made. O sweet Jesu, recognise what is Thine own, and wipe away from me what is not of Thee! O most kind Jesu, have pity on me, while it is the time of pity, and condemn me not when it is the time of judgment. The dead shall not praise Thee, Lord Jesu, nor will those who go down into hell. O most loving Jesus! O Jesu, most longed for by Thine own! O most gentle Jesu! Jesu, Jesu, Jesu, let me enter into the number of Thine elect. O Jesu, salvation of those who believe in Thee. Jesu, consolation of those who fly to Thee. Jesu, Son of Mary the Virgin, pour into me grace, wisdom, charity, chastity, and humility, that I may be able perfectly to love Thee, to praise Thee, to enjoy Thee, to serve Thee, and make my boast in Thee, and that all those who invoke Thy Name, which is Jesus, may join with me in these acts. Amen.

THE CHILD JESUS.

21. NOVENA PREPARATORY TO CHRISTMAS

In order to the devout preparation of ourselves for the glorious Birthday of our most loving Saviour, Jesus Christ, which the holy Church recalls to our memory every year on the 25th of December, and at the same time to render Him thanks for this great benefit, Pope Pius VII., by a Rescript of the *Segretaria* of the Memorials, dated August 12th, 1815 (which said Rescript is preserved in the *Segretaria* of the Vicariate), granted to all faithful Christians who, being contrite in heart, should prepare themselves for that great solemnity by a novena, consisting of pious exercises, prayers, acts of virtue, &c. -
i. An indulgence of 300 days each day of the said novena, and -
ii. A plenary indulgence to be gained on Christmas day, or on some day in its octave, by those who, after Confession and Communion, shall have made the said novena every day, and who shall pray according to the intentions of the Sovereigns Pontiff: and note that the Confession and Communion may be made on any one of the days of the said novena, provided the novena is correctly kept. This was declared by Pope Pius VIII., of holy memory, by means of the S. Congr. of Indulgences, July 9, 1830. These indulgences were extended by the above-named Pius VII. to one other time in the year, besides the the specified, when any one should make the aforesaid novena in honour of the Child Jesus.

22. ANOTHER NOVENA IN PREPARATION FOR THE TWENTY-FIFTH DAY OF EVERY MONTH.

In order to call to mind more frequently the august Mystery of the Incarnation and Birth of the Divine Word made Man, his Holiness the Sovereign Pontiff Pius IX., by a decree of the S. Congr. of Indulgences, dated Sept. 23, 1846, grants -
An indulgence of one year, to be gained each day of the following novena, which may be made either in public or private, nine days previous to the 25th day of any month provided that the faithful assist at it with a contrite heart.

The Novena is to be begun on the 16th day of every month.

i. *Offering.* Eternal Father, I offer to Thy honour and glory, and for my own salvation, and for the salvation of all the world, the mystery of the Birth of our Divine Saviour.

Gloria Patri, &c.

ii. *Offering.* Eternal Father, I offer to Thy honour and glory, and for my eternal salvation, the sufferings of the most holy Virgin and of St. Joseph in that long and weary journey from Nazareth to Bethlehem; I offer Thee their anxiety of heart when they found no place wherein to shelter themselves, when the Saviour of the world was to be born.

Gloria Patri, &c.

iii. *Offering.* Eternal Father, I offer to Thy honour and glory, and for my eternal salvation, the stable where Jesus was born, the hard straw which served Him for a bed, the cold He suffered, the swaddling clothes which bound Him, the tears he shed, and His tender infant cries.

Gloria Patri, &c.

iv. *Offering.* Eternal Father, I offer to Thy honour and glory, and for my eternal salvation, the pain which the holy Child Jesus felt in His tender infant body when He submitted it to the keen knife of circumcision; I offer Thee that Precious Blood which then first He shed for the salvation of the whole race of man.

Gloria Patri, &c.

v. *Offering.* Eternal Father, I offer to Thy honour and glory, and for my eternal salvation, the humility, mortification, patience, charity, all the virtues of the Child Jesus; and I thank Thee, and I love Thee, and I bless Thee without end, for this ineffable mystery of the Incarnation of the Divine Word.

Gloria Patri, &c.

V. Verbum caro factum est.
R. Et habitavit in nobis.

Oremus.
Deus, cujus Unigenitus in substantia nostra carnis apparuit; praesta quaesumus, ut per Eum, quem similem nobis foris agnovimus, intus reformari mereamur. Qui tecum vivit et regnat in saecula saeculorum. Amen.

V. The Word was made Flesh.
R. And dwelt amongst us.

Let us pray.

O God, whose only begotten Son was made manifest to us in the substance of our flesh; grant, we beseech Thee, that through Him our souls may be internally renewed, whom we acknowledge externally like unto ourselves. Who liveth and reigneth with Thee for ever and ever. Amen.

23. FOR ASSISTING AT OR SAYING THE DIVINE OFFICE ON CHRISTMAS DAY.

In order to increase the devotion of all faithful Christians towards the feast of the birthday of our Divine Saviour Jesus Christ, and that they may celebrate it with spiritual profit to their souls, Pope Sixtus V., by his brief, Ut fidelium devotio, dated Oct. 22, 1586, granted the following Indulgences, viz.:
i. The indulgence of 100 years to all those who, being truly penitent, having Confessed and Communicated, shall recite the Divine Office on that day, or assist in person in any church where Matins and Lauds are said;
ii. One hundred years indulgence for the Mass, and the same for first and second Vespers;
iii. The indulgence of forty years for each of the hours of Prime, Tierce, Sext, None, and Compline.

24. MYSTERIES OF THE HOLY CHILDHOOD.

In order that Christians might meditate mere frequently on the Incarnation, Birth, and all the other mysteries relating to the holy Childhood of our Divine Saviour Jesus Christ, and might render Him meet and worthy thanks, as well as imitate those virtues which lie in his Childhood has taught us by His example, Pope Pius VII., of holy memory, by a decree of the S. Congr. of Indulgences, dated Nov. 23, 1519, granted -
i. The plenary indulgence, on the 25th of every month, to all those who, being penitent, having Confessed and Communicated, should be present at any church or public oratory in which is practised the pious exercise in honour of the Child Jesus, and who shall then, in veneration of the mysteries of His Sacred Infancy, say the following prayers revised and approved by the S. Congr. of Rites; provided also they pray according to the intentions of the Sovereign Pontiff.
ii. The indulgence of 300 days, once a day, to those who, in private, with a contrite heart, devoutly practise this pious exercise.

THE MYSTERIES.

V. Deus in adjutorium meum intende.
R. Domine ad adjuvandum me festina.

V. Gloria Patri, et Filio, et Spiritui Sancto.
R. Sicut erat in principio, et nunc et semper, et in saecula saeculorum. Amen.

Pater noster.

i. Jesu Infans dulcissime e Sinu Patris propter nostram salutem descendens, de Spiritu Sancto conceptus, Virginis uterum non horrens, et Verbum caro factum formam servi accipi nos, miserere nostri.
R. Miserere nostri, Jesu Infans, miserere nostri.

Ave Maria.

ii. Jesu Infans dulcissime per Virginem Matrem tuam visitans Elisabeth, Joannem Baptistam praecursorem tuum Spiritu Sancto replens, et adhuc in utero Matris suae sanctificans, miserere nostri.
R. Miserere, &c.

Ave Maria.

iii. Jesu Infans dulcissime novem mensibus in utere clausum, summis votis a Maria Virgine, et a Sancto Joseph expectatum, et Deo Patri pro salute mundi oblatus, miserere nostri.
R. Miserere, &c.

Ave Maria.

iv. Jesu Infans dulcissime in Bethlehem ex Virgine Maria natus, pannis involutus, in praesepio reclinatum, ab Angelis annuntiatum, et a Pastoribus visitatus, miserere nostri.
R. Miserere, &c.

Ave Maria.

Jesu tibi sit gloria,
Qui natus es deVirgine,
Cum Patre et Sancto Spiritu.
In sempiterna saecula. Amen.

V. Christus prope est nobis.
R. Venite adoremus.

Pater noster.

v. Jesu Infans dulcissime in circumcisione post dies octo vulneratus, glorioso Jesu uonsiae vocatus, et in nomine simul et sanguine Salvatoris officio praesignatus, miserere nostri.
R. Miserere, &c.

Ave Maria.

vi. Jesu Infans dulcissime stella duco tribis Magis demonstratus, in sinu Matris adoratus, ut mysticis muneribus auro, thure et myrrha donatus, miserere nostri.
R. Miserere, &c.

Ave Maria.

vii. Jesu Infans dulcissime in Templo a Matre Virgine presentatus, inter brachia a Simeone amplexatus, et ab Anna prophetissa Israeli revelatus, miserere nostri.
R. Miserere, &c.

Ave Maria.

viii. Jesu Infans dulcissime ab iniquo Herode ad mortem quaesitus, a Sancto Joseph in Aegyptum cum Matre deportatus, a crudeli caede sublatus, et a praeconiis martyrum innocentium glorificatus, miserere nostri.
R. Miserere, &c.

Ave Maria.

Jesu tibi sit gloria, &c.

V. Christus, &c.
Pater noster.

ix. Jesu Infans dulcissime in Aegypto cum Maria sanctissima, et patriarcha Sancto Joseph usque ad obitum Herodis commoratus, miserere nostri.
R. Miserere, &c.

Ave Maria.

x. Jesu Infans dulcissime ex Aegypto cum parentibus in terram Israel reversus, multos labores in itinere perpessus, et in civitatem Nazareth ingressus, miserere nostri.
R. Miserere, &c.

Ave Maria.

xi. Jesu Infans dulcissime in sancta Nazarena domo subditus parentibus sanctissime commoratus, paupertate at laboribus fatigatus, in sapientia, aetatis, et gratia profectu confortatus, miserere nostri.
R. Miserere, &c.

Ave Maria.

xii. Jesu Infans dulcissime in Jerusalem duodennis ductus, a parentibus cum dolore quaesitus, et post triduum cum gaudio inter doctores inventus, miserere nostri.
R. Miserere, &c.

Ave Maria.

Jesu tibi sit gloria, &c.

For the Nativity and its Octave.

V. Verbum caro factum est. Alleluia.
R. Et habitavit in nobis. Alleluia.

Throughout the rest of the year the Alleluia *is omitted.*

For the Epiphany and its Octave.

V. Christus manifestavit se nobis. Alleluia.
R. Venite adoremus. Alleluia.

Oremus.
Omnipotens sempiterne Deus, Domino coeli et terrae, qui te revelas parvulis, concede quaesumus ut flos sacrosancta Filii tui Infantis Jesu mysteria digno honore recolentes, ac digna imitatione sectantes; ad regnum coelorum promissum parvulis pervenire valeamus. Per eumdem, &c. R. Amen.

TRANSLATION OF THE MYSTERIES.

V. Incline unto my aid, O God.
R. O Lord, make haste to help mc.
V. Glory be to the Father, &c.

Pater noster.

The Incarnation.
i. Jesu, sweetest Child, who didst come down from the bosom of the Father for our salvation, who wast conceived by tile holy Ghost, who didst not abhor the Virgin's womb, and, as the Word made flesh, didst take upon Thee the form of a servant; have mercy upon us.
R. Have mercy on us, O Lord, have mercy on us.

Ave Maria.

The Visitation.
ii. Jesu, sweetest Child, who, through Thy Virgin Mother, didst visit Saint Elisabeth, and fill Thy forerunner the holy Baptist with the Holy Ghost, sanctifying him whilst yet in his mother's womb; have mercy upon us.
R. Have mercy, &c.

Ave Maria.

The Expectation of the Birth.
iii. Jesu, sweetest Child, who, shut up for nine months in lily Mother's womb, wast looked for with eager expectation by Mary and by Joseph, and wast

offered to God the Father for the salvation of tile world; have mercy upon us.
R. Have mercy, &c.
Ave Maria.

The Birth.
iv. Jesu, sweetest Child, born in Bethlehem of Mary ever Virgin, swathed in rags, laid in the manger, announced by angels, visited by shepherds ; have mercy upon us.
R. Have mercy, &c.

Ave Maria.

O, Jesu, born of Virgin bright,
Immortal glory be to Thee;
Praise to the Father Infinite,
And Holy Ghost eternally.

V. Christ is at hand.
R. Come, let us worship.

Pater noster.

The Circumcision.
v. Jesu, sweetest Child, wounded in Thy circumcision the eighth day, called by the glorious Name of Jesus, and at once by Thy Name and Thy Blood foreshown as thin Saviour of the world ; have mercy upon us.
R. Have mercy, &c.

Ave Maria.

The Adoration of the Magi.
vi. Jests, sweetest Child, made known to the three Magi by a star, adored in the arms of Thy Mother, presented with the mystic gifts of gold, frankincense, and myrrh; have mercy upon us.
R. Have mercy, &c.

Ave Maria.

The Presentation.
vii. Jesu, sweetest Child, who wrist presented in the Temple by Thy Virgin Mother, who wast embraced by Simeon, and revealed to Israel by Anna the prophetess; have mercy upon us.
R. Have mercy, &c.

Ave Maria.

The Flight into Egypt.
viii. Jesu, sweetest Child, whom wicked Herod sought to slay, whom Joseph

carried with Mary into Egypt, who wast withdrawn from a cruel death and wast glorified by the blood of innocents; have mercy upon us.
B. Have mercy, &c.

Ave Maria.

O Jesu, &c. *as above. V. and R. as above.* Pater noster, &c.

The Sojourn in Egypt.
ix. Jesu, sweetest Child, who didst dwell in Egypt with most holy Mary and the Patriarch holy Joseph until the death of Herod; have mercy upon us.
B. Have mercy, &c.
Ave Maria.

The Return out of Egypt.
x. Jesu, sweetest Child, who, after Herod's death, didst return out of Egypt into the hand of Israel, who didst suffer many toils by the way, and didst enter into thin city of Nazareth; have mercy upon us.
B. Have mercy, &c.

Ave Maria.

Early Life.
xi. Jesu, sweetest Child, who, in time holy house at Nazareth, subject to Thy parents, didst dwell most holily, wast wearied by poverty and labours, and didst advance iii wisdom, age, and grace; have mercy upon us.
R. Have mercy, &c.

Disputation with the Doctors.
xii. Jesu, sweetest Child, at twelve years old brought to Jerusalem, sought for by Thy parents with sorrow, and found with joy after three days amongst the doctors; have mercy upon us.
R. Have mercy, &c.

Ave Maria.

O Jesu, &c. *as above.*

For Christmas-day and its Octave.

V. The Word was made flesh. Alleluia.
R. And dwelt amongst us. Alleluia.

The Alleluia *is omitted during the year.*

For the Epiphany and its Octave.

V. Christ hath manifested Himself to us. Alleluia.
R. Come, let us adore. Alleluia.

Let us pray.

Almighty and everlasting God, Lord of Heaven and earth, who dost reveal Thyself to little ones; grant, we beseech Thee, that we, duly honouring the holy mysteries of Thy Son the infant Jesus, and daily imitating Him in our lives, may come to the kingdom of heaven promised by Thee to little children. Through the same Jesus Christ, &c.

APPENDIX

169. PRAYER BEFORE THE HOLY CRIB, WHICH IS VENERATED IN THE LIBERIAN BASILICA (ST. MARY MAJOR), "I ADORE THEE, O WORD INCARNATE," ETC.

In order to increase in the souls of the faithful devotion and homage towards the Crib of our Lord Jesus Christ, which is religiously preserved in the Patriarchal Basilica of St. Mary Major, the Sovereign Pontiff Pius IX., by a Brief of Oct. 1, 1861, granted to all the faithful who with contrite heart and devotion shall say, on any day in the above-named Basilica of St. Mary Major, the following prayer, in any language, provided the translation be faithful - 200 days of indulgence.

Moreover, to those also who shall say it in any other place, and on any day, be granted - 100 days of indulgence.

THE PRAYER.

I adore Thee, O Word Incarnate, true Son of God from all eternity, and true Son of Mary ever Virgin in the fullness of time. Whilst, then, I adore Thy Divine Person, and the Humanity which is thereunto united, I cannot but venerate the poor manger which welcomed Thee when an Infant, and which was truly the throne of Thy love. Let me prostrate myself before it, with the simplicity of the shepherds, with the faith of Joseph, with the love of Mary! Let me incline myself in lowly veneration of this precious memorial of our salvation with the same spirit of mortification, poverty, and humility with which Thou, though the Lord of heaven and of earth, didst choose for Thyself a manger as a receptacle of Thy poor infant limbs. And Thou, O Lord, who in Thine Infancy didst deign to lay Thyself in this manger, vouchsafe at the same time to pour into my heart one drop of that joy which both the sight of Thy lovely Infancy, and the miracles which accompanied Thy Birth, must needs have caused. In virtue of that holy Birth, here I now implore Thee to grant to all the world peace and good-will; and I desire, in the name of the whole human race, to render all thanks and all honour to the Father, and to the Holy Spirit, who with Thee liveth and reigneth one God world without end. Amen.

JESUS CRUCIFIED.

25. VISIT TO THE "SCALA SANTA" (THE SACRED STAIRS).

The *Scala Santa* is one of the sacred memorials of the Passion of our Lord Jesus Christ; and it is worthy of our reverence and devotion, for upon its steps our blessed Saviour trod, and that more than once, and it was consecrated by His Precious Blood, shed there in the last hours of His life on earth. This hallowed relic was brought from Jerusalem to Rome by the Empress Saint Helena, about the year 326, and deposited near the patriarchal basilica of St. John Lateran; afterwards Sixtus V., in the year 1580, set it up with much magnificent decoration in front of the famous chapel called the *Sancta Sanctorum*. It has always been, and still is, a devotional practice of the faithful of every rank and condition to mount it devoutly in a kneeling posture. In order to give a greater impulse to this devout and appropriate spiritual exercise, the Sovereign Pontiff Leo IV. about the year 850, and Paschal II. by his Bull of Aug. 5, 1100 (the original of which is kept in the far-famed basilica of St. John Lateran), granted the indulgence of nine years for each of the twenty-eight steps of the said *Scala Santa*, to all the faithful, every time they shall ascend them with a contrite heart and on their knees, praying and meditating on the Passion of their Lord.

26. VISIT TO THE "VIA CRUCIS," OR WAY OF THE CROSS.

Among those devotional exercises which help us to meditate upon the Passion, Cross, and Deaths of our Lord and Saviour Jesus Christ (the sovereign medicine for the conversion of sinners, for the renovation of the tepid, and for the sanctification of the just), one of the chief has ever been the exercise of the Way of Calvary, commonly called the *Via Crucis*.[1] This devotion, continued in an unbroken tradition from the time Jesus Christ ascended into heaven, [2] arose first in Jerusalem amongst the Christians who dwelt there, out of veneration for those sacred spots which were sanctified by the sufferings of our Divine Redeemer; and from the very times of the Gospel, as we learn from St. Jerome, [3] Christians were wont to visit the holy places in crowds; and the gathering of all persons, he says, even from the farthest corners of thee earth, to visit the holy places, continued to his own times.

From Jerusalem this devout exercise was introduced into Europe by various pious and holy persons, who had travelled to the Holy Land to satisfy their devotion. Amongst others we read of the blessed Alvarez of the order of Friars Preachers, (4) who, after he returned to his own convent of St. Dominic in Cordova, built several little chapels, to serve as so many separate stations, in which he had painted the principal events which took place on our Lord's way to Mount Calvary. Afterwards, more formally, the Fathers Minorite Observants of the Order of St. Francis, as soon as ever, on the foundation of their order, they were introduced into the Holy Land, and more especially from the time that, in the year 1542, they had their house in Jerusalem, and the custody of the sacred places, began both in Italy and elsewhere, in short, throughout the whole Catholic world, to spread the devotion of the *Via Crucis*. This they did by erecting in all their own churches fourteen separate stations, in visiting which, it was said that "the faithful, like the devout pilgrims who go in person to visit the holy places in Jerusalem, do themselves also make this journey in spirit, whilst they meditate on all that our Lord Jesus Christ vouchsafed to suffer for our eternal salvation at those holy places in the last hours of His life." (5)

This wholesome devotion has met with the repeated approvals of the Holy Church: in the Constitutions, for instance, of the venerable pontiff Innocent XI., of Innocent XII., (6) of the two Benedicts XIII. and XIV., (7) and of Clement XII.(8) By this last Pope it was extended to the whole Catholic world; and it is now in constant use with persons of every quality, being moreover enriched with most generous indulgences. For instance, those who perform devoutly the *Via Crucis* may gain all the Indulgences which have ever been granted by Popes to the faithful who visit in person the sacred places in Jerusalem. All, however, who wish to gain these Indulgences by means of this devotion, must bear in mind, that it is indispensably required of them to meditate, according to their abilities, on the Passion of our Lord and Saviour Jesus Christ, and to go from one station to the other so far as the number of persons engaged in the devotion, and the space where the fourteen stations are erected, will admit. So much is evident from the Apostolical Constitutions above named. This, then, is all that is required for the Indulgences, and so the words *V. Adoramus te, Christe, &c.*, the *Pater noster*, the *Ave Maria*, with the *V. Miserere nostri, Domine, &c.*, are nothing more than a pious and praiseworthy custom introduced by devout persons into the devotion of the Via Crucis. This the S. Congr. of Indulgences itself declared in their Instructions for performing the exercise of the *Via Crucis*, Nos. VI. and IX., published by order of, and with the approbation of Popes Clement XII., April 3, 1731, and Benedict XIV., May 10, 1742. These instructions, by the way, prohibit all catechists, preachers, and others, from *specifying* the indulgences which may be gained by the devotion of the *Via Crucis*, and bid them conform themselves in this respect to whatever the before-named Popes have declared and confirmed on this subject.

All, however, who are sick, all who are in prison, or at sea, or *in partibus infidelium*, or prevented in any other way from visiting the stations of the *Via Crucis* erected in churches or public oratories, may gain the said Indulgences by reciting fourteen *Pater noster's* and fourteen *Ave Maria's*, and at the end of these five *Pater noster's* and five *Ave Maria's,* and five times *Gloria Patri*, and one *Pater, Ave*, and *Gloria* besides for the Pope, "holding in their hands the while a brass crucifix" which has been blessed by the Most reverend the Father-General of the entire order of the Friars Minor Observants at the Convent of Ara Coeli, or else by the Father-Provincial, or any Father Guardian, subject of the said Father-General. This favour was granted by Pope Clement XIV., Jan. 26, 1773, at the prayer of the Reformed Minorites of the Retreat of St. Bonaventure here in Rome, who keep this decree in their Archivium. It is also to be observed, that these crucifixes, so indulgenced, after they have been blessed, cannot be sold or given away, or lent to any one for the purpose of enabling them to gain the Indulgences of the *Via Crucis,* as appears from repeated decrees to this effect of the S. Congr. of Indulgences above named.

NOTES.

(1) Benedict XIV., in the brief *Cum tanta*, dated Aug. 30, 1741.
(2) Apology for the Via Crucis. By F. Irenaeus Affo, Minorite Observant. Parma, 1783, page 14, and following. *Vid.* also the work of F. Flaminius da Latera, Min. Obs. cap. iii. &c.
(3) St. Jerome, epist. 46, *alias* 17.
(4) In the Office of the B. Alvarez, of the order of Preachers, Feb. 21, lect. ii. noct.
(5) Benedict XIII., in the Bull *Inter plurima et maxima*, March 3, 1726, § 1.
(6) The Ven. Innocent XI., brief Sept. 5, 1686. Innocent XII, brief *Ad ea per quae*, Dec. 24, 1692; and another, *Sua nobis*, Dec. 26, 1695.
(7) Brief above named, in the notes 1 and 5.
(8) Clement XII., in the brief *Exponi nobis*, Jan. 16, 1731, in which he confirmed the above-named brief of Benedict XIII.

DEVOTIONS WHICH MAY BE USED FOR THE VIA CRUCIS

[The pious reader may use any other devotions which are more to his mind.]

Begin with an act of contrition.

STATION I.

Jesus is condemned to death.

V. Adoramus Te Christe, et benedicimus Tibi.
R. Quia per sanctam Crucem tuam redimisti mundum.

My Jesus, oft have I signed Thy death-warrant by my sins; save me by Thy death from that death eternal I deserve.

Pater, Ave, &c.

V. Miserere nostri, Domine.
R. Miserere nostri.

STATION II.

Jesus is laden with the cross.

V. Adoramus, &c.

My Jesus, who by Thine own will didst take on Thee the heavy cross which I made for Thee by my sins; O make me know the weight of them, and sorrow for them ever while I live.

Pater, &c. V. Miserere &c.

STATION III.

Jesus falls the first time beneath the cross.

V. Adoramus, &c.

My Jesus, the heavy burden of my sins has made Thee fall down beneath the cross. My Jesus, I loathe them, I detest them, I beseech Thee to pardon them; aided by Thy grace I will never commit them more.

Pater, &c. V. Miserere &c.

STATION IV.

Jesus meets His Mother.

V. Adoramus, &c.

Jesus most suffering! Mary, Mother most sorrowful! if for the past by sin I have caused you pain and sorrow, yet by divine grace it shall be so no more, but I will love you faithfully until death.

Pater, &c. V. Miserere &c.

STATION V.

Simon of Cyrene helps Jesus to carry the cross.

V. Adoramus, &c.

My Jesus, happy was that man of Cyrene who aided Thee to bear the cross. Happy shall I be, if I too aid Thee to bear the cross, by suffering with patience and good-will the crosses Thou shalt send me during life. My Jesus, give me grace to do so.

Pater, &c. V. Miserere &c.

STATION VI.

Jesus and Veronica.

V. Adoramus, &c.

Jesus most compassionate, who didst deign to print Thy sacred countenance upon the cloth with which Veronica wiped the sweat from off Thy brows; print in my soul deep, I pray Thee, the lasting memory of Thy most bitter pains.

Pater, &c. V. Miserere &c.

STATION VII.

Jesus falls a second time.

V. Adoramus, &c.

My Jesus, oft have I sinned, and by sin often made Thee fall beneath the cross. Help me to use such efficacious means of grace, that I may never fall again into Sin.

Pater, &c. V. Miserere &c.

STATION VIII.

Jesus comforts the women of Jerusalem.

V. Adoramus, &c.

My Jesus, who didst comfort the pious women of Jerusalem, who wept to see Thee so tormented; comfort my soul with Thy mercy, for in Thy mercy alone is my sole trust; O may I never frustrate it!

Pater, &c. V. Miserere &c.

STATION IX.

Again a third time Jesus falls.

V. Adoramus, &c.

My Jesus, by all Thy bitter woes Thou didst endure, when a third time Thou didst fall beneath the heavy cross, O never, never let me fall away; but rather let me die than ever mortally sin again!

Pater, &c. V. Miserere &c.

STATION X.

Jesus stripped and drenched with gall.

V. Adoramus, &c.

My Jesus, who wast stripped of Thy clothes, and drenched with gall, strip me of love for things of earth, and make me loathe all that savours of the world and sin.

Pater, &c. V. Miserere &c.

STATION XI.

Jesus nailed to the cross.

V. Adoramus, &c.

My Jesus, by those agonising pains Thou didst endure when the hated nails pierced Thy tender hands and feet, and fixed them to the cross, O make me ever crucify my flesh with the spirit of true Christian penance.

Pater, &c. V. Miserere &c.

STATION XII.

Jesus dies upon the cross.

V. Adoramus, &c.

My Jesus, three hours didst Thou hang in agony upon the cross, and then didst die for me; let me die before I sin again, and if I live, may I live to love Thee and to serve Thee faithfully.

Pater, &c. V. Miserere &c.

STATION XIII.

Jesus taken from the cross and laid in Mary's bosom.

Mary, Mother most sorrowful, the sword of grief went through thy soul when thou didst see thy dear Son Jesus lying lifeless in thy bosom; ask for me hatred of sin, which was the cause of His death, and made thee suffer so much; and then obtain for me grace to live a true Christian life, and save my soul.

Pater, &c. V. Miserere &c.

STATION XIV.

Jesus laid in the tomb.

V. Adoramus, &c.

My Jesus, with Thee in the tomb I desire that I may ever remain as one dead; and if I live, I wish to live only to Thee, that so one day I may come with Thee to taste the bliss of heaven, the fruit of Thy Passion and most painful death. Amen.

Pater, &c. V. Miserere &c.

Oremus.
Deus, qui Unigeniti Filii tui pretioso sanguine vivificae crucis vexillum sanctificare voluisti; concede quaesumus, eos, qui ejusdem sanctae crucis gaudent honore, tua quoque ubique protectione gaudere. Per eumdem Christum Dominum nostrum.

Let us pray.
God, who by the Precious Blood of Thy only-begotten Son didst sanctify the standard of the cross; grant, we beseech Thee, that those whose joy is in the glory of the same Holy Cross, may rejoice also everywhere in Thy protection. Through the same Christ our Lord.

End with one Pater, Ave, and Gloria, for the intention of the Sovereign Pontiff.

---

27. FIVE PATER NOSTER'S AND FIVE AVE MARIA'S ON FRIDAYS AT THREE O'CLOCK, ETC.

In the Second Provincial Council held by St. Charles Borromeo, archbishop of Milan, it was decreed (decr. x.) that in all the churches of the Archdiocese the church-bell should ring every Friday at Nones, to remind the faithful of the

Passion of Jesus Christ at that hour, and Forty days' Indulgence was granted to every one who should then say three *Pater noster*'s and three *Ave Maria*'s. This pious and appropriate devotion on the day and hour when our Lord suffered for us was afterwards introduced into other places; and Pope Benedict XIV. was desirous of extending the usage uniformly and for ever to the whole Catholic world. Accordingly, on the 23rd of Dec. 1740, in his brief, *Ad Passionis*, he commanded all superiors of churches, in virtue of holy obedience, to have the bells of their churches rung every Friday at three o'clock in the afternoon; and he granted -

The indulgence of 100 days to every one of the faithful who should then kneel down and say five *Pater noster*'s and five *Ave Maria*'s in memory of the Passion and Agony of our Lord and Saviour Jesus Christ, with the intention of praying according to the mind of his Holiness, and for the conversion of sinners. The same Pope Benedict XIV. caused a special notice to be issued of this Indulgence; and it was confirmed afresh by a decree of the S. Congr. of Indulgences, dated Sept. 24, 1838.

28. DEVOTION IN MEMORY OF THE AGONY OF JESUS.

Pops Pius VII., by a Rescript of August 26, 1814, issued through his Eminence the Cardinal-Prefect of the S. Congr. of Rites, gave his approbation to the following devotion in memory of the Agony of our Lord and Saviour Jesus Christ; granting at the same time an indulgence of 300 days to all the faithful every time they devoutly say it.

This original Rescript is preserved amongst the acts of the S. Congr. of Rites, and an authentic copy of it is kept in the *Segretaria* of the S. Congr. of Indulgences.

THE DEVOTION.

V. Deus in adjutorium meum intende.
R. Domine ad adjuvandum me festina.
V. Gloria Patri, &c.

WORDS OF JESUS ON THE CROSS.

FIRST WORD.

Father, forgive them; for they know not what they do.

V. Adoramus Te Christe, et benedicimus Tibi.
R. Quia per sanctam Crucem tuam redimisti mundum.

Jesus, my Love! who for love of me didst hang in agony upon the cross, there by Thy pains to pay the penalty of my sins, and didst open Thy divine mouth to obtain for me the pardon of them from Eternal Justice; O Jesus, pity all the faithful who are now in their last agony, and pity me when I too shall be in mine. By the merits of Thy most Precious Blood shed for our salvation, vouchsafe unto us all such lively sorrow for our sins, that when we have sent forth our last breath we may at once repose in the bosom of Thy infinite mercy.

Three Gloria Patri's, *&c.*

Miserere nostri, Domine, miserere nostri.

My God, in Thee I believe, in Thee I hope, Thou art my love. I repent of my sins, because by them I have offended Thee.

SECOND WORD.

This day shalt thou be with me in Paradise.

V. Adoramus, &c.

Jesus, my Love! who for love of me didst hang in agony upon the cross, and with such readiness and bounty didst meet the faith of the good thief, when in Thy humiliations he acknowledged Thee to be the Son of God, and didst make him sure of the paradise prepared for him; O, pity all the faithful who are in their last agony, and pity me when I too shall be in mine. By the merit of Thy most Precious Blood, stir up in our souls such firm and steadfast faith as shall never waver under any suggestion of the evil one; that so we also may obtain the blessed prize of Paradise.

Three Gloria Patri's, *&c.*

Miserere, &c.

My God, in Thee I believe, in Thee I hope, Thou art my love. I repent of my sins, because by them I have offended Thee.

THIRD WORD.

Behold thy Mother! Behold thy Son!

V. Adoramus, &c.

Jesus, my Love! who for love of me didst hang in agony upon the cross, and unmindful of Thine own sorrows didst leave us Thy own most holy Mother as the pledge of Thy love, that through her intercession we might seek Thee with confidence in our greatest straits; have pity on all the faithful who are in their last agony, and pity me when I too shall be in mine. By the inward martyrdom of Thy dear Mother, quicken in our hearts a firm hope in the infinite merits of Thine own most Precious Blood, that so we may escape the sentence of eternal death, which we know we well merit for our sins.

Three Gloria Patri's, *&c.*

V. Miserere, &c.

My God, in Thee I believe, in Thee I hope, Thou art my love. I repent of my sins, because by them I have offended Thee.

FOURTH WORD.

My God, My God, why hast Thou forsaken Me?

V. Adoramus, &c.

Jesus, my Love! who for love of me didst hang in agony upon the cross, and, whilst suffering after suffering was heaped upon Thee, didst bear with infinite patience the most afflicting desolation of spirit in addition to the pain of body, being forsaken by Thine Eternal Father; pity all the faithful who are in their last agony, and pity me when I too shall be in mine. By the merits of Thy most Precious Blood, grant us all Thy grace that we may suffer with patience every pain and anguish of our agony, that so joining our pains with Thine, we too may be made partakers of Thy glory in Paradise.

Three Gloria Patri's, *&c.*

V. Miserere, &c.

My God, in Thee I believe, in Thee I hope, Thou art my love. I repent of my sins, because by them I have offended Thee.

FIFTH WORD.

I thirst.

V. Adoramus, &c.

Jesus, my Love! who for love of me didst hang in agony upon the cross, and who, insatiable in Thy thirst for insults and sufferings, didst will yet more and more to suffer, that all men might be saved, showing thereby that all the torrent of Thy Passion was not enough to quench the thirst of Thy most loving Heart; pity all the faithful who are in their last agony, and pity me when I too shall be in mine. By the merits of Thy most Precious Blood, so kindle in our hearts the fire of charity that they may desire exceedingly to be united with Thee for all eternity.

Three Gloria Patri's, *&c.*

V. Miserere, &c.

My God, in Thee I believe, in Thee I hope, Thou art my love. I repent of my sins, because by them I have offended Thee.

SIXTH WORD.

It is finished.

V. Adoramus, &c.

Jesus, my Love! who for love of me didst hang in agony upon the cross, and from that pulpit of truth didst announce that the work of our redemption was finished, that work through which, from children of wrath and perdition we became God's children and the heirs of heaven; pity all the faithful who are in their last agony, and pity me when I too shall be in mine. By the merits of Thy most Precious Blood, detach us wholly from the world and from ourselves, and at the moment of our agony grant us grace to offer Thee with all our hearts the sacrifice of our life, in expiation for our sins.

Three Gloria Patri's, *&c.*

V. Miserere, &c.

My God, in Thee I believe, in Thee I hope, Thou art my love. I repent of my sins, because by them I have offended Thee.

SEVENTH WORD.

Father, into Thy hands I commend my spirit.

V. Adoramus, &c.

Jesus, my Love! who for love of me didst hang in agony upon the cross, and who in accomplishment of the great sacrifice didst accept the will of Thine Eternal Father, commending Thy spirit into His hands, and so didst bow Thy head and die; pity all the faithful who are in their agony, and pity me when I too shall be in mine. By the merits of Thy most Precious Blood, give us in our agony an entire conformity to Thy divine will, that, ready to live or die as it please Thee, we may desire nothing but that Thine adorable will may ever find its full accomplishment in us.

Three Gloria Patri's, *&c.*

V. Miserere, &c.

My God, in Thee I believe, in Thee I hope, Thou art my love. I repent of my sins, because by them I have offended Thee.

PRAYER TO THE HOLY VIRGIN, MOTHER OF SORROWS.

Most Holy Mother of sorrows, by that intense martyrdom which thou didst suffer at the foot of the cross during the three hours of the agony of Jesus; deign to aid us all, who are the children of thy sorrows, in our last agony, that by thy prayers we may pass from our bed of death to adorn thy crown in Paradise.

Three Ave Maria's, *&c.*

Maria mater gratiae,
Mater misericordiae,
Tu nos ab hoste protege,
Et mortis hora suscipe.

V. A subitanea et improvisa morte,
R. Libera nos, Domine.
V. Ab insidiis diaboli,
R. Libera nos, Domine.
V. A morte perpetua,
R. Libera nos, Domine.

Oremus.

Deus, qui ad humani generis salutem in dolorosissima Filii tui morte, exemplum et subsidium constituisti: concede, quaesumus, ut in extremo mortis nostrae periculo tantae charitatis effectum consequi, et ipsius Redemptoris gloriae consociari mereamur. Per eumdem Christum, etc. R. Amen.

Mother of mercy, Mother of grace,
Mary, help a fallen race.
Shield us when the foe is nigh,
And receive us when we die.

V. From sudden and unprepared death,
R. Deliver us, O Lord.
V. From the snares of the devil,
R. Deliver us, O Lord.

V. From everlasting death,
R. Deliver us, O Lord.

Let us pray.
God, who for the salvation of the human race hast, in the most bitter death of
Thy Son, made for us both an example and a refuge; grant, we beseech Thee,
that in the last peril, at the hour of our death, we may be made worthy to
experience the effect of this great charity, and so to be associated in the glory
of the Redeemer Himself. Through the same Jesus Christ Thy Son.

End with the three ejaculations,

Jesus, Mary, Joseph, I offer you my heart and my soul.
Jesus, Mary, Joseph, assist me in my last agony.
Jesus, Mary, Joseph, may I breath forth my soul with you in peace.

29. DEVOTION FOR THE SEVEN FRIDAYS IN LENT AND THROUGHOUT THE YEAR.

Pope Pius VII., of holy memory, by a Rescript given through the *Segretaria* of
the Memorials, dated April 6, 1816, the original of which is in the *Segretaria* of
the S. Congr. of Indulgences, grants to all the faithful who, on the seven
Fridays in Lent (on which days we specially call to mind the Passion and
Death of our divine Lord Jesus Christ), shall use certain devotional exercises
collected in the little book first published in Rome in the year 1816, by
Michael Puccinelli -
i. An indulgence of 300 days, for each Friday in Lent.
ii. A plenary indulgence once on any of one these Fridays, provided that, after
Confession and Communion, they shall pray for our holy mother the Church,
&c.
iii. An indulgence of 300 days to every one who shall make use of these
devotions on any other Friday in the year.
iv. A plenary indulgence, if he shall practise them on seven consecutive Fridays
at any time in the year; to be gained on any one of those Fridays under the
above-named condition.
This little book is a collection of affectionate colloquies for each of the seven
Fridays, addressed to Jesus in His Passion, calling to the mind all He suffered
for love of us, from His agony in the garden of Gethsemane to His death on
Mount Calvary. To these colloquies are added the virtues to be practised on
each of these Fridays, as well as certain ejaculatory prayers.
N.B. Those who cannot read, or who have not in their possession the above-
named book, may supply the want of it by visiting any church or public oratory

73

on any one of the aforesaid Fridays, and praying for the intention of the Pope, and devoutly reciting seven times *Pater noster, Ave Maria*, and *Gloria Patri*, before any image or picture of Jesus crucified, in memory of all that He suffered for our redemption. This grant was made by Gregory XVI., of holy memory, by a Rescript of the S. Congr. of Indulgences, dated August 4, 1837, in which Rescript he also confirmed afresh the above-named Indulgences.

30. THE THREE HOURS' AGONY ON GOOD FRIDAY AND ANY OTHER FRIDAY.

In order to animate all faithful Christians to a grateful correspondence with the love of Jesus, who for our redemption suffered three hours of most bitter agony upon the cross, and to renew in our minds the memory of that day and those very hours on which He suffered for love of us; the servant of God, Father Alphonsus Messia, of the Company of Jesus, who died on January 4, 1732, in the city of Lima in Peru, many years before his death devised and practised this devotion in those cities, beginning it on Good Friday at midday, and continuing it on for the three following hours, up to that moment when we make the yearly remembrance of the death of our Divine Redeemer. This tender devotion was introduced into Rome about the year 1788, and is now spread over the whole Catholic world. The more to increase this devotion, with the greatest fruit to the souls of the faithful, Pope Pius VII., *motu proprio*, by a decree of the S. Congr. of Indulgences, dated Feb. 14, 1815, granted for ever -
i. The plenary indulgence to all the faithful who, being truly penitent, having Confessed and Communicated on Holy Thursday, or intending to Communicate in Easter week, praying also for the intention of the Sovereign Pontiff, shall, either in public or private, alone or in company with others, under the direction of a priest or sacred minister, or with the aid of some book approved for this purpose, practise this devotional exercise on Good Friday for three hours together either by meditating according to their abilities on the sufferings of Jesus Christ, during the three hours He hung on the cross, and on the seven words He then uttered, or else, instead of meditation, by reciting certain psalms, hymns, or other prayers.
ii. The indulgence of 200 days, any Friday in the year, to every one who, in remembrance of, and out of devotion to, the agony of our Blessed Lord, shall spend some time in prayer in a church, praying as above.
iii. The plenary indulgence once every month to every one who, having meditated and prayed every previous Friday in the month, in the way just mentioned, shall, after Confession and Communion, * renew on the last Friday this devotion of the Three Hours' Agony of Jesus Christ in the way already

indicated for Good Friday.
(* This Communion may be made in the following week.)

31. PRAYERS TO THE MOST HOLY WOUNDS.

Pope Pius VII., by a Rescript of time S. Congr. of Indulgences, dated Sept. 29, 1807, granted -
i. The indulgence of 100 days, daily, to all the faithful who shall devoutly recite the following prayers to the Five Sacred Wounds of Jesus Christ.
ii. The plenary indulgence, besides the above partial Indulgence, twice a year, - that is, on the two feasts, first, that of the Invention (May 3), and, secondly, that of the Exaltation, of the holy Cross (Sept. 14), - to all who shall say these prayers at least ten times a month, if, after having Confessed and Communicated on the above-named feast, they shall visit a church, and pray there according to the mind of the Sovereign Pontiff.
iii. The indulgence of seven years and seven quarantines, daily, to those who say these prayers from Passion Sunday to Holy Saturday, inclusive. Plenary on Easter Day, if, after Confession and Communion on that day, they should visit and pray as aforesaid.

THE PRAYERS.

Act of Contrition.

As I kneel before Thee on the cross, most loving Saviour of my soul, my conscience reproaches me with having nailed Thee to that cross with these hands of mine, as often as I have fallen into mortal sin, wearying Thee with my monstrous ingratitude. My God, my chief and most perfect Good, worthy of all my love, for the many blessings Thou hast ever bestowed upon me; I cannot now undo my misdeeds as I would most willingly; but I will loathe them, grieving greatly for having offended Thee who art Infinite Goodness! And now, kneeling at Thy feet, I will try at least to compassionate Thee, to give Thee thanks, to ask of Thee pardon and contrition; wherefore with heart and lips I say:

To the first Wound, of the Left Foot.
Holy wound of the Left Foot of my Jesus! I adore Thee, I compassionate Thee for the most bitter pain which Thou didst suffer. I thank Thee for the love whereby Thou wast wearied in overtaking me on the way to ruin, and didst bleed amid the thorns and brambles of my sins. I offer to the Eternal Father the pain and love of Thy most holy humanity, in atonement for my sins, all

75

which I detest with sincere and bitter contrition.

Pater noster. Ave Maria. Gloria Patri.

Holy Mother, pierce me through,
In my heart each wound renew
Of my Saviour crucified.

To the Second Wound, of the Right Foot.
Holy wound of the Right Foot of my Jesus! I adore Thee, I compassionate Thee for the bitter pain which Thou didst suffer. I thank Thee for that love which pierced Thee with such torture and shedding of blood in order to punish my wanderings and the guilty pleasures I have granted to my unbridled passions. I offer the Eternal Father all the pain and love of Thy most holy humanity, and I pray unto Thee for grace to weep over my transgressions with burning tears, and to enable me to persevere in the good which I have begun, without ever swerving again from my obedience to the commandments of my God.

Pater noster. Ave Maria. Gloria Patri.

Holy Mother, &c.

To the Third Wound, of the Left hand.
Holy wound of the Left Hand of my Jesus! I adore Thee, I compassionate Thee for the bitter pain which Thou didst suffer. I thank Thee for having, in Thy love, spared me the scourges and eternal damnation which my sins had merited. I offer to the Eternal Father the pain and love of Thy most holy humanity, and I pray Thee to teach me how to turn to good account my span of life, and bring forth in it worthy fruits of penance, and so disarm the justice of God, which I have provoked.

Pater noster. Ave Maria. Gloria Patri.

Holy Mother, &c.

To the Fourth Wound, of the Right Hand.
Holy wound of the Right Hand of my Jesus! I adore Thee, I compassionate Thee for the bitter pain which Thou didst suffer. I thank Thee for Thy graces lavished on me with such love, in spite of all my most perverse obstinacy. I offer to the Eternal Father all the pain and love of Thy most holy humanity, and I pray Thee to change my heart and its affections, and make me do all my actions in accordance with the will of God.

Pater noster. Ave Maria. Gloria Patri.

Holy Mother, &c.

To the Fifth Wound, of the Sacred Side.
Holy wound in the side of my Jesus! I adore Thee, I compassionate Thee for the cruel insult Thou didst suffer. I thank Thee, my Jesus, for the love which suffered Thy side and heart to be pierced, that so the last drops of blood and water might issue forth, making my redemption to abound. I offer to the Eternal Father this outrage, and the love of Thy most holy Humanity, that my soul may enter once for all into that most loving Heart, eager and ready to receive the greatest sinners, and never more depart.

Pater noster. Ave Maria. Gloria Patri.

Holy Mother, &c.

TO THE MOST HOLY VIRGIN, MOTHER OF SORROWS.

Mary, Virgin Mother of God, Martyr of love and sorrow, in witnessing the pains and torments of Jesus: truly didst thou concur in the great work of my redemption, first by thy innumerable afflictions, and then by the offering thou didst make to the Eternal Father of His and thy Only-begotten for a holocaust and victim of propitiation for my sins. I compassionate thee for the bitter pain which thou didst suffer, I thank thee for that love, well-nigh infinite, through which thou didst bereave thyself of the fruit of thy womb, very God and very Man, to save me, a sinner; let thy intercession, which never returneth to thee void, be ever interposed with the Father and the Son for me; that I may steadily amend my evil ways, and never, by further faults, crucify afresh my loving Saviour; that so, persevering in His grace until death, I may obtain eternal life, through the merits of His dolorous Passion and Death upon the cross.

Three Ave Maria's.

Oremus.
Domine Jesu Christe, qui hora sexta pro redemptione mundi crucis patibulum ascendisti, et Sanguinem tuum pretiosum in remissionem peccatorum effudisti: te humiliter deprecamur, ut post obitum nostrum Paradisi januas nos gaudenter introire concedas.

Interveniat pro nobis, quaesumus Domino Jesu Christe, nunc et in hora mortis nostrae apud tuam clementiam Beata Virgo Maria Mater tua, cujus sacratissimam animam in hora tuae Passionis doloris gladius pertransivit. Per te, Jesu Christe Salvator mundi, qui cum Patre et Spiritu Sancto vivis et regnas in saecula saeculorum. R. Amen.

TRANSLATION.

Let us pray.
O Lord Jesus Christ, who at the sixth hour of the day didst, for the redemption of the world, mount the gibbet of the cross, and shed Thy Precious Blood for the remission of sins; we humbly beseech Thee to grant us, after our deaths, a joyful entrance into the gates of Paradise.

Grant, we beseech Thee, O Lord Jesus Christ, that now, and at the hour of our death, blessed Mary ever Virgin, Thy Mother, may intercede for us, through whose most holy soul the sword passed in the hour of Thy Passion. Through Thee, Jesus Christ, Saviour of the world, who with the Father and the Holy Ghost livest and reignest for ever and ever. Amen.

32. CHAPLET OF THE FIVE WOUNDS.

At the prayer of the Congregation of Discalced Clerks of the Passion of our Lord Jesus Christ here in Rome, in the Retreat of SS. John and Paul, Pope Leo XII, of holy memory, by a decree of the S. Congr. of Indulgences, dated Dec. 20, 1823, granted the following Indulgences to all the faithful who, being contrite of heart, shall say with devotion the Chaplet of the Five Wounds of our Divine Redeemer, Jesus Christ, at the same time meditating upon them.
i. An indulgence of one year, to be gained once a day by saying this chaplet.
ii. A plenary indulgence (besides the above partial Indulgence) three times a year, that is on any one Friday in March, on the Feast of the Invention, and of the Exaltation of the Holy Cross, or on any one day in the octave of these feasts, to all who shall have practised the devotion of saying this Chaplet at least ten times each month provided that on the aforesaid day, being truly penitent, having confessed and received the Holy Communion, they shall pray according to the intention of the Sovereign Pontiff.
The Sovereign Pontiff Pius IX., by a decree of the S. Congr. of Indulgences, dated August 11, 1851, extended this Plenary Indulgence to the feasts of this Nativity, Circumcision, and Epiphany of our Lord Jesus Christ, the feasts of His Most Holy Name, Easter Sunday, the Ascension, Corpus Christi, and the Transfiguration, or any one day in the octaves of these feasts, on the same conditions as above.
iii. An indulgence of seven years and seven quarantines to all who shall say this Chaplet from Passion Sunday to holy Saturday inclusive; and the plenary indulgence, when they fulfil the Paschal precept.
The condition of gaining all these Indulgences is, that the Chaplet used should be blessed by the most reverend the Father-General of the said Congregation,

or by some other priest of the Congregation to whom the General has communicated the faculty received by him in virtue of the above-named decree; after they have been blessed, they cannot be sold or lent, or given away to others, &c., for the purpose of communicating to them the Indulgences, according to the general decrees of the S. Congr. of Indulgences, dated Feb. 6, 1657, June 5, 1721, and Feb. 9, 1820. This chaplet consists of five sets, of five beads each; and at each one of these beads, in memory of the Five Wounds of Jesus Christ, one *Gloria Patri*is to be said; and at the end of each set of five, one *Ave Maria* is added in devotion to our Lady's sorrows.

33. THE PRAYER, "DEUS QUI PRO REDEMPTIONE", ETC., WITH FIVE "PATER NOSTER'S" "AVE MARIA'S" AND "GLORIA PATRI'S."

Pope Pius VII., by a decree of the S. Congr. of Indulgences, dated Aug. 25, 1820, granted to all the faithful who should say with contrition the above-named prayer, composed by St. Augustine, with five *Pater noster's*, five *Ave Maria's*, and five *Gloria Patri's*, in memory of the Passion and Death of Jesus Christ -
i. An indulgence of 300 days, once a day.
ii. A plenary indulgence to all who shall have said it every day for a month to be granted on any one of the three last days of the month, when, after Confession and Communion, they shall pray for the intention of the Sovereign Pontiff.
The prayer, which may also be said for a soul in its agony, is to be found above; to it are to be added five *Pater noster's*, five *Ave Maria's*, and five *Gloria Patri's*.

34. PRAYER, "EN EGO," ETC., BEFORE A CRUCIFIX.

Pope Pius VII., by a decree of the S. Congr. of Indulgences, dated April 10, 1821, granted -
A plenary indulgence to all who shall devoutly say the following prayer before any representation of Jesus crucified, with contrite hearts, praying for the wants of Holy Church, after Confession and Communion.

En ego, O bone et dulcissime Jesu, ante conspectum tuum genibus me provolvo ac maximo animi ardore te oro atque obtestor ut meum in cor vividos fidei, spei, et charitatis sensus, atque veram peccatorum meorum poenitentiam, eaque emendandi firmissimam voluntatem velis imprimere: dum magno animi affectu et dolore, tua quinque Vulnera mecum ipse considero, ac mente contemplor, illud prae oculis habens, quod jam in ore ponebat suo David Propheta de Te, O bone Jesu: "Foderunt manus Meas et pedes Meos; dinumeraverunt omnia ossa Mea."

O good and sweetest Jesus, before Thy face I humbly kneel, and with all fervour of soul I pray and beseech Thee to vouchsafe to fix deep in my heart lively sentiments of faith, hope, and charity, true contrition for my sins, and a most firm purpose of amendment; whilst I contemplate with great sorrow and love Thy five Wounds, and ponder them over in my mind, having before my eyes the words which, long ago, David the prophet spoke in his own person concerning Thee, my Jesus: "Foderunt manus Meas et pedes Meos; dinumeraverunt omnia ossa Mea," - They digged My hands and My feet; they numbered all My bones." Ps. xxi. 17,18.

APPENDIX

170. VISIT TO THE TWO STAIRS PLACED RESIDE THE SCALA SANTA OR HOLY STAIRCASE.

By a Brief of December 9, 1856, the Sovereign Pontiff Pius IX. grants to all the faithful who, after Confession and Communion, shall, on the Feast of All Saints, and on any day during the Octave of the Commemoration of the Faithful Departed, or on any day from Christmas Day to the Feast of the Epiphany inclusive, as well as during the whole time of Lent, mount upon their knees the stairs placed on either side of the said Holy Staircase, and who, whilst doing so, shall pray according to custom, or meditate on the Passion of our Lord Jesus Christ, the same Indulgences, collectively and individually, as would be gained if they actually ascended the Holy Staircase itself on their knees. See above.

171. PRAYER OF ST. PIUS V., "O MY LORD JESUS CHRIST CRUCIFIED," ETC.

His Holiness Pope Pius IX., by a Rescript of May 24, 1859, which is preserved in the Secretary's Office of the Holy Congregation of Indulgences, vouchsafed to grant -
The indulgence of 60 days to all the faithful every time that, with contrite heart and devotion, they shall say the following prayers, composed by the Holy Pontiff Pius V., and which he was accustomed to say at the time of his labours

and business of importance: provided that the faithful when they say these prayers (known commonly as the Five *Credo's* of St. Pius V.) intend to apply them to peace and concord amongst Christian princes, to the extirpation of heresies, and the exaltation of our holy Mother the Church, &c. Moreover, to those who for a month together shall have said them every day he granted - The plenary indulgence, to be gained on that day when, having Confessed and Communicated, they shall apply them as above directed.

THE PRAYERS.

i. O my Lord Jesus Christ crucified, Son of the most Blessed Virgin Mary, open Thy ears, and listen to me as Thou didst listen to Thy eternal Father upon Mount Tabor.
Say then a Credo.

ii. O my Lord Jesus Christ crucified, Son of the most Blessed Virgin Mary, open Thine eyes, and look upon me as Thou didst look from the tree of the Cross upon Thy dear Mother sorrowing and afflicted.
Credo.

iii. O my Lord Jesus Christ crucified, Son of the most Blessed Virgin Mary, open Thy blessed mouth, and speak as Thou didst speak to St. John when Thou gavest him for son to Thine own most beloved Mother.
Credo.

iv. O my Lord Jesus Christ crucified, Son of the most Blessed Virgin Mary, open Thine arms, and embrace me as Thou didst open them upon the Cross to embrace the whole human race.
Credo.

v.   O my Lord Jesus Christ crucified, Son of the Blessed Virgin Mary, open Thy Heart, and receive therein my heart, and hear me in all that I ask of Thee, if so be it be agreeable to Thy most holy will.
Credo.

PRECIOUS BLOOD OF JESUS

35. CHAPLET.

Pope Pius VII., in order to inflame the hearts of the faithful with devotion to the Precious Blood of Jesus Christ, wherewith we were redeemed, granted by two Rescripts, one of May 31, 1809, kept in the acts of the Congregation of Rites, the other of Oct. 18, 1815, in the Archivium of the Archconfraternity of the Precious Blood, erected at St. Nicholas in Carcer, here in Rome -

i. An indulgence of seven years and seven quarantines, once a day, to all who shall say with devotion the Chaplet in honour of the Precious Blood of Jesus Christ.

ii. A plenary indulgence, once a month, to all who, having said it every day for a month, shall Confess and Communicate, and pray for the holy Church, &c.

iii. Three hundred days indulgence, daily, to all who say the prayer, "Most Precious Blood, &c.," for which see below.

This Chaplet is composed of seven Mysteries, in which we meditate upon the seven times in which Jesus Christ for love of us shed blood from His most innocent Body; at each Mystery, except the last, we are to say five *Pater noster's* and one *Gloria Patri*; and at the last, three *Pater noster's* only and one *Gloria Patri*; thus making up the number of thirty-three *Pater noster's* in remembrance of the thirty-three years during which the Precious Blood of Jesus flowed in His veins, before it was all poured out for our salvation. The Chaplet ends with the devout prayer, "Most Precious Blood, &c."

THE CHAPLET.

V. Deus in adjutorium meum intende.
R. Domine ad adiuvandum me festina.
V. Gloria Patri, &c.
R. Sicut erat, &c.

FIRST MYSTERY.

The first time our loving Saviour shed His Precious Blood for its was on the eighth day after His birth, when He was circumcised in order to accomplish the law of Moses. While, then, we reflect that Jesus did this to satisfy the justice of God for our dissolute lives, let us excite ourselves to true sorrow for them, and promise, with the help of his all-powerful grace, to be henceforth truly chaste in body and in soul.

Five Pater noster's *and one* Gloria Patri.

V. Te ergo quaesumus tuis famulis subveni, quos pretioso Sanguine redemisti.
We beseech Thee, therefore, help Thy servants, whom Thou hast redeemed with Thy Precious Blood.

SECOND MYSTERY.

Next, in the Garden of Olives, Jesus shed His Blood for us in such quantity that it bathed the earth around. Thus took place at the sight of the ingratitude with which men would meet His love. O, let us, then, repent sincerely because we have hitherto corresponded so ill with the innumerable benefits of our God, and resolve to make good use of His graces and holy inspirations.

Five Pater noster's *and one* Gloria Patri.

V. Te ergo quaesumus, &c.

THIRD MYSTERY.

Next, in His cruel scourging, Jesus shed His Blood, when His flesh was so torn that rivers of Blood flowed from His body in every part, all of which He offered all the time to His Eternal Father in payment of our impatience and our delicacy. How is it, then, we do not curb our anger and our self-love? Henceforth we will indeed try our very best to bear our troubles well, and, despising ourselves, to take peacefully the injuries which men may do us.

Five Pater noster's *and one* Gloria Patri.

V. Te ergo quaesumus, &c.

FOURTH MYSTERY.

Again, from the sacred Head of Jesus Blood poured down when it was crowned with thorns, in punishment of our pride and evil thoughts. Shall we, then, continue to nurture haughtiness, foster foul imaginations, and feed the wayward will in our minds? Henceforth let there be ever before our eyes our utter nothingness, our misery, and our weakness; and with generous hearts let its resist all the wicked suggestions of the devil.

Five Pater noster's *and one* Gloria Patri.

V. Te ergo quaesumus, &c.

FIFTH MYSTERY.

But O! how much of His Precious Blood did our loving Lord pour forth from His veins when laden with the heavy wood of the cross. He made His mournful way to Calvary, so that the streets and ways of Jerusalem, through which He passed, were watered with it! this was done in satisfaction for the scandals and the bad examples by which His own creatures had led others astray on the way to ruin. Who can tell how many of us are of this unhappy number? Who knows how many he himself alone has by his own bad example brought down to hell? And have we done anything to remedy this evil? L et us henceforth at least endeavour all we can to save souls by word and by example, making ourselves a pattern to all of good and holy life.

Five Pater noster's *and one* Gloria Patri.

V. Te ergo quaesumus, &c.

SIXTH MYSTERY.

Still more copiously the Redeemer of mankind shed Blood in His barbarous Crucifixion; when His veins being rent and arteries burst, there gushed forth in a torrent, from His hands and His feet, that saving balm of life eternal, to pay for all the crimes and enormities of the universe. Who ever after this would continue in sin, and so renew the cruel crucifixion of the Son of God? Let us weep bitterly for our bad deeds, and let us detest them at the feet of the sacred minister of God; let us amend our evil ways, and henceforth begin a truly Christian life, with the thought ever in our hearts of all the Blood which our eternal salvation cost the Saviour of men.

Five Pater noster's *and one* Gloria Patri.

V. Te ergo quaesumus, &c.

SEVENTH MYSTERY.

Last of all, after His death, when His sacred Side was opened by the lance and His loving Heart was wounded, Jesus shed Blood, and with the Blood there came forth water, to show us how the Blood was all poured out to the last drop for our salvation. O the infinite goodness of our Redeemer! Who will not love Thee, my Saviour? What heart will not consume itself away for love of Thee, who hast done all this for our redemption? The tongue wants words to praise Thee: let us, then, invite all creatures upon earth, all angels and all saints in Paradise, and, most of all, our dear Mother Mary, to bless, to praise, and to celebrate Thy most Precious Blood. Glory to the Blood of Jesus! Glory to the Blood of Jesus now and ever throughout all ages. Amen.

At this last Mystery three Pater noster's *and one* Gloria Patri *are to be said, to make up the number of thirty-three.*

V. Te ergo quaesumus, &c.

Then say the following

PRAYER.

Most Precious Blood of life eternal! price and ransom of the whole universe! drink and bath of the soul! ever pleading the cause of man before the throne of heavenly Mercy; I adore Thee most profoundly: I would, if I were able, make Thee some compensation for the outrages and wrongs Thou dost ever suffer from men, and especially from those who in their rashness dare to blaspheme Thee. Who will not bless this Blood of value infinite? who does not feel himself inflamed with the love of Jesus, who shed it all for us? What should I be but for this Blood, which hath redeemed me? And who drew it out of the veins of my Lord, even unto the last drop? It was love. O immense love, which gave to us this saving Balsam! O Balsam beyond all price, streaming forth from the Fount of immeasurable love! Give to all hearts, all tongues, power to praise, celebrate, and thank Thee, now and ever, and throughout all eternity. Amen.

V. Redemisti nos, Domine, in Sanguine tuo.
R. Et fecisti nos Deo nostro regnum.

Oremus.
Omnipotens sempiterne Deus, qui Unigenitum Filium tuum mundi Redemptorem constituisti, ac ejus Sanguine placari voluisti: concede nobis, quaesumus, salutis nostrae pretium ita venerari, atque praesentis vitae malis ejus virtute defendi in terris, ut fructu perpetuo laetemur in coelis. Qui tecum vivit et regnat in unitate, &c. Amen.

TRANSLATION.

V. Then hast redeemed us, O Lord, with Thy Blood.
R. And hast made us a kingdom to our God.

Let us pray.
Almighty and Everlasting God, who hast appointed Thine only-begotten Son the Saviour of the world, and hast willed to be appeased with His Blood; grant us, we beseech Thee, so to venerate this Blood, the price of our salvation, and so to be defended by its power upon earth from the evils of this present life, that in heaven we may enjoy its everlasting fruit. Who liveth and reigneth with Thee in the Unity of the Holy Ghost, world without end. Amen.

85

36. SEVEN OFFERINGS, WITH SEVEN "GLORIA PATRI'S."

Pope Pius VII., of holy memory, by a Rescript of the *Segretaria* of the Memorials of Sept. 22, 1817, kept in the Archivium of the Archconfraternity of the Precious Blood, granted -

i. An indulgence of 300 days to all the faithful who, with contrite hearts, shall make to the Eternal Father the following offerings of the Precious Blood of His well-beloved Son Jesus Christ, together with seven *Gloria Patri's*, and an ejaculation with the intention of making thereby a compensation for all the outrages which are done to the Precious Blood, which is the price and ransom of our souls.

ii. A plenary indulgence to all who say them for a month together, on any one day, once in the month, when, after Confession and Communion, they shall pray according to the intention of the Sovereign Pontiff.

THE OFFERINGS.

I. Eternal Father! I offer Thee the merits of the Precious Blood of Jesus, Thy well-beloved Son, my Saviour and my God, for the propagation and exaltation of my dear Mother Thy holy Church, for the safety and prosperity of her visible head, our chief pastor the Bishop of Rome; for the cardinals, bishops, and pastors of souls, and for all the ministers of the sanctuary.

Then say one Gloria Patri, *and the ejaculation,*

Blessed and praised for evermore be Jesus, who hath saved us with His Blood.

II. Eternal Father! I offer Thee the merits of the Precious Blood of Jesus, Thy well-beloved Son, my Saviour and my God, for the peace and concord of Catholic kings and princes, for the humiliation of the enemies of our Holy Faith, and for the welfare of all Christian people.

One Gloria Patri, *and* Blessed and praised, *&c.*

III. Eternal Father! I offer Thee the merits of the Precious Blood of Jesus, Thy well-beloved Son, my Saviour and my God, for the repentance of unbelievers, the uprooting of heresy, and the conversion of sinners.

One Gloria Patri, *and* Blessed and praised, *&c.*

IV. Eternal Father! I offer Thee the merits of the Precious Blood of Jesus, Thy well-beloved Son, my Saviour and my God, for all my relations, friends, and enemies; for the poor, the sick, and the afflicted, and for all those for whom Thou my God knowest that I ought to pray, or wouldst have me pray.

One Gloria Patri, *and* Blessed and praised, *&c.*

V. Eternal Father! I offer Thee the merits of the Precious Blood of Jesus, Thy well-beloved Son, my Saviour and my God, for all who this day are passing to the other life; that Thou wouldst save them from the pains of Hell, and admit them quickly to the possession of Thy glory.

One Gloria Patri, *and* Blessed and praised, *&c.*

VI. Eternal Father! I offer Thee the merits of the Precious Blood of Jesus, Thy well-beloved Son, my Saviour and my God, for all those who love this great treasure, for those who join with me in adoring it and honouring it, and for those who strive to spread devotion to it.

One Gloria Patri, *and* Blessed and praised, *&c.*

VII. Eternal Father! I offer Thee the merits of the Precious Blood of Jesus, Thy well-beloved Son, my Saviour and my God, for all my wants, spiritual and temporal, in suffrage for the holy souls in purgatory, and chiefly for these who were most devout to this Blood, the price of our redemption, and to the sorrows and pains of our dear Mother, most holy Mary.

One Gloria Patri, *and* Blessed and praised, *&c.*

Glory be to the Blood of Jesus, new and for ever, and throughout all ages. Amen.

37. PRAYER. DEVOUT ASPIRATIONS.

The same Pope Pius VII., by a Rescript of Oct. 18, 1815, kept in the same Archivium as the above, granted -
The Indulgence of 300 days for the prayer given above, Most Precious Blood, &c.
He granted also by the same Rescript the Indulgence of 100 days daily, to every one who makes the following aspirations.

THE ASPIRATIONS.

Viva, Viva Jesù!

Glory be to Jesus!
Who in bitter pains

Pour'd for me the life-blood
From His sacred veins.

Grace and life eternal
In that Blood I find;
Bless'd be His compassion,
Infinitely kind!

Bless'd through endless ages
Be the precious stream,
Which from endless torment
Doth the world redeem.

There the fainting spirit
Drinks of life her fill;
There, as in a fountain,
Laves herself at will.

O the Blood of Christ!
It soothes the Father's ire;
Open the gate of heaven,
Quells eternal fire.

Abel's blood for vengeance
Pleaded to the skies;
But the Blood of Jesus
For our pardon cries.

Oft as it is sprinkled
On our guilty hearts,
Satan in confusion
Terror-struck departs.

Oft as earth exulting
Wafts its praise on high,
Hell with terror trembles,
Heaven is filled with joy.

Lift ye, then, your voices;
Swell the mighty flood;
Louder still and louder,
Praise the Precious Blood.

38. EJACULATION OR OFFERING.

The same Pope Pius VII., by a Rescript signed with his own hand, March 22, 1817 (kept in the Archivium of the Congregation of Passionist Fathers at their retreat of SS. John and Paul, here in Rome), granted -
The Indulgence of 100 days to all the faithful, every time they nay the following Ejaculation, or Offering of the Precious Blood of Jesus Christ to the Eternal Father.

Eternal Father! I offer Thee the Precious Blood of Jesus, in satisfaction for my sins, and for the wants of Holy Church.

39. ANOTHER OFFERING, WITH ONE "PATER NOSTER," "AVE MARIA," AND " GLORIA PATRI."

Pope Leo XII., of holy memory, by his Rescript of Oct. 25, 1825 (kept in the Archivium of the FF. Minor Observants of Ara Coeli, here in Rome), granted to all the faithful -
i. The indulgence of 100 days every time they devoutly say the following Offering of this Most Precious Blood of our Lord Jesus Christ to the Eternal Father, to obtain His heavenly blessing, with one *Pater noster,* one *Ave Maria,* and one *Gloria Patri,* to the most Holy Trinity, in thanksgiving for blessings received.
ii. The Plenary indulgence to those who say it daily for a month, at the end of this month, on any one day when, after having Confessed and Communicated, they shall pray according to the intention of the Sovereign Pontiff.

THE OFFERING.

Eternal Father! we offer Thee the most Precious Blood of Jesus, shed for us with such great love and bitter pain from His Right Hand; and through the merits and the efficacy of that Blood, we entreat thy Divine Majesty to grant us Thy Holy benediction, in order that we may be defended thereby from all our enemies, and be set free from every ill; whilst we say, "Benedictio Dei omnipotentis, Patris et Filii et Spiritus Sancti, descendat super nos, et maneat semper. Amen."

Pater, Ave, *and* Gloria, *as before mentioned.*

40. SHORT CHAPLET OF THE PRECIOUS BLOOD.

By a grant of Pope Gregory XVI., of July 5, 1843, the Indulgence mentioned above, for saying the Chaplet of the Precious Blood, may all be gained by saying the following short Chaplet; and any one who cannot meditate, may gain them by only saying devoutly the thirty-three *Pater noster's* which make up the Chaplet.

THE SHORT CHAPLET.

V. Deus in adjutorium meum intende.
ii. Domine ad adjuvandum me festina.
Gloria Patri, &c.

First Mystery.
Jesus shed Blood in His Circumcision.

Five Pater noster's, *one* Gloria, *and*

Te ergo quaesumus tuis famulis subveni, quos pretioso Sanguine redemisti. We beseech Thee, therefore, help Thy servants, whom Thou hast redeemed with Thy Precious Blood.

Second Mystery.
Jesus shed Blood in the Agony in the Garden.

Five Pater noster's, *one* Gloria.
Te ergo quaesumus &c.

Third Mystery.
Jesus shed Blood in His Scourging.

Five Pater noster's, *one* Gloria.
Te ergo quaesumus &c.

Fourth Mystery.
Jesus shed Blood in His crowning with Thorns.

Five Pater noster's, *one* Gloria.
Te ergo quaesumus &c.

Fifth Mystery.
Jesus shed Blood in carrying His Cross.

Five Pater noster's, *one* Gloria.
Te ergo quaesumus &c.

Sixth Mystery.
Jesus shed Blood in His Crucifixion.

Five Pater noster's, *one* Gloria.
Te ergo quaesumus &c.

Seventh Mystery.
Jesus shed Blood and Water from His wounded Side.

Five Pater noster's, *one* Gloria.
Te ergo quaesumus &c.

PRAYER.

Most Precious Blood, &c., <u>as above.</u>

V. Redemisti, &c.
R. Et fecisti nos, &c.

Oremus.
Omnipotens sempiterne Deus, &c.
<u>*All as above.*</u>

41. DEVOTION OF THE MONTH CONSECRATED TO THE BLOOD OF JESUS CHRIST.

Pope Pius IX., by a Rescript of June 4, 1850, kept in the Archivium of the Congregation of Missionaries of the Precious Blood, granted to all the faithful
-
i. An indulgence of seven years and seven quarantines, for every day of "the month consecrated to the Blood of Jesus Christ," on whatever day the month may begin by the custom of any public church or oratory, the condition of gaining the Indulgence being to assist at the devotion with contrition.
ii. A plenary indulgence to all who shall assist at it at least ten times in the month; which they may gain in the course of the said month, or on one of the seven days immediately following it, if, having Confessed and Communicated, they shall visit a church or public oratory, and pray there for a time according to the mind of the Sovereign Pontiff.
iii. An indulgence of 300 days to those who shall practise this devotion in private, with devout prayers and good actions in honour of the Precious Blood.
iv. A plenary indulgence, if they shall practise it for a month together, provided that on the last day of the month, or one of the seven following days, they go to Confession and Communion, visit a church, and pray as aforesaid.

42. FEAST OF THE MOST PRECIOUS BLOOD.

The same Pope Pius IX., by the same Rescript of June 4, 1850, granted to all the faithful -
A plenary indulgence, (1) for the first Sunday of July (the day appointed for the Feast of the Precious Blood), and (2) for the Friday after the Fourth Sunday in Lent (when the Church recites the Office of the Precious Blood), beginning from the first vespers of those days, provided that they go to Confession and Communion, and visit the Church of the Archconfraternity or Confraternity of the Precious Blood, or else the church where has been established the Confraternity or Pious Union aggregated to the principal Archconfraternity, and bearing the same title.

43. THREE OFFERINGS OF THE PRECIOUS BLOOD.

At the prayer of several devout members of the Pious Union erected in Rome, under the protection of the Immaculate Conception of our Blessed Lady, the same Pope Pius IX., by an autograph Rescript of June 18, 1851, kept in the *Segretaria* of the S. Congr. of Indulgences, granted certain indulgences to all who say the following Offering of the Precious Blood of our Lord Jesus Christ to the Most Holy Trinity, in thanksgiving for the gifts and privileges with which the most holy Virgin Mary, Mother of God, was enriched, most especially those which she received in her Immaculate Conception, viz.
i. An indulgence of 300 days every time they are said with contrition, together with the accompanying prayer to the Blessed Virgin.
ii. A plenary indulgence to all who say them every day for an entire month, to be gained on that day when, after Confession and Communion, they shall visit a church or public oratory, and pray there for a time according to the intention of his Holiness.

THE OFFERINGS.

i. Eternal Father! in Union with the most Holy and Immaculate Virgin and in her name, and in union with and in the name of all the Blessed in heaven and of all the elect upon earth, I offer Thee the most Precious Blood of Jesus Christ in thanksgiving for the gifts and privileges with which Thou hast enriched Mary, as Thy most obedient Daughter, particularly in her Immaculate Conception. I offer Thee also His Precious Blood for the conversion of poor sinners, for the propagation and exaltation of Thy Holy Church, for the safety and prosperity of our chief pastor the Bishop of Rome, and according to his intentions.

Gloria Patri, &c.

ii. Eternal and Incarnate Word! in union with the most Holy and Immaculate Virgin and in her name, and in union with and in the name of all the Blessed in heaven and of all the elect upon earth, I offer Thee Thine own most Precious Blood in thanksgiving for the gifts and privileges with which Thou hast enriched Mary, as Thy most loving Mother, particularly in her Immaculate Conception. I offer Thee also this Precious Blood for the conversion of poor sinners, for the propagation and exaltation of Thy holy Church, for the safety and prosperity of our chief pastor the Bishop of Rome, and according to his intentions.

Gloria Patri, &c.

iii. Holy and Eternal Spirit! in union with the most Holy and Immaculate Virgin and in her name, and in union with and in the name of all the blessed in heaven and of all the elect upon earth, I offer Thee the most Precious Blood of Jesus in thanksgiving for the gifts and privileges with which Thou hast enriched Mary, as Thy most faithful Spouse, particularly in her immaculate Conception. I offer Thee also this Precious Blood for the conversion of poor sinners, for the propagation and exaltation of Thy Holy Church, for the safety and prosperity of our chief pastor the Bishop of Rome, and according to his intentions.

Gloria Patri, &c.

PRAYER TO THE MOST HOLY VIRGIN.

Mary, Mother of God, most Holy and Immaculate Virgin, by the love thou dost ever bear to God, by the gratitude thou hast towards him, for the manifold graces and favours with which thou wast enriched by Him, particularly for the privilege granted to thee alone of thy Immaculate Conception, and by the infinite merits of Jesus Christ, thy Divine Son our Lord, we pray thee most earnestly to obtain for us a most perfect and constant devotion towards thyself, and a full trust that through thy most mighty intercession we shall receive all the graces which we ask; certain therefore now of obtaining them from thy great goodness, with hearts overflowing with joy and thankfulness we venerate thee, repeating the salutation which the holy archangel Gabriel made to thee.

Ave Maria, &c.

44. FEAST AND OCTAVE OF CORPUS CHRISTI.

Pope Urban IV. in his Constitution *Transiturus*, of Aug. 11, 1264, established the Feast of Corpus Christi, with an octave, to be celebrated throughout the whole Catholic world, in remembrance of the institution of the adorable Sacrament of the Most Holy Eucharist by our Blessed Saviour before His Passion, which is commemorated by the Church only in the Mass of Holy Thursday. This holy Pontiff, being desirous that all the faithful should give God due thanks for this inestimable benefit, and be excited to meet their Lord's love in this most holy Sacrament with grateful hearts, granted in the said Constitution several Indulgences to the faithful, which were again augmented by Pope Martin V. in his Constitution *Ineffabile*, of May 26, 1429. Afterwards Pope Eugenius IV., in his Constitution *Excellentissimum*, of May 20, 1433, confirmed the Indulgences of Martin V., and added others, as follows -
i. An indulgence of 200 days, on the vigil of the Feast of Corpus Christi to all who, being truly contrite and having confessed, shall fast, or do some other good work enjoined them by their confessor.
ii. An indulgence of 400 days, on the feast itself, to all who, being contrite and having Confessed, shall devoutly assist at or be present at any of the following functions: First or Second Vespers, Matins, and Mass. An indulgence of 160 days for each of the Little hours, Prime, Terce, Sext, None, and Compline.
iii. An indulgence of 200 days, during the octave, for each Vespers, Matins, and Mass. An indulgence of 80 days for each of the Little Hours.
iv. An indulgence of 200 days for accompanying the procession of the Blessed Sacrament, which takes place on the Feast or during the Octave, to every priest who has said Mass, and to every layman who has gone to Communion on any one of these days, and who shall pray for the Holy Church, &c.
v. Ann indulgence of 200 days for accompanying the procession made by the Confraternity of the Blessed Sacrament on the third Sunday of the month, and on Holy Thursday.

N.B. Members of Confraternities of the Blessed Sacrament enjoy many other Indulgences which have been granted to them by Pope Paul V., in the Brief *Cum certas uniquique*, of Nov. 3, 1606, wherever these Confraternities have been, or shall be, canonically erected; which Indulgences were confirmed by the same Pope Paul V., by a decree of the S. Congr. of Indulgences, Feb. 15, 1608, and by Pope Clement X., by a decree of the same S. Congr., April 23, 1677. And the Sovereign Pontiff, Pius IX., by a decree of the S. Congr. of Indulgences of June 14, 1853, extended these Indulgences, and added many more besides to time Pious Union canonically erected in Rome in the year 1852, for accompanying the most holy Viaticum.

45. THE "HOUR SANCTIFIED" ON HOLY THURSDAY, ON CORPUS CHRISTI, AND ANY OTHER THURSDAY.

In order to awaken the gratitude of the faithful towards their Lord and Saviour Jesus Christ, for His institution of the holy Eucharist, on those days when time Church commemorates that act of His love, Pope Pius VII., by two Rescripts delivered through the medium of the *Segretaria* of the Memorials, dated Feb. 14, 1815, and April 6, 1816, kept in the*Segretaria* of the S. Congr. of Indulgences, granted -
i. A plenary indulgence to all who on Holy Thursday, either in public or private, shall, for one hour, practise some devotion in remembrance of the institution of the Most Holy Eucharist; to be gained after Confession and Communion on that day, or some day in the following week.
ii. A plenary indulgence, on the same conditions, on the Feast of Corpus Christi.
iii. An indulgence of 300 days on any other Thursday, on practising this devotion with a contrite heart.

46. PRAYERS TO BE SAID BY PRIESTS BEFORE MASS.

Pope Gregory XIII. granted -
An indulgence of 50 years to all priests, secular and regular, who, before celebrating the Holy Sacrifice of the Mass, shall say the following prayer:

Ego volo celebrare Missam, et conficere Corpus et Sanguinem Domini nostri Jesu Christi juxta ritum Sanctae Romanae Ecelesiae ad laudem omnipotentis Dei, totiusque curiae triumphantis, ad utilitatem meam, totsiusque curiae militantis; pro omnibus, qui se commendarut orationibus meis in genere et in specie, ac pro felici statu Sanctae Romanae Ecclesiae. Amen.

Gaudium cum pace, emendationem viae, spatium verae poenitentiae, gratiam et consolationem Sancti Spiritus, perseverantiae in bonis operibus tribuat nobis omnipotens et misericors Dominus. Amen.

TRANSLATION.

I purpose to celebrate Holy Mass, and to consecrate the Body and Blood of our Lord Jesus Christ according to the rite of the Holy Roman Church, to the praise of Almighty God and of all the Church triumphant, for the good of myself and of all the Church militant, for all who have recommended themselves to my prayers in general or in particular, and for the happy estate of the Holy Roman Church. Amen.

May the almighty and merciful Lord God grant unto us all joy and peace, amendment of our lives, time for true penance, the grace and the comfort of the Holy Ghost, and perseverance in every good work. Amen.

And Pius VII., of holy memory, granted, through his Eminence the Cardinal Vicar, by a Rescript kept in the *Segretaria* of his tribunal, dated Sept. 23, 1802 -

An indulgence of one year to all priests, secular and regular, who, before Mass, shall say devoutly the following prayer in honour of St. Joseph, the pure spouse of most holy Mary.

O felicem virum beatum Joseph, cui datum est Deum, quem multi reges voluerunt videre et non viderunt, audire et non audierunt; non solun videre et audire, sed portare, deosculari, vestire, et custodire,

V. Ora pro nobis, B. Joseph.
R. Ut digni, &c.

Oremus.
Deus, qui dedisti nobis regale sacerdotium; praesta quaesumus, ut sicut Beatus Joseph Unigenitum Filium tuum natum ex Maria Virgine suis manibus reverenter tractate meruit, et portare, ita nos facias cum cordis munditia et operis innocentia tuis sanctis altaribus deservire, sit sacrosanctum Filii tui Corpus et Sanguinem hodie digne sumamus, et in futuro saeculo praemium habere mereamur aeternum. Per Christum Dominum nostrum. R. Amen.

TRANSLATION.

Thrice-happy man, blessed Joseph to whom it was granted to see and hear that which many Kings desired to see, and yet saw not; to hear, and yet heard not; and not only to see and hear, but to carry, to caress, to clothe, and to guard.

V. Pray for us, O blessed Joseph.
R. That we may be made worthy of the promises of Christ.

Let us pray.
O God, who hast given to us Thy servants a royal priesthood; grant, we beseech Thee, that like as blessed Joseph was made worthy reverently to touch with his hands, and to bear in his arms, Thine only-begotten Son, born of Mary the Virgin, so Them wouldest make us to serve at Thy holy altars with cleanness of heart and innocency of life, that we may this day worthily receive the holy Body and Blood of Thy Son, and in the world to come may merit an eternal reward. Through Christ our Lord. Amen.

47. PRAYER TO BE SAID BY PRIESTS AFTER MASS.

Our Sovereign Pontiff Pius IX., at the prayer of many priests of the clergy of Rome, granted, by a decree of the S. Congr. of Indulgences, dated Dec. 11, 1846, to all priests who, after celebration of Mass, shall say the following prayer, *Obsecro &c.,*
An indulgence of three years. Moreover, he directed that the decree of this grant should be set up in the sacristy of every church and public oratory, until by the publication of fresh cards of Preparation for Mass the error should be rectified which occurs in several of these cards concerning certain apocryphal Indulgences.

THE PRAYER.

Obsecro te, dulcissime Domine Jesu Christe, ut Passio tua sit mihi virtus, qua muniar, protegar, atque defendar: vulnera tua sint mihi cibus potusque, quibus pascar, inebrier, atque delecter; aspersio Sanguinis tui sit mihi ablutio omnium delictorum meorum, mors tua sit mihi gloria sempiterna. In his sit mihi refectio, exultatio, sanitas, et dulcedo cordis mei. Qui vivis et regnas in saecula saeculorum. Amen.

TRANSLATION.

I beseech Thee, most sweet Lord Jesus, let Thy Passion be to me strength, to guard me, protect me, and defend me; Thy wounds my meat and drink, to feed me, inebriate me, and delight me; the sprinkling of Thy Blood on me the cleansing away of all faults; and Thy Death my everlasting glory. In these be my food, my rejoicing, my health, the sweetness of my heart. Who livest and reignest for ever and ever. Amen.

---

48. THE ANIMA CHRISTI, OR INVOCATIONS TO BE SAID AFTER MASS OR COMMUNION, OR ANY OTHER TIME.

Pope Pius IX., at the prayer of several ecclesiastics, secular and regular, revoking, by a decree of the S. Congr. of Indulgences of Jan. 9, 1854, all other grants of Indulgences which might ever have been made to any who should say the following Invocations of St. Ignatius, made a new grant of -
i. An indulgence of 300 days to all the faithful, every time they shall say them with contrite heart.
ii. An indulgence of seven years and seven quarantines to all priests who shall say them after Mass, and to all the faithful who shall say them after Holy Communion.
iii. A plenary indulgence, once a month, to all who have the good custom of saying them at least once a day; to be gained on that day when, after

97

Confession and Communion, they shall visit some church or public oratory, and pray there for some time according to the intention of his Holiness.

THE INVOCATIONS.

Animas Christi, sanctifica me.
Corpus Christi, salva me.
Sanguis Christi, inebria me.
Aqua lateris Christi, lava me.
Passio Christi, conforta me.
O bone Jesu, exaudi me.
Intra tua vulnera absconde me.
Ne permittas me separari a Te.
Ab hoste maligno defende me.
In hora mortis meae voca me,
Et jube me venire ad Te,
Ut cum sanctis tuis laudem Te
In saecula saeculorum. Amen.

TRANSLATION.

Soul of Christ, be my sanctification;
Body of Christ, be my salvation;
Blood of Christ, fill all my veins;
Water of Christ's side, wash out my stains;
Passion of Christ, my comfort be;
O good Jesu, listen to me;
In Thy wounds I fain would hide,
Ne'er to be parted from Thy side;
Guard me, should the foe assail me;
Call me when my life shall fail me;
Bid me come to Thee above,
With Thy saints to sing Thy love
World without end. Amen.

49. FREQUENT COMMUNION.

Pope Gregory XIII., in his Constitution dated April 10, 1580, *Ad excitandum*, granted -
i. An indulgence of five years to the faithful, every time on festival-days they Confess, Communicate, and pray for the Sovereign Pontiff.
ii. An indulgence of ten years, every time they Communicate, to those who have the good habit of Communicating at least once a month, on the

Solemnities of our Lord, on the Festivals of the Blessed Virgin, of all the holy Apostles, and on the birthday of St. John Baptist.

iii. A plenary indulgence, one a year, on the day when the principal feast of the city or country where they live is celebrated: on condition of their going to Confession and Communion on this day, and praying as above.

50. ADORATION OF THE BLESSED SACRAMENT AT THE ELEVATION IN THE MASS, AT THE RINGING OF THE HOUR-BELL WHEN THERE IS SOLEMN EXPOSITION AND AT BENEDICTION.

The same Pope Gregory XIII., in the above-named Constitution, granted to the faithful -

i. An indulgence of one year, every time that, at the sound of the bell for the Elevation of the Blessed Sacrament at High Mass, Conventual Mass, or Parochial Mass, they adore on their knees Jesus Christ in the Blessed Sacrament, saying at the same time some short prayer.

ii. An indulgence of two years, if they then go into church for this object, and adore the Blessed Sacrament there during the Elevation as aforesaid.

Pope Pius VII., moreover, by a decree of the S. Congr. of Indulgences, dated Dec. 7, 1819, granted -

iii. An indulgence of 100 days, every time any one assisting at Mass shall, at the Elevation of both the sacred species, adore Jesus Christ in the Blessed Sacrament, and say devoutly and with contrition the well-known Ejaculation, or eucharistic tribute of praise:

Blessed and praised every moment
Be the most holy and divine Sacrament!

or,

O Sacrament most holy! O Sacrament divine!
All praise and all thanksgiving be every moment Thine.

Lastly, the same Pope Pius VII., wishing always to promote more and more the frequent use of acts of adoration to Jesus in the Blessed Sacrament, granted, by a decree of the same Congr. of Indulgences, of date prior to the last, viz. June 30, 1818 -

iv. An indulgence of 100 days to the faithful, every time they adore their Lord in the Blessed Sacrament, saying, with contrite hearts and devotion, the above ejaculation, "Blessed and praised," &c. at the ringing of the bell at the hours in churches where there is Solemn Exposition, either for the Forty Hours or for any other occasion, and at Benediction given with the Blessed Sacrament in a church.

51. ACCOMPANYING THE BLESSED SACRAMENT TO THE SICK.

It often happens that the Blessed Sacrament has to be carried to the sick as Viaticum; and in order to induce the faithful to accompany Jesus Christ upon this occasion, the Sovereign Pontiff Paul V., on Nov. 3, 1606, and the Venerable Innocent XI., on Oct. 1, 1688, granted certain Indulgences, which were confirmed and extended by Pope Innocent XII., in his Constitution *Debitum Pastoralis Officii*, of Jan. 5, 1695. These Indulgences are -

i. An indulgence of seven years and seven quarantines to all who accompany the Blessed Sacrament with a lighted taper or any other light.
ii. An indulgence of five years and five quarantines to those who accompany it without a light.
iii. An indulgence of three years and three quarantines to those who, being lawfully hindered from going themselves. send some one in their stead to carry a light in attendance upon the most holy Viaticum.
iv. An indulgence of 100 days to those who cannot go themselves with the Blessed Sacrament, provided they say one *Pater noster* and one *Ave Maria* for the intention of the Pope when they see it carried to the sick. This Indulgence was again confirmed, by Pope Clement X., by a decree of the S. Congr. of Indulgences, April 23, 1676.

N.B. These Indulgences continue in force in the holy year of Jubilee, by the declaration of Benedict XIV., in the Bull *Cum nos nuper*, of May 17, 1749, for the holy year 1750, by Clement XIV. in a similar Bull of May 15, 1774, for the holy year 1775, and lastly, by Leo XII., in his Bull of June 20, 1824, for the holy year 1825.

---

52. VISIT TO THE BLESSED SACRAMENT WHEN EXPOSED FOR THE FORTY HOURS' PRAYER.

The Prayer for forty hours together before the Blessed Sacrament, in memory of the forty hours during which the sacred Body of Jesus was in the Sepulchre, began in Milan about the year 1534.(1) Thence it spread into other cities of Italy, and was introduced into Rome for the first Sunday in every month by the Archconfraternity of the Most Holy Trinity of the Pilgrims (founded by St. Philip Neri in the year 1548), and for the third Sunday in the month by the Archconfraternity of our Lady of Prayer called *La Morte*, in the year 1551. This Prayer of the Forty Hours, practised often in one church or other at various times of the year out of devotion, was established for ever by Pope Clement VIII. for the whole course of the year, in a regular prescribed continuous succession from one church in Rome to another, commencing on the first Sunday in Advent with the chapel in the Apostolical Palace. (See the

Constitution of Clement VIII., *Graves et diuturnae*, of Nov. 25, 1592.) This Pope was minded to establish this devotion by reason of the public troubles of the Holy Church, in order that day and night the faithful might appease their Lord by prayer before the Blessed Sacrament in Solemn Exposition, imploring there His divine mercy; and to this end, he granted holy Indulgences to those who should pray there during the said solemn exposition. Afterwards Paul V., by his Brief *Cum felicis recordationis*, May 10, 1606, confirmed the Indulgences which had been granted by his predecessor. They are -

i. A plenary indulgence to all who, after having Confessed and Communicated, shall devoutly visit any church during the Exposition of the Blessed Sacrament there, and pray as long as they conveniently can.

ii. An indulgence of ten years and as many quarantines for every visit made with firm intention of Confession.

iii. Indulgence of the privileged Altar to all the altars of these churches during the time of exposition. This is granted by a Rescript of May 12, 1817, kept in the *Segretaria* of the Vicariate.(2)

NOTES.

(1) Gardellini in Commentariis ad Institutionem Clementis XI. latam prima vice die 21 Jan. 1705, pro Expositione Sanctissimi Sacramenti in oratione xl. horarum. Romae, apud Bourliè, 1819, p. 4.

(2) In November 1810, a Pious Union of worshippers of the Blessed Sacrament was instituted for the purpose of keeping up a watch all night in the churches where there is Exposition. Pope Pius VII. approved of this Pious Union, and granted to all its members, both those who made the prayer themselves, as well as those who contributed to the expenses of the Exposition, several privileges and Indulgences, for which see his Rescript of August 6, 1814, kept in the *Segretaria* of the Vicariate.

---

53. VISIT TO THE EXPOSITION OF THE BLESSED SACRAMENT DURING THE WEEKS FOLLOWING SEPTUAGESIMA SUNDAY TO ASH WEDNESDAY.

The devotions has been long introduced, not only in Rome but in other places, of exposing the Blessed Sacrament for the adoration of the Forty hours from the week following Septuagesima Sunday to Ash Wednesday, in order to make reparation by prayer for all the offences which are committed against the Divine Majesty during the Carnival, and also to ask for the help of God and His mercy. To animate the faithful to the practice of this holy exercise, so pleasing to Almighty God, Pope Clement XIII., by a decree of the S. Congr. of Indulgences, July 23, 1765, granted -

A plenary indulgence to all who, after Confession and Communion, shall visit the Blessed Sacrament when exposed for three days in any church in Christendom on one or all of the weeks from Septuagesima up to Ash Wednesday; and the same Indulgence to those who shall visit it when exposed only on the Thursday after Sexagesima Sunday, the day commonly called in Rome "Giovedì grasso."

54. VISIT TO THE HOLY SACRAMENT ON HOLY THURSDAY AND GOOD FRIDAY.

The practice of the faithful to make a visit on Holy Thursday or Good Friday to Jesus Christ in the Blessed Sacrament, represented as enclosed in the Holy Sepulchre, will always be considered a praiseworthy custom, very conformable to the spirit of our holy religion. In order that these visits may be made in the true spirit of our faith, and to our greater spiritual profit, Pope Pius VII., by a Rescript through the S. Congr. of Indulgences, of March 7, 1815, granted to all the faithful who should visit the Holy Sepulchre on the two aforenamed days, and remain there for a time praying according to the intention of the Sovereign Pontiff, the same Indulgences which are gained for visiting the Blessed Sacrament during the Exposition of the Forty Hours; viz. -
i. A plenary indulgence, on condition of Confession and Communion on Holy Thursday or in Easter Week.
ii. An indulgence of ten years and ten quarantines for visiting it with a firm resolution of Confession.

55. VISIT TO THE BLESSED SACRAMENT ON THURSDAYS, AND PRAYER "RESPICE, DOMINE," ETC.

Pope Pius VI, by a Rescript of the *Segretaria* of the Memorials, dated Oct. 17, 1796, granted -
i. A plenary indulgence to all the faithful who, being contrite, and having confessed and gone to Communion on tine first Thursday in the month, shall on that day visit the Blessed Sacrament, either at Exposition time or when enclosed in the Tabernacle, and say there the following prayer, *Respice, Domine,* &c. (composed, it is said, by St. Caietan, founder of the Theatines, in order to implore tine mercy of God), praying also for the good estate of the Church, &c.
ii. An indulgence of seven years and seven quarantines every Thursday in the year, to all who, after Confession and Communion, shall say the above prayer, on their knees, before the Blessed Sacrament.
iii. An indulgence of 100 days for saying it, with contrite heart, before the

Blessed Sacrament, on any day whatever.

The Rescript granting these Indulgences is kept in the Archivium of the Venerable Congregation of Clerks Regular of the Theatine Order, at St. Andrea della Valle in Rome, who first prayed for this grant.

THE PRAYER.

Respice, Domino, de sanctuario tuo et de excelso coelorum habitaculo, et vide hanc sacrosanctam Hostiam, quam Tibi offert magnus Pontifex noster Sanctus Puer tuus Dominus Jesus pro peccatis fratrum suorum; et esto placabilis super multitudinem malitiae nostrae. Ecce vox Sanguinis fratris nostri Jesu clamat ad Te de Cruce. Exaudi, Domine; placare, Domine; attende, et fac, ne moreris propter temetipsum, Deus meus, quia nomen tuum invocatum est super civitatem istam, et super populum tuum; et fac nobiscum secundum misericordiam tuam. Amen.

TRANSLATION.

Look down, O Lord, from Thy sanctuary, and from Heaven Thy dwelling-place on high, and behold this sacred Victim which our great High-Priest, Thy holy Child, our Lord Jesus, offers up to Thee for the sins of This brethren; and be appeased for the multitude of our transgressions. Behold the voice of the Blood of Jesus, our Brother, cries to Thee from the Cross. Give ear, O Lord! be appeased, O Lord! hearken, and do not tarry for Thine own sake, O my God, for Thy Name is invoked upon this city and upon Thy people; and deal with us according to Thy mercy. Amen.

---

56. THE HYMN "PANGE LINGUA" AND "TANTUM ERGO."

Pope Pius VII., in order to inflame the devotion of the faithful towards Jesus in the Blessed Sacrament, that they might adore Him in spirit and in truth, giving Him thanks for the inestimable benefits bestowed upon them by His offering Himself to be their food in this most awful Sacrament, granted, at the prayer of many bishops and the college of the Parish Priests of Rome, by a decree of the S. Congr. of Indulgences, Aug. 25, 1818 -

i. An indulgence of 300 days, once a day, to all the faithful who, devoutly and with a contrite heart, say the hymn *Pange lingua gloriosi,* &c., with the Versicle and Response, and Prayer of the most Holy Sacrament.

ii. An indulgence of 100 days to those who say the "Tantum ergo," &c. only, with the said Versicles and Prayer.

iii. A plenary indulgence every year on Holy Thursday, Corpus Christi, or one day in its octave, and any one other day, on condition of visiting some church, after Confessing and Communicating on those days, and praying there for the intention of the Sovereign Pontiff.

THE HYMN.

Pange lingua gloriosi
Corporis Mysterium,
Sanguinisque pretiosi,
Quem in mundi pretium,
Fructus ventris generosi
Rex effudit gentium.

Nobis datus, nobis natus
Ex intacta Virgine,
Et in mundo conversatus
Sparso verbi semine,
Sui moras incolatus
Miro clausit ordine.

In supremae nocte coenae
Recumbens cum fratribus,
Observata lege plene
Cibis in legalibus,
Cibum turbae duodenae
Se dat suis manibus.

Verbum caro, panem verum
Verbo carnem efficit;
Fitque Sanguis Christi merum
Et si sensus deficit,
Ad firmandum cor sincerum
Sola fides sufficit.

Tantum ergo Sacramentum
Veneremur cernui:
Et antiquum documentum
Novo cedant ritui:
Praestet fides supplementum
Sensuum defectui.

Genitori Genitoque
Laus et jubilatio,
Salus, honor, virtus quoque
Sit et benedictio,

Procedenti ab utroque
Compar sit laudatio. Amen.

V. Panem de coelo praestitisti eis.
R. Omne delectamentum in se habentem.

Oremus.
Deus, qui nobis sub Sacramento mirabili, Passionis tuae memoriam reliquisti: tribue, quaesumus, ita nos Corporis et Sanguinis tui sacra mysteria venerari, ut redemptionis tuae fructum in nobis jugiter sentiamus. Qui vivis et regnas, &c.

TRANSLATION.

Sing, my tongue, the Saviour's glory,
Of His Flesh the mystery sing;
Of the Blood, all price exceeding,
Shed by our immortal King,
Destin'd for the world's redemption,
From a noble womb to spring.

Of a pure and spotless Virgin
Born for us on earth below,
He, as Man with man conversing,
Stay'd, the seeds of truth to sow;
Then He clos'd in solemn order
Wondrously his life of woe.

On the night of that Last Supper,
Seated with His chosen band,
He the paschal victim eating,
First fulfils the Law's command;
Then as food to all His brethren
Gives Himself with His own hand.

Word made Flesh, the bread of nature
By his word to Flesh he turns;
Wine into his Blood He changes -
What though sense no change discerns?
Only be the heart in earnest,
Faith her lesson quickly learns.

[Tantum ergo Sacramentum.]

Down in adoration failing,
Lo! the sacred Host we hail;
Lo! o'er ancient forms departing,
Newer rites of grace prevail;

Faith for all defects supplying,
Where the feeble senses fail.

To the everlasting Father,
And the Son who reigns on high,
With the Holy Ghost proceeding
Forth from each eternally,
Be salvation, honour, blessing,
Might, and endless majesty.

V. Thou gavest them Bread from heaven.
R. And therein was sweetness of every kind.

Let us pray.
O God, who under this wonderful Sacrament hast left unto us the memorials of Thy Passion; grant us, we beseech Thee, so to venerate the sacred mysteries of Thy Body and Thy Blood, that we may constantly experience within us the fruit of Thy redemption, Who livest and reignest, &c.

---

57. EJACULATION, "BLESSED AND PRAISED," ETC.

Pope Pius VI, by a Rescript of the *Segretaria* of the Memorials, May 21, 1776, granted -
i. An indulgence of 100 days, once a day, to all the faithful who, with contrite hearts, say the Ejaculation in honour of the Blessed Sacrament.

Blessed and praised every moment
Be the most holy and divine Sacrament.

ii.　　　An indulgence of 300 days, every Thursday in the year, and in the octave of Corpus Christi to those who shall say it three times.
iii. A plenary indulgence, once a month, on anyone day, to those who, having said it every day for a month, shall, after Confession and Communion, pray for the Holy Church, &c.
These Indulgences were confirmed afresh by Pope Pius VII., by a decree of the S. Congr. of Indulgences, June 30, 1818 and he extended the indulgence of 100 days to all who say the above Ejaculation at Exposition, Benediction, and the Elevation in the Mass. See above.

58. ACTS OF ADORATION, WITH FIVE "PATER NOSTER'S," FIVE "AVE MARIA'S," AND FIVE "GLORIA PATRI'S," ETC.

Pope Pius VII., by a Rescript of Aug. 26, 1814, issued through his Eminence the Cardinal Prefect of the S. Congr. of Rites, kept in the Acts of the said S. Congr. of Rites, and of which there is an authentic copy in the *Segretaria* of the S. Congr. of Indulgences, declared his approbation of the following Acts of Adoration and Reparation to Jesus in the Blessed Sacrament, and granted to all the faithful -

An indulgence of 300 days, every time they are said devoutly, with five *Pater noster's*, five *Ave Maria's*, and five *Gloria Patri's*, &c.

ACTS OF ADORATION AND REPARATION TO JESUS IN THE BLESSED SACRAMENT.

i. I adore Thee profoundly, my Jesus, in the Blessed Sacrament; I acknowledge Thee true God and true Man. By this my act of adoration I intend to make Thee reparation for the coldness of so many of Thy people, who pass before Thy churches, nay, before Thy very tabernacle, where hour after hour Thou dost deign to dwell in loving impatience to communicate Thyself to Thy faithful; yet do not even bow the knee before Thee, but, like the Israelites in the wilderness, seem by their indifference to loathe this heavenly manna. I offer Thee Thine own most Precious Blood which Thou didst shed from the wound in Thy Left Foot, in reparation for this hateful coldness, and, entering therein, I say, and will never cease to say:

Blessed and praised every moment
Be the most holy and divine Sacrament.

Pater noster. Ave Maria. Gloria Patri.

ii. I adore Thee profoundly, my Jesus; I acknowledge Thee present in the most holy Sacrament. By this act of adoration, I would make amends for the forgetfulness of so many Christian people, who, when they see Thee go to the poor sick, to be their strength in their great journey to eternity, leave Thee unescorted, and hardly give Thee even one outward sign of homage. I offer Thee, in reparation for this coldness, that most Precious Blood which Thou didst shed from the wound in Thy Right Foot, and, entering therein, I say and will never cease to say:

Blessed and praised every moment
Be the most holy and divine Sacrament!

Pater noster. Ave Maria. Gloria Patri.

iii. I adore Thee profoundly, my Jesus, true Bread of life eternal; and by this my act of adoration I would make Thee compensation for all the wounds with which Thy Sacred Heart bleeds daily to see the profanation of those churches wherein Thou dost vouchsafe to abide beneath the sacramental species, to receive the love and adoration of Thy people. I offer Thee, in reparation for all those irreverences, that most Precious Blood which Thou didst shed from the wound in Thy Left Hand, and, entering therein, I say every moment:

Blessed and praised every moment
Be the most holy and divine Sacrament

Pater noster. Ave Maria. Gloria Patri.

iv. I adore Thee profoundly, my Jesus, the Living Bread which has come down from heaven; and by this act of adoration I would make amends for all the acts of irreverence which Thy people day by day commit whilst they assist at Holy Mass, in which bloodless Sacrifice Thou dost renew the very Sacrifice which once Thou didst consummate on Calvary for our salvation. I offer Thee, in reparation for all this ingratitude, that most Precious Blood which Thou didst shed from the wound in Thy Right Hand; and, entering therein, I unite my voice with the voices of the holy angels who adore around Thy throne:

Blessed and praised every moment
Be the most holy and divine Sacrament!

Pater noster. Ave Maria. Gloria Patri.

v. I adore Thee profoundly, my Jesus, true Victim of expiation for our sins; and I offer Thee this act of adoration in compensation for the sacrilegious outrages Thou dost receive from so many of Thy ungrateful people, who dare to draw nigh to Thee and receive Thee in Communion with mortal sin upon their souls. In reparation for these hateful sacrileges, I offer Thee those last drops of They most Precious Blood which Thou didst shed from the wound in Thy Side; and, entering therein, I approach Thee with acts of adoration, love, and thanksgiving, and with all holy souls who are devout to Thee in the most Holy Sacrament, I say:

Blessed and praised every moment
Be the most holy and divine Sacrament.

Pater noster. Ave Maria. Gloria Patri.

Tantum ergo Sacramentum, &c. *as above.* V. Panem de coelo, &c. *Prayer,* Deus qui nobis, &c.

59. REPARATION AND EJACULATIONS.

Pope Pius VII., at the prayer of the nuns of the Convent of the Perpetual Adoration of the Blessed Sacrament in Rome, granted by a Rescript of Jan. 20, 1815 -
An indulgence of 200 days to every one who, with contrition for his sins and with devotion, says the following Act of Reparation to Jesus in the Blessed Sacrament, which it is the practice of the religious of this order to say each in her turn in the hour of her adoration. This Indulgence was confirmed by Pope Leo XII., by an autograph Rescript of Aug. 13, 1828, kept in the Archivium of the said monastery.

THE REPARATION

Jesus, my God, my Saviour, true God and true Man, with that most profound homage with which the faith itself inspires me, I adore and love Thee with my whole heart, enclosed in the most august Sacrament of the Altar, in reparation for all the acts of irreverence, profanation, and sacrilege, which I may ever have been so unhappy as to have committed, as well as for all such like acts that ever have been done, or which may be done, though God forbid they should be, in ages yet to come. I adore Thee, therefore, my God, not indeed as Thou deservest, nor as much as I am bound to adore, but as far as I am able; and I would that I could adore Thee with all the perfection of which all reasonable persons are capable. Meantime I purpose now and ever to adore Thee, not only for those Catholics who adore Thee not, and love Thee not, but also in the stead of, and for the conversion of all heretics, schismatics, impious atheists, blasphemers, impostors, Mahometans, Jews, and idolaters. Jesus, my God, mayest Thou be ever known, adored, loved, and praised every moment, in the most holy and divine Sacrament. Amen.

EJACULATIONS.

I adore Thee every moment, O living Bread of Heaven, Great Sacrament!

Jesus, Heart of Mary, I pray Thee send Thy blessing on my soul.

Holiest Jesu! loving Saviour! I give Thee my heart.

The same Pope Leo XII., by the came Rescript, granted -
An indulgence of 100 days to every one who says the above Ejaculations with contrition, adding the following:

May all know, adore, and praise every moment, always, the most holy and divine Sacrament.

60. PRAYER TO THE HOST HOLY SACRAMENT AND TO THE SACRED HEART OF JESUS.

Pope Pius VI., of holy memory, by a Rescript of Nov. 7, 1787, granted -
An indulgence of 100 days, once a day, to all the faithful who say devoutly the following Prayer, " Behold, my most loving Jesus," to the Most Holy Sacrament and the most loving Heart of Jesus. Pope Pius VII., by another Rescript of the *Segretaria* of the Memorials, dated Feb. 9, 1818, confirmed this Indulgence. This Rescript is kept here in Rome, in the Archivium of the Pious Union of the Sacred Heart of Jesus at S. Maria in Capella, now transferred. to S. Maria della Pace.

THE PRAYER.

Behold, my most loving Jesus, to what an excess Thy boundless love has carried Thee. Of Thine own Flesh and Precious Blood Thou hast made ready for me a banquet in order to give me all Thyself. What was it that impelled Thee to this transport of love for me? It was Thy Heart, Thy loving Heart. O Adorable Heart of my Jesus! burning furnace of Divine Love! within Thy most sacred wound receive Thou my soul; that in this school of charity I may learn to requite the love of that God who has given me such wondrous proofs of his love. Amen.

APPENDIX

172. PRAYERS FOR A VISIT TO THE MOST HOLY SACRAMENT OR TO MOST HOLY MARY (FROM ST. ALPHONSO DE' LIQUORI).

The Sovereign Pontiff Pius IX., by a Rescript of Sept. 7, 1851, which is preserved in the venerable house of the Oblates of Torre de' Specchi, granted for ever -
300 days of indulgence to the faithful every time they shall say the following prayers, composed by St. Alphonso for a visit to the most holy Sacrament, before the tabernacle, where our Lord is enclosed, or to the Blessed Virgin Mary before her image.
The plenary indulgence, moreover, to be gained once a month, when, having used one or other of these devotions in the manner above indicated, they shall, having Confessed and Communicated, pray for the wants of the holy Church, according to the intention of the Sovereign Pontiff.

THE PRAYER FOR THE VISIT TO THE MOST HOLY SACRAMENT.

O my Lord Jesus Christ, who for the love which Thou dost bear men dost remain night and day in this Sacrament all full of tenderness and love, expecting, inviting, and receiving all those who come to visit Thee; I believe Thee present in the Sacrament of the Altar; I adore Thee in the depths of my own nothingness; and I thank Thee for all the graces which Thou hast granted me, especially for having vouchsafed to bestow Thyself upon me in this Sacrament, for having given me Thy own most holy Mother Mary for my advocate, and for having invited me to visit Thee in this church. I pay my homage this day to Thy adorable Heart, and I do so for these three intentions: first, in thanksgiving for this great gift itself; secondly, for a reparation for all the injuries which Thou hast received from all Thy enemies in this Sacrament; thirdly, I intend by this visit to adore Thee in all those places where Thou, sacramentally present, art least reverenced and most abandoned. My Jesus, I Jove Thee with my whole heart. I repent of having so many times heretofore displeased Thy infinite goodness. By Thy grace I resolve never to offend Thee more for the time to come; and at this present moment, poor sinner as I am, I consecrate myself wholly to Thee. I renounce for myself, and I give to Thee, my will, my affections, my desires, every thing that I call my own. From this day forth do Thou with me, and with every thing that belongs to me, whatever pleases Thee. I ask Thee only, and I wish only, for Thy holy love, for final perseverance, and the perfect fulfilment of Thy will. I commend to Thee the souls in purgatory, especially those who were most devoted to the most holy Sacrament, and to Mary most holy. Moreover, I commend to Thee all poor Sinners. For this intention I unite, O my dear Saviour Jesus, all my affections with the affections of Thy most loving Heart; and thus united, I offer them to thy Eternal Father, and I entreat Him, in Thy Name and for Thy love, to accept and answer them.

THE PRAYER FOR A VISIT TO THE MOST HOLY MARY.

O most holy Virgin, Immaculate Mary my Mother, to thee, who art the Mother of my Lord, the Queen of the world, the advocate, hope and refuge of sinners, I, most wretched sinner, have recourse this day; and I give thee thanks for all the favours thou hast bestowed on me up to this moment, especially for having freed us from hell, which I have so many times deserved. I love thee, O most loving Mother, and for the love which I bear thee I promise to be ready always to serve thee, and to do my best to make thee beloved by others. In thee I let all my hopes repose, all my salvation; accept me for thy servant, and gather me beneath thy robe, O Mother of mercy. And since thou art so powerful with God, free me from all temptations, or, at any rate, obtain for me strength to overcome them up to the moment of my death. O my Mother, for the love thou bearest to God, I pray thee to aid me always, but most in the last moment of my life. Leave me not till thou dost see me safe in heaven, there to bless thee and sing thy mercies for all eternity. Amen. This is my hope. Amen.

SACRED HEART OF JESUS

61. THE FEAST.

The most loving Heart of our Saviour Jesus Christ has ever been the object of the special devotion of the greatest saints; and in our own times it may be said to have become also the devotion of all holy persons without exception, from the time that our Lord Jesus Christ Himself chose a holy Salesian nun, the Venerable Sister Margaret Mary Alacoque, of the convent of Parài le Monial, in the diocese of Autun, in Burgundy, to originate this devotion, and to establish and propagate it in the Church through her. This we learn from the acts of the process of her beatification. This devotion was accordingly established and approved with public rite by the Sovereign Pontiff; and at the present day it is extended to the whole Catholic world; the Feast of the Sacred Heart being every where celebrated on the first Friday after the octave of Corpus Christi. Pope Pius VII., by a Rescript of the *Segretaria* of the Memorials, July 7, 1815, granted -

A plenary indulgence on this feast to all the faithful who, after Confession and Communion, shall visit a church or public oratory where the feast is celebrated, and pray there according to the intention of the Pope. He gave permission also that this feast might be transferred to any other day in the year with leave of the ordinary, and that the proper Mass, &c. might be celebrated on the day of the transferred feast.

The original of this Rescript is kept in the Archivium of the Pious Union of the Sacred Heart of Jesus, at the church of S. Maria in Capella, afterwards transferred to the church of S. Maria della Pace, where many other Rescripts and Briefs are kept regarding the devotion of the Sacred Heart of Jesus, to which reference will be made in the following pages.

62. VISIT TO A REPRESENTATION OF THE SACRED HEART.

Pope Pius VI, to increase devotion to the Sacred Heart of Jesus, granted, by a Rescript dated from Florence, Jan. 2, 1799, to all the faithful in the whole Catholic world -

An indulgence of seven years and seven quarantines, as often as, with contrite hearts and devotion, they visit a representation of the Sacred Heart of Jesus, exposed for public veneration at any church, oratory, or altar, and pray there for a time according to the intention of the Pope.

The original Rescript is kept in the Archivium of the Episcopal Palace of Fiesole at Florence, near S. Maria in Campo, where it was deposited by the pious persons who prayed the Holy Father for the grant of this Indulgence; and an authentic copy of it is kept in the Archivium of the Pious Union of the Sacred Heart above named.

63. "PATER NOSTER" "AVE MARIA," "CREDO," WITH THE EJACULATION, "SWEET HEART OF MY JESUS."

Pope Pius VII., by the Rescripts of March 7, 1801; March 20 and November 13, 1802; July 12 and 15, 1803; July 7, 1815; Sept. 26, 1817, granted to all the faithful who shall say devoutly every day one *Pater noster*, one *Ave Maria*, one *Credo*, and the Ejaculation,

Sweet Heart of my Jesus,
Make me love Thee ever more and more!

i. Two Plenary Indulgences: one on the first Friday or first Sunday in every month, the other on any one other day in the month, provided that on these days they, after Confession and Communion, pray according to the intention of the Sovereign Pontiff.

ii. A plenary Indulgence on the Feast of the Sacred Heart, i.e. the Friday or Sunday after the octave of Corpus Christi, provided that on one of those days they pray, &c., as aforesaid.

iii. An Indulgence of seven years and seven quarantines on the four Sundays immediately preceding the Feast of the Sacred Heart.

iv. An Indulgence of 60 days for every good work done devoutly by the faithful who have the pious custom of saying these prayers.

v. A plenary indulgence, in the article of death, to all who have been accustomed during life to say these prayers, provided that being penitent they invoke the Holy Name of Jesus, at least with their heart, if not able to do so with their lips.

Moreover the same Pope granted, by a Rescript of Sept. 10, 1814 -

i. An indulgence of 300 days to all who say three times a day, morning, noon, and evening, three *Gloria Patri's* in thanksgiving to the Most Holy Trinity for the particular privileges granted to the Blessed Virgin, and above all for her Assumption into heaven.

ii. An indulgence of 100 days each time these prayers are said, and -

iii. A plenary indulgence, once a month, to all who say them three times a day for a month together, on any one day after Confession and Communion.

N.B. The general condition for all these indulgences, besides the prayers above-named, is, Enrolment in the Pious Union of the Sacred Heart of Jesus canonically erected in Rome, Feb. 14, 1801, in S. Maria in Capella, transferred to S. Maria della Pace, or else in some other Congregation of the Sacred Heart out of Rome aggregated to this Pious Union.

64. OTHER DEVOTIONS.

The same Pope Pius VII., besides the indulgences already mentioned, granted, by two Briefs of April 2, 1805, to all members associated as above -

i. The Indulgences of the Stations at Rome, for visiting the church of their Congregation on the days of the Stations, as specified in the Roman Missal, and praying there according to the intention of the Pope. These Indulgences are granted in a decree of the S. Congr. of indulgences of July 9, 1777, which will be referred to again in its proper place.

ii. A plenary indulgence, on the Feasts of the Immaculate Conception of the B.V.M., the Nativity of the B.V.M., the Annunciation of the B.V.M., the Purification of the B.V.M., the Assumption of the B.V. M., of St. Joseph, the Holy Apostles SS. Peter and Paul, St. John the Evangelist, and all Saints, and also on All Souls' Day, provided that the members of the association, after Confession and Communion, visit the church of their Congregation.

iii. An indulgence of seven years and seven quarantines on all other feasts of our Lady and of the Apostles, on condition of visiting the church of the Congregation.

iv. An indulgence of seven years and seven quarantines, by another Rescript of March 4, 1806, to all members of these Congregations who shall keep a devout novena before the Feast of the Sacred Heart, visiting with contrite heart the church or public oratory where the feast is kept, and praying there for the intention of the Sovereign Pontiff; to be gained each day of the said novena.

v. A plenary indulgence each of the six Sundays or Fridays before the feast, to all who, after having Confessed and Communicated, visit the church or oratory where the feast is kept, and pray there as before. And observe, that in order that all these indulgences may be the more easily gained, the two Pontifical

114

Rescripts quoted above, which are in force both in Rome and out of Rome, state that if, on the days of the said novena, or the said six Sundays and Fridays before the feast, the faithful are not able to make the visit there enjoined to the church of the Pious Union or Congregation where they are enrolled; or if they cannot visit the church or public oratory where the feast is celebrated, through sickness, absence from home, or any other sufficient reason, - they may still gain all the above-named indulgences on condition of their performing on the days stated some good work enjoined them by their own confessor.

Furthermore, the same Pope Pius VII., by another Rescript of the *Segretaria* of the Memorials of May 15, 1816, made the additional concession that all the above-named indulgences for members of the Pious Union of the Sacred Heart of Jesus might be gained by all the faithful, wherever in the whole world they might be residing, where no confraternities or pious unions can be erected, or where, for any sufficient reason, it may be difficult for them to aggregate themselves to the Pious Union here in Rome, provided they only perform the other pious works enjoined and mentioned above.

Again, Pope Leo XII., of holy memory, by a Rescript of the S. Congr. of Indulgences, May 21, 1828, granted to all the members of the Pious Union as above, who keep devoutly a Triduo upon the Feast of the Sacred Heart of Jesus -

vi. An indulgence of seven years and seven quarantines, every day of the Triduo, on condition of visiting with a contrite heart the church or public oratory where the feast is kept, and praying there according to the intention of the Sovereign Pontiff.

Further, in order to keep up a continual "cultus" or worship of the Sacred Heart of Jesus, that there may always be some one to adore It, to glorify It, and to give It some special homage, every member of the said Pious Union may also have himself enrolled for the Perpetual Adoration, choosing one or more fixed days in the year whereon to dedicate himself to the Most Sacred Heart of Jesus in the following manner:

1. By Confession and Communion. 2. By visiting a church or public oratory, and praying there for a time. - i. For the intention of the Sovereign Pontiff, and for all the sacred ministers of the altar; ii. For the conversion of sinners; iii. For all the associates of this pious practice, and the souls in purgatory. 3. By making mental or vocal prayer, either for one whole *hour continuously*, or else at intervals during the day, provided there he a good reason for so doing; and also by offering up frequently during the day some ejaculatory prayers in honour of the Sacred Heart of Jesus. 4. By renewing to our Blessed Lord the promises made in baptism, as well as any other particular promises made during life. On all days when any one of the associations shall practise this exercise, it shall gain -

vii. The plenary indulgence, granted by Pope Leo XII., at the prayer of the priests of the said Pious Union, by a decree of the S. Congr. of Indulgences.

Feb. 18, 1826.

Lastly, Pope Gregory XVI., of blessed memory, by a Brief of June 20, 1834, kept in the Archivium of the said Pious Union, confirmed anew for ever all these Indulgences for the associates as above; and, in addition to the above, granted them -

viii. The plenary indulgence, on the feast of Pope Gregory the Great (March 12), commencing with First Vespers; provided that, after Confession and Communion, they visit the church or oratory of their Congregation, and pray there for our holy mother the Catholic Church, &c.

65. OFFERING.

Pope Pius VII., by Rescripts of June 9, 1807, and Sept. 26, 1817, issuing from the *Segretaria* of the Memorials, granted -

i. A plenary indulgence, once a month, and remission of all sins, to all the faithful who, every day for a month, shall say the following offering to the Most Sacred Heart of Jesus before a representation of the Sacred Heart, to be gained on any one day when, after Confession and Communion, they shall pray according to the intention of the Sovereign Pontiff.

ii. An indulgence of 100 days, once a day, to all who shall make this offering with contrite hearts.

THE OFFERING.

My loving Jesus, out of gratitude to Thee, and to make reparation for my unfaithfulness to grace, I (N. N.) give Thee my heart, and I consecrate myself wholly to Thee; and with Thy help I purpose never to sin again.

66. PRAYERS, WITH THREE "PATER NOSTER'S," ETC.

The same Pope Pius VII., at the prayer of several bishops, priests, and devout lovers of the Sacred Heart of Jesus, confirmed for ever by a Rescript of Feb. 12, 1808 -

i. An indulgence of 300 days, granted previously, once a day, to all the faithful who shall say with devotion the following prayers to the Sacred Heart of Jesus, with three *Pater noster's*, three *Ave Maria's*, and three *Gloria Patri's*. He added the grant of -

ii. A plenary indulgence, once a month, to all who shall have said them daily for a month, on any one day when, after Confession and Communion, they shall pray to God for the wants of the Church, &c.

THE PRAYERS.

i. Verbum caro factum est, et habitavit in nobis.
The Word was made Flesh, and dwelt amongst us.

Eternal Word, made Man for love of us, humbly kneeling at Thy feet we adore Thee with the deepest veneration of our soul; and in order that we may make reparation of our ingratitude for this great benefit of Thy Incarnation, we unite ourselves to the hearts of all those who love Thee, and together with them we offer Thee our humble loving thanksgiving. Touched with the great humility, goodness, and sweetness which we behold in Thy Divine Heart, we beseech Thee to give us Thy grace, that in our lives we too may imitate these virtues so dear to Thee.

Pater noster. Ave Maria. Gloria Patri.

ii. Crucifixus etiam pro nobis, sub Pontio Pilato passus, et sepultus est.
He was crucified also for us, suffered under Pontius Pilate, and was buried.

Jesus, our loving Saviour, humbly kneeling at Thy feet we adore Thee with the deepest veneration of our soul; and in order that we may give Thee proof of the sorrow we feel for our insensibility to the outrages and sufferings which Thy loving heart made Thee undergo for our salvation in Thy painful Passion and Death, we here unite ourselves with the hearts of all those who love Thee, and together with them we give thanks unto Thee with our whole soul. We wonder at the boundless patience and the generosity of Thy Divine Heart; and we entreat Thee to fill our hearts with such a spirit of Christian penance as may enable us courageously to embrace suffering, and to make Thy cross our great comfort and all our glory.

Pater noster. Ave Maria. Gloria Patri.

iii. Panem de coelo praestitisti eis,
Omne delectamentum in se habentem.
Thou didst give them bread from heaven to eat,
Containing in itself all sweetness.

Jesus, who dost burn with love for us, humbly kneeling at Thy feet we adore Thee with the deepest veneration of our soul; and in order to make Thee recompense for the outrages which Thy Divine Heart daily receives in the most holy Sacrament of the Altar, we unite ourselves with the hearts of all those who love Thee and give Thee tender thanks. We love in Thy Divine heart this incomprehensible fire of love towards Thy Eternal Father; and we entreat Thee to inflame our hearts with ardent charity towards Thee and towards our neighbours.

Pater noster. Ave Maria. Gloria Patri.

Lastly, O most loving Jesu, we entreat Thee, by the sweetness of Thy Divine Heart, to convert the sinner, to console the afflicted, to help the dying, to lighten the pains of the souls in purgatory. Make all our hearts one in the bonds of true peace and charity, deliver us from sudden and unforeseen death, and grant us a death which shall be holy and peaceful. Amen.

V. Cor Jesu, flagrans amore nostri,
R. Inflamma cor nostrum amore Tui.

Oremus.
Concede quaesumus, omnipotens Deus, ut qui in Sanctissimo dilecti Filii tui Corde gloriantes, praecipua in nos charitatis ejus beneficia recolimus; eorum pariter et actu delectemur et fructu. Per eumdem Christum, &c.

V. Heart of Jesus, burning with love of us,
R. Inflame our hearts with love of Thee.

Let us pray.
Grant, we beseech Thee, Almighty God, that we who glory in the Most Sacred Heart of Thy well-beloved Son, and call to mind the great benefits of His heavenly charity towards us, may be gladdened by the operation and fruit of those graces in our souls. Through the same Christ our Lord.

O Divine Heart of my Jesus! I adore Thee with all the powers of my soul; I consecrate them to Thee for ever, together with all my thoughts, my words, my works, and my whole self, and I purpose to offer to Thee, as far as I am able, acts of adoration, love, and glory, like unto those which Thou dost offer to Thine Eternal Father. I beseech Thee, make reparation for my transgressions, be the Protector of my life, my refuge and asylum in the hour of my death. By Thy sighs and by that sea of bitterness in which Thou wast immersed for me throughout the whole course of Thy mortal life, grant me true contrition for my sins, contempt of earthly things, an ardent longing for the glory of heaven, trust in Thy infinite merits, and final perseverance in Thy grace.

Heart of Jesus, all love! I offer Thee these humble prayers for myself and for all who unite with me in spirit to adore Thee; vouchsafe of Thy infinite goodness to receive and to answer them, and especially for that one of us who shall first end this mortal life. Sweet Heart of my Saviour, pour down upon him in the agony of death Thine inward consolations; receive him within Thy sacred wounds; cleanse him from every stain in that Furnace of Love, that so Thou mayest open to him speedily the entrance into Thy glory, there to intercede with Thee for all those who yet tarry in this their land of exile.

Most Holy Heart of my most loving Jesus, h purpose to renew these acts of adoration and these prayers for myself, miserable sinner, as well as for all who are associated with me in adoring Thee, and to offer them to Thee every moment while I live, down to the last instant of my life. I recommend to Thee, my Jesus, the Holy Church, Thy well-beloved Spouse, our own true Mother, all just souls, all poor sinners, the afflicted, the dying, and all men over the face of the whole earth: let not Thy Blood be shed in vain for them; and vouchsafe lastly to apply it to the relief of the souls in purgatory, and above all to those who in the course of their life were wont devoutly to adore Thee.

Most loving Heart of Mary, who, amongst the hearts of all creatures of God, art at once the most pure, most inflamed with love for Jesus, and most compassionate towards us poor sinners, gain for us from the heart of Jesus our Redeemer all the graces which we ask of thee. Mother of mercies, one sigh, one movement of thy heart inflamed with love towards the Heart of Jesus, has power perfectly to console us. Grant us, then, this favour, and then the Heart of Jesus, full of that filial love It had for thee and will ever have, will not fail to hear and answer our request. Amen.

67. LITTLE CHAPLET AND PRAYERS.

Pope Pius VII., in order to extend throughout the Christian world the devotion to the Sacred Heart of Jesus, granted, by a decree of the S. Congr. of indulgences, of March 20, 1815, and Rescript of the *Segretaria* of the Memorials of September 26, 1817 -
i. An indulgence of 300 days, once a day, to all the faithful who, with contrition and devotion, say the following little Chaplet, or rather prayers, to the Sacred Heart of Jesus.
ii. A plenary indulgence, once a month, to all who say them once a day for an entire month; to be gained on that day, when, after Confession and Communion, they shall pray for the intention of the Sovereign Pontiff.

THE CHAPLET AND PRAYERS

V. Deus in adjutorium meum intende.
R. Domine ad adjuvandum me festina.
Gloria, &c.

i. My most loving Jesus, my own heart is glad when I think upon Thy most Sacred Heart, all tenderness and sweetness for sinners, and I am filled with confident hope of Thy kind welcome. But O, my sins! how many and how great are they! Grieving now, like Peter and like Magdalene, I bewail and abhor them, because they are an offence to Thee, my Sovereign Good. O, grant me pardon for them all. Would that I might die before I offend Thee again! I pray Thee, by Thy Sacred Heart, that I may live only to requite Thy love.

Say one Pater, *and five* Gloria Patri's *in honour of the Sacred Heart, then -*

119

Sweet Heart of my Jesus,
Make me love Thee ever more and more.

ii. My Jesus, I bless Thy most humble Heart; and I give thanks unto Thee, who by making It my model dost not only give me strong and urgent inducement to imitate It, but also, at the cost of so many humiliations, dost vouchsafe Thyself to point out, and to smooth for me the way to follow Thee. Cool and ungrateful that I am, how have I wandered far away from Thee! Pardon me, my Jesus! Take from me all hateful pride and ambition, that with lowly heart I may follow Thee, my Jesus, amidst humiliations, and so obtain peace and salvation. Strengthen me, Thou who canst, and I will ever bless Thy Sacred Heart.

One Pater *and five* Gloria Patri's.

Sweet heart, &c.

iii. My Jesus, I admire Thy most patient Heart, and I give Thee thanks for all the wondrous examples of unwearied patience which Thou hast left us. It grieves me that these examples still have to reproach me for my extraordinary delicacy, which shrinks from every little pain. Pour, then, into my heart, O dear Jesus, a fervent and constant love of suffering and the cross, of mortification and of penance, that, following Thee to Calvary, I may with Thee attain to glory, and the joys of Paradise.

One Pater *and five* Gloria Patri's.

Sweet heart, &c.

iv. Dear Jesus, when I look first upon Thy most gentle Heart and then upon my own, I shudder to see how unlike mine is to Thine. How I am wont to fret and grieve when a hint, a look, or a word thwarts me! Pardon for the future all my violence; and give me grace to imitate in every contradiction Thy unalterable meekness, that so I may enjoy an everlasting and holy peace.

One Pater *and five* Gloria Patri's.

Sweet heart, &c.

v. Let me sing praises to Jesus for His most generous heart, the Conqueror of death and hell; for well it merits every praise. I am more than ever confounded whilst I look upon my coward heart, which dreads even a rough word or injurious taunt. But it shall be so with me no more. My Jesus, I pray Thee for such strength that, fighting and conquering on earth, I may one day rejoice triumphantly with Thee in heaven.

One Pater *and five* Gloria Patri's.

Sweet heart, &c.

Let us now have recourse to Mary; and dedicating ourselves wholly to her, and trusting in her maternal heart, let us say: By all the virtue of thy most sweet heart obtain for us, great Mother of God, our Mother Mary, a true and enduring devotion to the Sacred Heart of Jesus, thy Son, that, bound up in every thought and affection in union with his Heart, we may fulfil all our duties, serving our Jesus evermore with readiness of heart, and especially this day.

V. Cor Jesu, flagrans amore nostri,
R. Inflamma cor nostrum amore tui.

Oremus.
Illo nos igne, quaesumus Domine, Spiritus Sanctus inflammet, quem Dominus noster Jesus Christus e penetralibus cordis sui misit in terram, et voluit vehementer accendi. Qui tecum vivit et regnat in unitate ejusdem Spiritus Sancti Deus per omnia saecula saeculorum. Amen.

TRANSLATION.

V. Heart of Jesus, burning with love of us,
R. Inflame our heart with love of Thee.

Let us pray.
Lord, we beseech Thee, let Thy holy Spirit kindle in our hearts that fire of charity which our Lord Jesus Christ, Thy Son, sent forth from his inmost heart upon this earth, and willed that it should be kindled exceedingly. Who liveth and reigneth with Thee in the unity of the same Holy Spirit, God for ever and ever. Amen.

68. FATHER BORGO'S NOVENA.

The same Pope Pius VII., desirous of increasing the devotion of the faithful to the Sacred Heart of Jesus, granted, by a decree of his Eminence the Cardinal Pro-Vicar, of March 15, 1809 (kept in the *Segretaria* of his court), and a Rescript of the S. Congr. of indulgences of Jan. 13, 1818, to all the faithful who should make, with contrite hearts, the above-named Novena before the Feast of time Sacred Heart -
i. An indulgence of 300 days, each day of the said Novena, and -
ii. A plenary indulgence, to be gained either on the Feast of the Sacred Heart or on some one day in the Octave when, after having assisted at every day of the Novena, they shall pray, after Confession and Communion, for the intention of the Sovereign Pontiff.
This Novena may be used any one other time in the year, with power to gain these indulgences on the same conditions as above.
Any of the faithful who are not in possession of F. Alphonso Rodriguez's book

on Perfection, which F. Borgo's Novena assigns as spiritual reading during the Novena, may, by the permission of the same Pope Pius VII., use any other book of devotion or spiritual reading they like.

This Novena of F. Charles Borgo, S.J., is divided into several meditations, full of doctrine and spiritual unction; it had passed through three editions before it was printed by Bourliè in Rome, in the year 1809, who has also published several other editions of the work. Its idea was suggested by a devout exercise composed concisely by the Ven. Sister Margaret Mary Alacoque of the Visitation, already mentioned above, hearing for its title "The Life of Jesus Christ in the Blessed Sacrament, and the way of honouring Him throughout the Octave of His Feast." See her life, reprinted at Rome in 1768, book vii.

69. THE PRAYER, "BEHOLD, MY MOST LOVING JESUS," ETC.

This Prayer is to be found at the end of the Indulgences relating to the Blessed Sacrament, <u>above</u>.

MOST HOLY MARY

70. OFFICE

St. Pius V., in his Bull, *Quod a nobis,* of July 9, 1568, granted -
i. An indulgence of 100 days, to all the faithful who, being bound thereto by obligation, shall devoutly say the Office of the Blessed Virgin on the days prescribed in the rubric of the Roman Breviary.
ii. An indulgence of fifty days, by another Bull, *Superni omnipotentis,* April 5, 1574, to all the faithful who shall say this office out of devotion, and not of obligation.

71. ROSARY

St. Dominic, the founder of the order of Friar Preachers, having recourse to the Blessed Virgin in order to stem the flood of the Albigensian heresy, which was spreading itself like a plague over many countries, but especially over France, instituted, by special revelation from her, in the year 1206, and afterwards very effectually promulgated, the devotion of the holy Rosary, which ever since has produced now for many ages the most marvellous results in the Christian world. In order to animate all the faithful often to have recourse to the Blessed Virgin by using this devotion, Pope Benedict XIII. granted, by his Brief, *Sanctissimus,* of April 13, 1726, to all who say with contrition the whole Rosary of fifteen decades, or the third part of it of five decades -

i. An indulgence of 100 days for every *Pater noster* and every *Ave Maria.*

ii. A plenary indulgence to all who shall say the third part of it once every day for a year; on any one day in the year, after Confession and Communion.

The present Sovereign Pontiff Pius IX., by a decree of the S. Congr. of Indulgences of May 12, 1851, confirmed these Indulgences, and granted besides -

iii. An indulgence of seven years and seven quarantines to every one who with contrition shall say a third part of the Rosary in company with others, either in public or private.

iv. A plenary Indulgence, on the last Sunday in every month, to all who are in the habit of saying with others, at least three times a week, the said third part of the Rosary; provided that on that Sunday they shall, after Confession and Communion, visit a church or public oratory, and pray there for a time according to the mind of his Holiness.

To gain these Indulgences it is requisite that the Rosaries should be blessed by religious of the order of Friar-Preachers, and that, during the recital of the Rosary, meditation be made on the mysteries of the Birth, Passion, Death, Resurrection, &c. of our Lord Jesus Christ, according to the decree of the S. Congr. of Indulgences of August 12, 1726, approved by the above-named Pope Benedict XIII. Note, moreover, that our holy Father declared, in his Constitution *Pretiosus,* of May 16, 1727, § 4, that simple people who could not meditate might obtain the Indulgence by merely saying the Rosary devoutly. Observe also that all persons enrolled in the Confraternity of the Rosary, wherever It has been canonically erected, gain many other Indulgences when they say the Rosary, or do any other pious work. See the Brief of the venerable Pontiff Innocent XI., *Nuper pro parte,* of July 31, 1679; also another Brief of Pius VII., *Ad augendam,* of February 16, 1808, and the above-named decree of Pope Pius IX., of May 12, 1851.

THE MYSTERIES ON WHICH WE ARE TO MEDITATE WHILE WE SAY THE ROSARY.

The Joyful Mysteries.

1. In the First Joyful Mystery we meditate on the Annunciation made by the angel Gabriel to most holy Mary, that she was to conceive and bear a Son, our

Lord Jesus Christ.

One Pater noster, *ten* Ave Maria's, *and one* Gloria Patri; *so also in all the mysteries.*

2. In the Second Joyful Mystery we meditate how, when Mary heard that Elizabeth had conceived, she went to her house to visit her, and stayed with her three months.

3. In the Third Joyful Mystery we meditate how, when the full time of Mary's delivery was come, she brought forth our Saviour Jesus Christ at midnight, in the city of Bethlehem, and laid Him in a manger between two brute beasts.

4. in the Fourth Joyful Mystery we meditate how most Holy Mary, on the day of her Purification, presented Christ our Lord in the Temple, and placed Him in the arms of the holy old man Simeon.

5. In the Fifth Joyful Mystery we meditate how the Virgin Mary lost her Son, sought for Him three days, and at the end of the third day found Him in the Temple amid the doctors, both hearing them and asking them questions, at twelve years of age.

The Sorrowful Mysteries.

1. In the First Sorrowful Mystery we meditate how our Lord Jesus Christ prayed in the garden of Olivet, and sweated blood.

2. In the Second Sorrowful Mystery we meditate how our Lord Jesus Christ was cruelly scourged in Pilate's house with innumerable blows.

3. In the Third Sorrowful Mystery we meditate how our Lord Jesus Christ was crowned with sharp thorns.

4. In the Fourth Sorrowful Mystery we meditate how Jesus was condemned to die, and, for His greater ignominy and pain, the heavy tree of the cross was laid upon his shoulder.

5. In the Fifth Sorrowful Mystery we meditate how, when Jesus arrived at Calvary, He was stripped, and nailed with iron nails to the cross, and died thereon before the eyes of His afflicted Mother.

The Glorious Mysteries.

1. In the First Glorious Mystery we meditate how Jesus Christ our Lord rose again in glory, the third day after His Death and Passion, triumphant over death, and never more to die.

2. In the Second Glorious Mystery we meditate how Jesus Christ, the fortieth day after His Resurrection, ascended into heaven with great joy and triumph, in the presence of His most holy Mother and His disciples.

3. In the Third Glorious Mystery we meditate how Jesus Christ sat down on the right hand of the Father, and sent from thence the Holy Ghost into the room where the Apostles and the most holy Virgin were assembled.

4. In the Fourth Glorious Mystery we meditate how, twelve years after our Lord Jesus Christ rose from the dead, His Mother herself passed from this mortal life, and was carried into heaven by the angels.

5. In the Fifth Glorious Mystery we meditate how, in heaven, Mary was crowned by her Son; in this Mystery also we meditate upon the glory of the saints.

This Rosary may end with the Litanies of the B. Virgin.
See the indulgences for them below.

72. THE ROSARY HOUR

Pope Pius VII., by the Brief *Ad augendam,* of Feb. 16, 1808, granted -
A plenary indulgence once a year to all the faithful who, being truly penitent, should, after Confession and Communion, on the day and hour assigned to them, say with devotion the Rosary and other prayers.

73. THE ROSARY OR CHAPLET CALLED ST. BRIDGET'S

Pope Leo X., in a Bull of July 10, 1515, and Pope Clement XI., in a Bull *De salute Dominici gregis,* of Sept. 22, 1714, granted many Indulgences to all who carry with them, or who say, the Chaplet, called St. Bridget's because she first conceived the idea of it and promulgated the usage of it. These Indulgences were confirmed by Pope Benedict XIV., in a Brief of Jan. 15, 1743, wherein he added others, of all which a summary will now be given.

This Chaplet is said in honour of the sixty-three years which, it is said, the most holy Mary lived upon this earth: it is composed of six divisions, each division consisting of one *Pater noster,* ten *Ave Maria's,* and one *Credo.* After these, one *Pater noster* more is said, and three more *Ave Maria's:* thus in all there will be seven *Pater noster's,* to mark the number of her Seven Sorrows and Seven Joys; and the three *Ave Maria's* are added to make up the full number of sixty-three years. (See the Archivium of the *Segretaria* of the S. Congr. of Indulgences, tom. vi. p.144.) Moreover, it will be seen in the following summary that the same Indulgences may be gained by saying the fifteen decades, or five decades only, as is mentioned in the preceding Rosary.

It is requisite, in order to gain these Indulgences, that the Chaplet, being made, as has been said, of six decades, &c., should be blessed by the superiors of the monastic houses or other priests of the order of St. Saviour, sometimes called the order of St. Bridget, deputed for this purpose; and after they have been blessed they cannot be sold, or lent for the purpose of communicating the Indulgences to others, according to the express command of the said Pope Clement XI. in the Bull above named, and according to the general decrees of the S. Congr. of Indulgences, confirmed by Benedict XIV., under date Feb. 9, 1743.

SUMMARY OF INDULGENCES ANNEXED TO THE CHAPLET OF ST. BRIDGET.

i. An indulgence of 100 days for each *Pater,* 100 days for each *Ave,* and 100 days for each *Credo,* to all the faithful who say the Rosary or Chaplet of St. Bridget. Pope Leo X., July 10, 1515.
ii. An Indulgence or seven years and seven quarantines, besides the above, to every one who says the said Rosary or Chaplet of fifteen decades. Grant of the same Pope Leo.
(Whenever this Rosary is said with others, each person may gain the Indulgences i. and ii. precisely the same as when the said Rosary is said by one person alone. The same Pope Leo.)
iii. A plenary indulgence to all who shall say at least five decades daily for a year, on any one day in the year when, after Confession and Communion, they shall pray for the Holy Church. Pope Clement XI., Sept. 22, 1714.
iv. A plenary indulgence, on the Feast of St. Bridget (Oct. 8), to all who say the said Rosary of five decades at least once a week, and who on this day shall, after Confession and Communion, visit their own parish church or any other church, and pray to God there for the Church as above. Benedict XIV., Jan. 15, 1743.
v. A plenary indulgence to all who, having Confessed and Communicated, or being at least contrite, shall have been accustomed to say this Rosary, as in No. iv., when, *in articulo mortis,* recommending their soul to God, they say the holy name JESUS with their hearts, if unable to do so with their lips. Benedict XIV.
vi. A plenary indulgence, once a month, to all who say this Chaplet daily for a month, on any one day when, after Communion, they visit a church and pray as

above. Benedict XIV.

vii. An indulgence of forty days to all who carry this Rosary with them, if, at the tolling of the bell for a passing soul, they kneel down and pray for that soul. Benedict XIV.

viii. An indulgence of twenty days to all who carry this Rosary, whenever they make examination of conscience, and say three *Pater noster's* and three *Ave Maria's*. Ben. XIV.

ix. An indulgence of 100 days to all who carry this Rosary whenever they hear Mass (feast-day or ferial), or assist at a sermon, or accompany the Most Holy Viaticum, or bring back any sinner into the way of salvation, or do any other good work in honour of our Lord Jesus Christ, the Blessed Virgin, or St. Bridget, provided they say also three *Pater noster's* and three *Ave Maria's*. Benedict XIV., as before.

74. THE LITANIES

The Litanies commonly called " Litanies of our Lady" are named "Litanies of Loretto" in the Constitutions of several Sovereign Pontiffs, - viz. *Reddituri,* of Sixtus V., July11, 1687; *Sanctissimus,* of Clement VIII., Sept. 6, 1601; and *In supremo,* of Alexander VII., May 28, 1664 - by reason of their being sung with great solemnity every Saturday in the Holy House of Loretto. They are composed of humble supplications and devout prayers to Almighty and (this being the meaning of the word "Litanies"), offered up through the intercession of our Blessed Lady, who is honoured therein by the application to her of the mystic figures, high titles, and glorious appellations whereby she is invoked. That these Litanies, when said by the faithful, in church in public, or at home in private, might always remain word for word exactly as they have been handed down to us from ancient tradition, Pope Alexander VII., in the Constitution above named, strictly forbade the making of any alteration in them.

To encourage the faithful often to have recourse to the intercession of most holy Mary in their behalf with Almighty (and, and at the same time to do her honour, Pope Sixtus V., in the above-named Constitution, granted -

i. An indulgence of 200 days, every time these Litanies are said with devotion and contrition.

Pope Benedict XIII., by a decree of the S. Congr. of Indulgences, Jan. 12, 1728, confirmed this Indulgence; and Pope Pius VII., confirming it afresh by a decree of the same S. Congr. of Sept 30, 1817, extended it to 300 days.

He granted, moreover, to all who say them daily -

ii. A plenary Indulgence on the five Feasts of our Blessed Lady, of Obligation according to the Roman Calendar, viz, the Immaculate Conception, the

Nativity, the Annunciation, the Purification, and the Assumption, on condition that, being truly contrite for their sins, and after Confession and Communion, they visit a public church, and pray according to the intention of the Pope.

LITANY OF THE BLESSED VIRGIN;

Commonly called the Litany of Loretto.

Kyrie eleison.	Lord have mercy.
Kyrie eleison.	Lord have mercy.
Christe eleison.	Christ have mercy.
Christe eleison.	Christ have mercy.
Kyrie eleison.	Lord have mercy.
Kyrie eleison.	Lord have mercy.
Christe audi nos.	Christ hear us.
Christe exaudi nos.	Christ graciously hear us.
Pater de coelis Deus, miserere nobis.	God the Father of heaven, have mercy on us.
Fili Redemptor mundi Deus, miserere nobis.	God the Son, Redeemer of the world, have mercy on us.
Spiritus Sancte Deus, miserere nobis.	God the Holy Ghost, have mercy on us.
Sancta Trinitas, unus Deus, miserere nobis.	Holy Trinity, one God, have mercy on us.
Sancta Maria, ora pro nobis.	Holy Mary, pray for us.
Sancta Dei Genitrix, ora pro nobis.	Holy Mother of God, pray for us.
Sancta Virgo virginum, ora pro nobis.	Holy Virgin of virgins, pray for us.
Mater Christi, ora pro nobis.	Mother of Christ, pray for us.
Mater divinae gratiae, ora pro nobis.	Mother of divine grace, pray for us.
Mater purissima, ora pro nobis.	Mother most pure, pray for us.
Mater castissima, ora pro nobis.	Mother most chaste, pray for us.
Mater inviolata, ora pro nobis.	Mother inviolate, pray for us.
Mater intemerata, ora pro nobis.	Mother undefiled, pray for us.
Mater amabilis, ora pro nobis.	Mother most amiable, pray for us.
Mater admirabilis, ora pro nobis.	Mother most admirable, pray for us.
Mater Creatoris, ora pro nobis.	Mother of our Creator, pray for us.
Mater Salvatoris, ora pro nobis.	Mother of our Redeemer, pray for us.
Virgo prudentissima, ora pro nobis.	Virgin most prudent, pray for us.
Virgo veneranda, ora pro nobis.	Virgin most venerable, pray for us.
Virgo praedicanda, ora pro nobis.	Virgin most renowned, pray for us.
Virgo potens, ora pro nobis.	Virgin most powerful, pray for us.
Virgo clemens, ora pro nobis.	Virgin most merciful, pray for us.
Virgo fidelis, ora pro nobis.	
Speculum justitiae, ora pro nobis.	

Sedes sapientiae, ora pro nobis.
Causa nostrae laetitiae, ora pro nobis.
Vas spirituale, ora pro nobis.
Vas honorabile, ora pro nobis.
Vas insigne devotionis, ora pro nobis.
Rosa mystica, ora pro nobis.
Turris Davidica, ora pro nobis.
Turris eburnea, ora pro nobis.
Domus aurea, ora pro nobis.
Foederis area, ora pro nobis.
Janua coeli, ora pro nobis.
Stella matutina, ora pro nobis.
Salus infirmorum, ora pro nobis.
Refugium peccatorum, ora pro nobis.
Consolatrix afflictorum, ora pro nobis.
Auxilium Christianorum, ora pro nobis.
Regina Angelorum, ora pro nobis.
Regina Patriarcharum, ora pro nobis.
Regina Prophetarum, ora pro nobis.
Regina Apostolorum, ora pro nobis.
Regina Martyrum, ora pro nobis.
Regina Confessorum, ora pro nobis.
Regina Virginum, ora pro nobis.
Regina Sanctorum omnium, ora pro nobis.
Regina sine labe originali concepta, ora pro nobis.

Agnus Dei, qui tollis peccata mundi, Parce nobis, Domine.
Agnus Dei, qui tollis peccata mundi. Exaudi nos, Domine.
Agnus Dei, qui tollis peccata mundi, Miserere nobis.
Christe audi nos.
Christe exaudi nos.

V. Ora pro nobis, sancta Dei Genitrix.
R. Ut digni efficiamur promissionibus Christi.

Virgin most faithful, pray for us.
Mirror of justice, pray for us.
Seat of wisdom, pray for us.
Cause of our joy, pray for us.
Spiritual Vessel, pray for us.
Vessel of honour, pray for us.
Special Vessel of devotion, pray for us.
Mystical Rose, pray for us.
Tower of David, pray for us.
Tower of ivory, pray for us.
House of gold, pray for us.
Ark of the covenant, pray for us.
Gate of heaven, pray for us.
Morning star, pray for us.
Health of the sick, pray for us.
Refuge of sinners, pray for us.
Comforter of the afflicted, pray for us.
Help of Christians, pray for us.
Queen of Angels, pray for us.
Queen of Patriarchs, pray for us.
Queen of Prophets, pray for us.
Queen of Apostles, pray for us.
Queen of Martyrs, pray for us.
Queen of Confessors, pray for us.
Queen of Virgins, pray for us.
Queen of all Saints, pray for us.
Queen conceived without stain of original sin, pray for us.

Lamb of God, who takest away the sins of the world, Spare us, O Lord.
Lamb of God, who takest away the sins of the world, Graciously hear us, O Lord.
Lamb of God, who takest away the sins of the world, Have mercy on us.
Christ hear us,
Christ graciously hear us.

V. Pray for us, O holy Mother of God.

Oremus.
Gratiam tuam, quaesumus Domine, mentibus nostris infunde: ut qui, angelo nuntiante, Christi Filii tui Incarnationem cognovimus, per Passionem + ejus et Crucem ad resurrectionis gloriam perducamur. Per eumdem Christum Dominum nostrum. R. Amen.

V. Divinum auxilium maneat semper nobiscum. R. Amen.

R. That we may be made worthy of the promises of Christ.

Let us pray.
Pour forth, we beseech Thee, O Lord, Thy grace into our hearts; that we to whom the Incarnation of Christ Thy Son was made known by the message of an angel, may by His Passion + and Cross be brought to the glory of His resurrection. Through the same Christ our Lord. R. Amen.

V. May the divine assistance remain always with us. R. Amen.

75. THE "ANGELUS DOMINI," ETC., OR THE "REGINA COELI," ETC.

The seraphic Doctor St. Bonaventura, in the General Chapter of his Order, held at Pisa in the year 1262, directed his religious to exhort the faithful to say, at the sound of the church-bell at even, three times the *Ave Maria,* in veneration of the mystery of the Incarnation of the Son of God in the most pure womb of the Blessed Virgin, by the operation of the Holy Ghost. This same devotion, which bad been already introduced in the episcopal church of Saintes (the capital of Saintonge in Western France), was approved by Pope John XXII., by a bull dated from Avignon, Oct. 13, 1318, who granted several days of Indulgence to all who should practise it with contrition; and this grant was renewed by him, May 7, 1327, in the injunction he sent to his Cardinal Vicar, to give at even in Rome a signal, by the sounding of the church-bell, to remind all persons to say these three *Ave Maria's.* See F. Theodore a Spiritu Sancto, *de Indulgentiis,* part ii. art. iv. § v.
In later times Pope Benedict XIII. opened the treasury of the Church to bestow greater Indulgences in furtherance of this pious practice; being desirous that all the faithful, not once only but many times a day, should implore the protection of the Ever-blessed Virgin, and venerate the grand mystery of the Incarnation. Accordingly, by a universal Brief, *Injuncta nobis,* of Sept. 14, 1724, he granted to all Christians who, at the sound of the bell, morning, noon, and even, at

sunset, shall say on their knees daily the *Angelus Domini, &c.,* with three *Ave Marias, -*

i. A plenary indulgence and remission of all sins, once a month, on any one day when, after Confession and Communion, they pray for the Holy Church, &c.

ii. An indulgence of 100 days, every time that, being truly penitent, they say the *Angelus Domini,* as above.

These Indulgences are not suspended in the Holy Year, as the same Pope Benedict XIII. expressly declared, Jan. 10, 1725, and as other Popes afterwards, viz. Benedict XIV., Clement XIV., and Leo XII., have declared in their respective Bulls, quoted above, on the suspension of Indulgences in the Holy Year.

Afterwards Pope Benedict XIV., by a formal notice issued by his Cardinal-Vicar, published in the year 1742, April 20, confirmed the above-named Indulgences, at the same time declaring that the *Angelus Domini* was to be said standing, every Sunday in the year, beginning from first Vespers, that is, Saturday evening; and that in Paschal tide the *Regina coeli,* should be said in its stead, always standing, with its proper V., R., and prayer.

Note, that those who do not know the *Regina coeli* may obtain the same Indulgences by saying the *Angelus Domini* as above.

Observe also: i. That Religions of both sexes, or others who live in community, if they cannot say the *Angelus Domini* or *Regina coeli* at the sound of the bell as aforesaid, by reason of their being engaged upon some work prescribed by their rule or constitution, may obtain the above-named Indulgences, provided that immediately on the conclusion of their respective duties they say the *Angelus Domini* or *Regina coeli.* This is evident from the Papal Rescript of the S. Congr. of Indulgences of Sept. 5, 1727. And observe: ii. That all the faithful who happen to be dwelling where there is no such bell, may obtain the above-named Indulgences if, at the hours specified or thereabouts, they say the *Angelus Domini* or *Regina coeli,* according to the season. See the Rescript of Pope Pius VI. of March 18, 1781.

V. Angelus Domini nuntiavit Mariae, et concepit de Spiritu Sancto.
Ave Maria.

V. Ecce ancilla Domini, fiat mihi secundum verbum tuum.
Ave Maria.

V. Et verbum caro factum est, et habitavit in nobis.
Ave Maria.

The following ending may be added:

V. Ora pro nobis, Sancta Dei Genitrix.
R. Ut digni efficiamur promissionibus Christi.

Oremus.

Gratiam tuam, quaesumus Domine, mentibus nostris infunde: ut qui, angelo nuntiante, Christi Filii tui incarnationem cognovimus, per Passionem ejus et Crucem ad resurrectionis gloriam perducamur. Per eundem Christum Dominum nostrum. R. Amen.

TRANSLATION.

V. The angel of the Lord declared unto Mary, and she conceived of the Holy Ghost.
Ave Maria.

V. Behold the handmaid of the Lord; be it done unto me according to Thy word.
Ave Maria.

V. And the Word was made Flesh, and dwelt among us.
Ave Maria.

V. Pray for us, O Holy Mother of God.
R. That we may be made worthy of the promises of Christ.

Let us pray.
Pour forth, we beseech Thee, O Lord, Thy grace into our hearts; that we to whom the Incarnation of Christ Thy Son was made known by the message of an angel, may by His Passion and Cross be brought to the glory of His resurrection. Through the same Christ our Lord. R. Amen.

In Paschal-time, that is, from Holy Saturday at midday to midday on the Saturday preceding the Feast of the Most Most Trinity, inclusive, instead of saying the Angelus Domini the following is to be said, standing.

Regina coeli laetare. Alleluia.
Quia quem meruisti portare. Alleluia..
Resurrexit sicut dixit. Alleluia.
Ora pro nobis Deum. Alleluia.
V. Gaude et laetare, Virgo Maria. Alleluia.
R. Quia surrexit Dominus vere. Alleluia.

Oremus.
Dens, qui per resurrectionem Filii tui Domini nostri Jesu Christi mundum laetificare dignatus es; praesta quaesumus, ut per ejus Genitricem Virginem Mariam perpetuae capiamus gaudia vitae. Per eumdem Christum Dominum nostrum. R. Amen.

TRANSLATION.

Queen of heaven, rejoice. Alleluia.
For He whom thou wast made worthy to bear. Allehuia.
Hath arisen, as He said. Alleluia.
Pray for us to our God. Alleluia.
V. Rejoice and be glad, Virgin Mary. Alleluia.
R. For the Lord hath risen indeed. Alleluia.

Let us pray.
O God, who through the resurrection of Thy Son our Lord Jesus Christ hast vouchsafed to give joy to the whole world; grant, we beseech Thee, that, through the intercession of the Virgin Mary His Mother, we may obtain the joys of eternal life. Through the same our Lord Jesus Christ. Amen.

---

76. THE "SALVE REGINA," ETC., AND THE "SUB TUUM PRAESIDIUM," ETC.

Pope Pius VI., by a decree of the S. Congr. of Indulgences, April 5, 1786, after expressing his approbation of the following devout practice introduced and propagated by certain pious persons in Germany (as mentioned in the decree already quoted), granted -
i. An indulgence of 100 days, every day; and -
ii. An indulgence of seven years and seven quarantines, on all Sundays, to all the faithful who, being moved by a spirit of true religion to make some reparation for the injuries done to the honour of Mary, Mother of God, and to the saints by heretics, and to defend and propagate the worship *(cultus)* and veneration of their sacred images and pictures, shall to this end say at morn the *Salve Regina,* &c., with the VV. *Dignare me,* &c. and *Benedictus Deus in sanctis suis,* and at even the *Sub tuum praesidium,* &c. with the same versicles. Moreover, to all who say these prayers every day, he granted -
iii. A plenary indulgence twice a month, on any two Sundays when, after Confession and Communion, they shall pray according to the intention of the Sovereign Pontiff.
iv. A plenary indulgence, on the same conditions, on every Feast of our Blessed Lady, and on the Feast of All Saints.
v. A plenary indulgence at the hour of death to all who have been accustomed during life to say these prayers, provided they have been to Confession and Communion, or are at least contrite in heart.

AT MORN.

Salve regina, mater misericordiae, vita, dulcedo, et spes nostra, salve. Ad te clamamus exules filii Hevae; ad te suspiramus, gementes et flentes in hac lacrymarum valle. Eja ergo, advocata nostra, illos tuos misericordes oculos ad nos converte; et Jesum benedictum fructum ventris tui nobis post hoc exilium ostende, O clemens, O pia, O dulcis Virgo Maria.

V. Dignare me laudare te, Virgo sacrata.
R. Da mihi virtutem contra hostes tuos.
V. Benedictus Deus in sanctis suis.
R. Amen.

AT EVEN.

Sub tuum praesidium confugimus, Sancta Dei Genitrix; nostras deprecationes ne despicias in necessitatibus nostris, et a periculis cunctis libera nos, semper Virgo gloriosa et benedicta.

The VV. Dignare, *&c. as before.*

TRANSLATION.

AT MORN.

Hail, Holy Queen, Mother of Mercy, our Life, our Sweetness, and our Hope, all hail! To thee we cry, poor banished sons of Eve; to thee we send up our sighs, weeping and mourning in this vale of tears. Turn, then most gracious Advocate, thine eyes of mercy towards us; and after this our exile, show unto us the blessed Fruit of thy womb, Jesus, O merciful, O kind, O sweet Virgin Mary.

V. Make me worthy to praise Thee, Holy Virgin.
R. Give me strength against thine enemies.
V. Blessed be God in His saints.
R. Amen.

AT EVEN.

We fly to thy patronage, O Holy Mother of God; despise not thou our petitions in our necessities, but deliver us always from all dangers, O ever glorious and blessed Virgin.

V. Make me worthy, &c. *as before.*

77. EJACULATION IN HONOUR OF THE IMMACULATE CONCEPTION

Pope Pius VI., by a Rescript of Nov. 21, 1793, at the prayer of the seraphic order of St. Francis, granted to all the faithful, in order to increase the fervour of their devotion to the great mystery of the Immaculate Conception of most holy Mary -

An indulgence of 100 days, every time they say with devotion either of the following ejaculations:

Blessed he the Holy and Immaculate Conception of the Blessed Virgin Mary.

Or,

In conceptione tua, Virgo Maria, immaculata fuisti: ora pro nobis Patrem, cujus Filium Jesum de Spiritu Saucto conceptum peperisti.

TRANSLATION.

In thy Conception, O Mary, thou wast Immaculate. Pray for us to the Eternal Father, whose only-begotten Son Jesus, conceived in thy womb by the Holy Ghost, thou didst bring forth.

78. INVOCATION OF THE MOST HOLY NAME OF MARY

Mary is the name of our tender Mother, our loving Mediatrix, the Stewardess of God's graces, the Queen of the Universe, and Mother of God. This name has many mystic meanings - as, Star of the Sea, who dost illuminate the world, Princess; titles of glory to her, and consolation to us. The name of Mary, then, ought to be ever in our hearts, and often on our lips during life, and specially at the moment of our death. To animate the faithful often to invoke this name in union with the name of Jesus, Pope Sixtus V., in his Bull *Reddituri,* of July 11, 1587, granted many Indulgences afterwards confirmed by Benedict XIII. See above, Indulgences for the Most Holy Name of Jesus.

79. PSALMS IN HONOUR OF HER MOST HOLY NAME

Amongst the devout practices invented to honour the most holy name of Mary, our Mother and our Queen, one of the most ancient is that of saying Five Psalms whose initial letters compose her name. This devotion, well known in Italy and France, and in other kingdoms, has been much more extensively circulated ever since the Venerable Pope Innocent XI., in 1684, established throughout the whole Catholic world the Feast of this Glorious Name of Mary, at the same the that he instituted the archconfraternity of the Name of Mary, with power to aggregate to itself other confraternities out of Rome; to all of whose members who should recite these five psalms in honour of the name of the great Virgin, he granted certain Indulgences, confirmed by subsequent Popes.
Pope Pius VII., desirous that all the faithful should practise this devotion, by a

135

decree of the S. Congr. of Indulgences of June 13, 1815, granted the following fresh Indulgences:

i. The Indulgence or seven years and seven quarantines for each recitation of these psalms.

ii. A plenary indulgence once a month to all who recite them daily for a month, on any one day when, after Confession and Communion, they pray according to the intention of the Sovereign Pontiff.

iii. A plenary indulgence on the Sunday in the octave of our Lady's Nativity (the Feast of her Name), provided that on that day, after Confession and Communion, they pray as above.

THE FIVE PSALMS.

Ant. Mariae nomen.

M. *Cantic. B.V.M. Luc. I.*

Magnificat: * anima mea Dominum.
Et exsultavit spiritus meus: * in Deo, salutari meo.
Quia respexit humilitatem ancillae suae: * ecce enim ex hoc beatam me dicent omnes generationes.
Quia fecit mihi magna, qui potens est: * et sanctum nomen ejus.
Et misericordia ejus, a progenie in progenies: * timentibus eum.
Fecit potentiam in brachio suo: * dispersit superbos mente cordis sui.
Deposuit potentes de sede: * et exaltavit humiles.
Esurientes implevit bonis: * et divites dimisit inanes.
Suscepit Israel puerum suum: * recordatus misericordiae suae.
Sicut locutus est ad patres nostros: * Abraham, et semini ejus in saecula.
Gloria Patri, et Filio, * et Spiritui Sancto.
Sicut erat in principio, et nunc, et semper, * et in saecula saeculorum. Amen.

Ant. Mariae nomen cunctas illustrat ecclesias, cui fecit magna, qui potens est, et sanctum nomen ejus.

Ant. A solis ortu.

A. *Ps.* 119.

Ad Dominum cum tribularer clamavi: * et exaudivit me.
Domine, libera animam meam a labiis iniquis, * et a lingua dolosa.
Quid detur tibi, aut quid apponatur tibi * ad linguam dolosam?
Sagittae potentis acutae, * cum carbonibus desolatoriis.
Heu mihi, quia incolatus meus prolongatus est: habitavi cum habitantibus Cedar: * multum incola fuit anima mea.
Cum his, qui oderunt pacem, eram pacificus: * cum loquebar illis, impugnabant me gratis.

Gloria Patri, et Filio, * et Spiritui Sancto.
Sicut erat in principio, et nunc, et semper, * et in saecula saeculorum. Amen.

Ant. A solis ortu usque ad occasum laudabile nomen Domini, et Mariae matris ejus.

Ant. Refugium est.

R. *Ps.* 118.

Retribue servo tuo, vivifica me; * et custodiam sermones tuos.
Evela oculos meos, * et considerabo mirabilia tua.
Incola ego sum in terra, * non abscondas a me mandata tua.
Concupivit anima mea desiderare justificationes tuas * in omni tempore.
Increpasti superbos: * maledicti qui declinant a mandatis tuis.
Aufer a me opprobrium, et contemptum, * quia testimonia tua exquisivi.
Etenim sederunt principes, et adversus me loquebantur: * servus autem tuus exercebatur in justificationibus tuis.
Nam et testimonia tua meditatio mea est: * et consilium meum jumstificationes tuae.
Adhaesit pavimento anima mea: * vivifica me secundum verbum tuum.
Vias meas enuntiavi, et exaudisti me: * doce me justificationes tuas.
Viam justificationum tuarum instrue me, * et exercebor in mirabilibus tuis.
Dormitavit anima mea prae taedio: * confirma me in verbis tuis.
Viam iniquitatis amove a me, * et de lege tua miserere mei.
Viam veritatis elegi : * judicia tua non sum oblitus.
Adhaesi testimoniis tuis, Domine: * noli me confundere.
Viam mandatorum tuorum cucurri, * dum dilatasti cor meum.
Gloria Patri, et Filio, * et Spiritui Sancto.
Sicut erat in principio, et nunc, et semper, * et in saecula saeculorum. Amen.

Ant. Refugium est in tribulationibus Mariae nomen omnibus illud invocantibus.

Ant. In universa terra.

I. *Ps.* 125.

In convertendo Dominus captivitatem Sion: * facti sumus sicut consolati.
Tunc repletum est gaudio os nostrum: * et lingua nostra exsultatione.
Tunc dicent inter Gentes: * Magnificavit Dominus facere cum eis.
Magnificavit Dominus facere nobiscum: * facti sumus laetantes.
Converte, Domine, captivitatem nostram, * sicut torrens in austro.
Qui seminant in lacrimis, * in exsultatione metent.
Euntes ibant et flebant, * mittentes semina sua.
Venientes autem venient cum exsultatione, * portantes manipulos suos.

Gloria Patri, et Filio, * et Spiritui Sancto.
Sicut erat in principio, et nunc, et semper, * et in saecula saeculorum. Amen.

Ant. In universa terra admirabile est nomen tuum, O Maria.

Ant. Annuntiaverunt.

A. *Ps.* 122.

Ad te levavi oculos meos: * qui habitas in coelis.
Ecce sicut oculi servorum: * in manibus dominorum suorum.
Sicut oculi ancillae in manibus dominae suae: * ita oculi nostri ad Dominum,
Deum nostrum, donec misereatur nostri.
Miserere nostri, Domine, miserere nostri: * quia multum repleti sumus
despectione.
Quia multum repleta est anima nostra: * opprobrium abundantibus, et
despectio superbis.
Gloria Patri, et Filio, * et Spiritui Sancto.
Sicut erat in principio, et nunc, et semper, * et in saecula saeculorum. Amen.

Ant. Annuntiaverunt coeli nomen Mariae, et viderunt omnes populi gloriam
ejus.

V. Sit nomen Virginis Mariae benedictum.
R. Ex hoc nunc et usque in saeculum.

Oremus.
Concede quaesumus, omnipotens Deus, ut fideles tui, qui sub sanctissimae
Virginis Mariae nomine et protectione laetantur; ejus pia intercessione a
cunctis malis liberemur in terris, et ad gaudia aeterna pervenire mereantur in
coelis. Per Dominum, &c.

TRANSLATION.

V. Blessed be the name of Mary the Virgin.
R. From henceforth and for evermore.

Let us pray.
Grant, we beseech Thee, Almighty God, that Thy faithful people, wino rejoice
in the shelter of the name and protection of the most Holy Virgin Mary, may by
her loving intercession be delivered from all evils here on earth, and be made
worthy to attain eternal glory in the life to come. Through our Lord Jesus
Christ. Amen.

80. THE FORTY "AVE MARIA'S" IN HONOUR OF HER SACRED DELIVERY

The devotion commonly called the Forty *Ave Maria's* was first devised and afterwards continually practised by St. Catherine of Bologna; its object being to dispose the faithful during Advent for the devout celebration of the Sacred Delivery of Mary on Christmas Day. To further this devotion, Pope Pius VII., by a Rescript of the S. Congr. of Indulgences, Nov. 14, 1815, granted -
i. The indulgence of 100 days to the faithful, for each day that they practise this devotion fervently and with a contrite heart; and -
ii. The plenary indulgence to those who shall have practised it at least twenty times, provided that, being truly contrite, having Confessed and Communicated, they visit a church and pray there according to the intention of the Sovereign Pontiff.

Order to be observed in this devotion, commencing Nov. 29, and ending Dec. 23.

OFFERING AND PRAYER TO BE SAID EVERY DAY.

We kneel in lowly reverence at thy feet, great Mother of our God, most holy Mary, advocate of sinners; humbly praying thee by the merits of the Precious Blood of thy Divine Son, shed for us sinners, and by the intercession of thy well-beloved servant, Catherine, to gain for us by thy prayers true fervour of spirit in this holy exercise, and the grace to walk in the way of all thy virtues, after the example of St. Catherine, to the honour and glory of Jesus Christ, thine only Son our Saviour. Forget our monstrous ingratitude, look not upon our sins, but rather find for us a refuge in the depths of thy loving kindness; and remembering the love wherewith thou didst love thy faithful servant Catherine, obtain for us the remission of our sins, that so we may confidently hope to attain all that we desire for our spiritual wants. Amen.

For the first day.
In imitation of Saint Catherine, we purpose now to praise the great Mother of our God, honouring her Sacred Delivery, by saying to her forty Angelical Salutations and forty Benedictions, thereby to obtain her powerful aid at the hour of our death, and a true contrition for our sins, that so we may pass from this land of our pilgrimage to eternal joys.

For the other days.
Let us continue to praise the great Mother of our God, honouring her Sacred Delivery with forty Angelical Salutations and forty Benedictions, to obtain thereby her powerful aid at the hour of our death, and true contrition for our sins, that so we may pass from this land of our pilgrimage to eternal joys.

For the last day.

To-day we shall end this exercise praising the great Mother of our God, and honouring her Sacred Delivery, with forty Angelical Salutations and forty Benedictions, to obtain thereby her powerful aid at the hour of our death, and true contrition for our sins, that so we may pass from this land of our pilgrimage to eternal joys.

FOR THE FIRST DECADE.

Whilst saying the first ten *Ave Maria's* and ten Benedictions, we will meditate on the ineffable mystery of the Incarnation of the Eternal Word, and the great dignity of the Virgin who was elected to be the Mother of the Highest.

Ave Maria *ten times, and after each* Ave *say,*
O Mary, blessed be the hour when thou didst become Mother of Jesus, Son of God.

FOR THE SECOND DECADE.

Whilst saying the second ten *Ave Maria's* and ten Benedictions, we will meditate on the humility of the King of heaven, who chose for His birthplace a poor stable, and on the joy of Mary when first she saw the Only-begotten of the Father, the Fruit of her womb.

Ave Maria *ten times, and after each,*
O Mary, blessed be the hour when thou didst bring forth Jesus, Son of God.

FOR THE THIRD DECADE.

Whilst saying the third ten *Ave Maria's* and ten Benedictions, we will devoutly meditate upon the exact carefulness of Mary, fulfilling perfectly the offices both of Martha and of Magdalene, in that she both contemplated her Son as her Redeemer, and at the same time ministered to Him as her Child.

Ave Maria *ten times, and after each,*
O Mary, blessed be the hour when thou didst give suck to Jesus, Son of God.

FOR THE FOURTH DECADE.

Whilst saying the fourth ten *Ave Maria's* and ten Benedictions, we will devoutly meditate upon the great reverence with which Mary embraced and pressed more to her very heart than to her bosom, kissed and adored her God and ours, incarnate for love of us; and moved thereby with awe and devout affection we will say,

Ave Maria *ten times, and after each,*
Blessed be the hour, Mary, when thou didst embrace Jesus, Son of God.

Then say,
Praise be to our God, because in imitation of St. Catherine we
have begun *(first day)*
are continuing *(other days)*
have ended *(last day)*
this holy exercise.

We beseech the Queen of Angels that for these our thousand Ave Maria's and
thousand Benedictions which we are saying [have said (last day)], the Mother
may obtain of the Infant which is born of her these two blessings only, viz, the
first, in life, grace to repent us truly of our sins; the second, in death, certainty
of salvation. Wherefore let every one here present say heartily with St.
Catherine:
Eja ergo, advocata nostra, illos tuos misericordes oculos ad nos converte; et
Jesum benedictum fructum ventris tui nobis post hoc exilium ostende, O
clemens, O pia, O dulcis Virgo Maria.

TRANSLATION.

Come, then, most gracious Advocate, turn thine eyes of mercy towards us; and
after this our exile, show unto us the blessed Fruit of thy womb, Jesus, O
merciful, O kind, O sweet Virgin Mary.

Then say the Litanies B.V.M. &c., and then,
V. Dignare me laudare te, Virgo sacrata.
R. Da mihi virtutem contra hostes tuos.

Oremus.
Deus, qui de beatae Mariae Virginis utero Verbum tuum, angelo nuntiante,
carnem suscipere voluisti; praesta supplicibus tuis, ut qui vere eam Genitricem
Dei credimus, ejus apud te intercessionibus adjuvemur.

Conscientias nostras, quaesumus Domine, visitando purifica: ut veniens Jesus
Christus Filius tuus Dominus noster cum omnibus sanctis, paratam sibi in nobis
inveniat mansionem. Qui tecum vivit et regnat in saecula saeculorum. R.
Amen.

TRANSLATION.

V. Make me worthy to praise thee, holy Virgin.
R. Give me strength against thine enemies.

Let us pray.
God, who by the message of an angel didst will that Thy Divine Word should
take to himself human flesh in the womb of the Blessed Virgin Mary; grant
unto us Thy suppliants that we, who believe her to be verily and indeed Mother
of God, may be aided by her intercession with Thee.

Visit us, O Lord, we beseech Thee, and purify our hearts; that our Lord Jesus Christ Thy Son, when He comes with all his saints, may find a dwelling-place prepared for Himself within us. Who with Thee liveth and reigneth for ever and ever. Amen.

81. PRAYER TO THE IMMACULATE HEART OF MARY

The devotion to the Sacred Heart of Jesus having been firmly established in the Catholic world, it seemed fitting that a similar devotion should be established in honour of the Immaculate Heart of Mary. Accordingly Benedict XIV., with a Bull of March 7, 1753, erected in the church of the Most Holy Redeemer, near Ponte Sisto in Rome, the first Confraternity which took its name from the Immaculate Heart of Mary; and Pope Pius VII., whilst approving the devotion, by a decree of the S. Congr. of Rites of Aug. 31, 1805, granted also an office and Mass for the feast of it, to kindle thereby the love of the faithful towards it.

In the year 1807, in order still more to advance this devotion, he erected in Rome, in the deaconry of St. Eustachius, a "Primary Congregation *(Congregazione Primario)* of the Sacred Heart of Mary," granting to its members many Indulgences, with power to aggregate other confraternities out of Rome, which should also participate in the Indulgences. Moreover, in order that not only the members of both sexes of the said confraternities and congregations in Rome and elsewhere, but that all the faithful every where, might he moved to honour the Sacred Heart of Mary, the same Pope Pius VII., at the prayer of many bishops and priests, by Rescripts given from the Segretaria of the Memorials, Aug. 18, 1807, Feb. 1, 1816, and Sept. 26, 1817 (all of which are preserved in the Archivium of the Pious Union of the Sacred Heart of Jesus before named), granted -

i. The indulgence of sixty days, once a day, to all who say devoutly the following prayer to the Sacred Heart of Mary, with the act of praise to the SS. Hearts of Jesus and Mary; and -

ii. The plenary indulgence to those who say it every day for a year, on each of the following three feasts of our Lady, viz, the Nativity, Assumption, and her Immaculate Heart provided that, after Confession and Communion, they visit a church or altar dedicated to the Blessed Virgin, and pray there according to the Pope's intention.

Lastly, he granted -

iii. The plenary indulgence at the hour of death to all who in life shall not omit to say this prayer.

THE PRAYER.

Heart of Mary, Mother of God, our Mother, Heart most amiable, on which the Adorable Trinity ever looks with complacency, worthy of all the veneration and tenderness of angels and of men; Heart most like the Heart of Jesus, whose most perfect image thou art; heart full of goodness, ever compassionate towards our miseries, - vouchsafe to thaw our icy hearts, that they may be changed entirely to the likeness of the heart of Jesus. Infuse into them the love of thy virtues, inflame them with that blessed fire with which thou dost ever burn. In thee let the Holy Church find safe shelter; protect it, and be its sweet asylum, its tower of strength, impregnable against every inroad of its enemies. Be thou the road leading to Jesus; be thou the channel whereby we receive all graces needful for our salvation. Be thou our help in need, our comfort in trouble, our strength in temptation, our refuge in persecution, our aid in all dangers; but especially in the last struggle of our life, at the moment of our death, when all hell will be unchained against us to snatch away our souls, - in that dread moment, that hour so terrible, whereon our eternity depends, and, yes, most tender Virgin, do thou then make us feel how great is the sweetness of thy motherly Heart, and the strength of thy power with the Heart of Jesus, by opening for us a safe refuge in the very fount of mercy itself, whereby we too may one day join with thee in Paradise in praising that same Heart of Jesus for ever and for ever. Amen.

ACT OF PRAISE TO THE HEARTS OF JESUS AND MARY.

May the Divine Heart of Jesus and the Immaculate Heart of Mary be known, praised, blessed, loved, worshipped, and glorified always and in all places! Amen.

82. EJACULATION, "SWEET HEART"

As above

83. EJACULATION, "SWEET HEART OF MARY," ETC.

At the humble prayer of a pious promoter of the devotion to the Sacred Heart of Mary, our Sovereign Pontiff Pius IX., by a decree of the S. Congr. of Indulgences, dated Sept. 30, 1852, granted to the faithful -
i. An indulgence of 300 days, every time they say with contrition and devotion the following ejaculation.
ii. A plenary indulgence, once a month, to all who say it daily devoutly for a

month; provided that, after Confession and Communion, they visit a church or public oratory, and pray there according to the mind of his Holiness.

THE EJACULATION.

Sweet Heart of Mary, be my salvation.

---

84. PRAYERS FOR EVERY DAY OF THE WEEK, WITH THREE "AVE MARIA'S" ETC.

Pope Pius VII., of holy memory, at the prayer of the Chapter of the Basilica of St. Mary in Cosmedin here in Rome, by a Rescript of the S. Congr. of Indulgences, dated June 21, 1808, kept in the Archivium of the said Basilica, granted -
i. An indulgence or 300 days, once a day, to all the faithful who, with contrite hearts, say the following prayers to our Blessed Lady, extracted from the spiritual works of the holy Bishop Alphonsus Maria de' Liguori, each on that day of the week to which it has been assigned, together with three *Ave Maria's,* with the intention of making some reparation to her for the many blasphemies which have been, and are daily uttered against her, not only by unbelievers, but even by bad Christians.
ii. A plenary indulgence, once a month, to all who say these prayers, with three *Ave Maria's,* daily for a whole month, with the intention above named, on any one day when, after Confession and Communion, they shall pray to God for the Holy Church, &c.

PRAYER FOR SUNDAY.

Mother of my God, look down upon a poor sinner, who has recourse to thee, and puts his trust in thee. I am not worthy that thon shouldst even cast thine eyes upon me; but I know that thou, beholding Jesus thy Son dying for sinners, dost thyself yearn exceedingly to save them. O Mother of Mercy, look on my miseries and have pity upon me. I hear it said by all that thou art the refuge of the sinner, the hope of the desperate, the aid of the lost; be thou, then, my refuge, hope, and aid. It is thy prayers which must save me. For the love of Jesus Christ be thou my help; reach forth thy hand to the poor fallen sinner who recommends himself to thee. I know that it is thy consolation to aid the sinner when thou canst do so; help me then, thou who canst help. By my sins I have forfeited the grace of God and my own soul. I place myself in thy hands; O, tell me what to do that I may regain the grace of God, and I will do it. My Saviour bids me go to thee for help; He wills that I should look to thy pity; that so, not only the merits of thy Son, but thine own prayers also, may unite to save me. To thee, then, I have recourse: pray thou to Jesus for me; and make me experience how great good thou canst do for one who trusts in thee. Be it done unto me according to my hope. Amen.

Then say three Ave Maria's *to the Blessed Virgin Mary in reparation for the blasphemies uttered against her.*

PRAYER FOR MONDAY.

Most holy Mary, Queen of heaven, I who was once the slave of the Evil One now dedicate myself to thy service for ever; and I offer myself, to honour and to serve thee as long as I live. Accept me for thy servant, and cast me not away from thee as I deserve. In thee, O my Mother, I place all my hopes. All blessing and thanksgiving be to God, who in His mercy giveth me this trust in thee. It is true that in past time I have fallen miserably into sin; but by the merits of Jesus Christ, and thy prayers, I hope that God has pardoned me. But this is not enough, my Mother. One thought terrifies me; it is, that I may yet lose the grace of God. Danger is ever nigh; the devil sleeps not; fresh temptations assail me. Protect me, then, my Queen; help me against the assaults of my spiritual enemy. Never suffer me to sin again, or to offend Jesus thy Son. Let me not by my sin lose my soul, heaven, and my God. This one grace, Mary, I ask of thee; this is my desire; may thy prayers obtain this for me. Such is my hope. Amen.

The three Ave Maria's *as before.*

PRAYER FOR TUESDAY.

Most holy Mary, Mother of Goodness, Mother of Mercy; when I reflect upon my sins and upon the moment of my death, I tremble and am confounded. O my sweetest Mother, in the Blood of Jesus, in thy intercession, are my hopes. Comforter of the sad, abandon me not at that hour; fail not to console me in that great affliction. If even now I am so tormented by remorse for the sins I have committed, the uncertainty of my pardon, the danger of a relapse, and the strictness of the judgment, how will it be with me then? O my Mother, before death overtake me, obtain for me great sorrow for my sins, a true amendment, and constant fidelity to God for the remainder of my life. And when at length my hour is come, then do thou, Mary, my hope, be thyself my aid in those great troubles wherewith my soul will be encompassed. Strengthen me, that I may not despair when the enemy sets my sins before my face. Obtain for me at that moment grace to invoke thee often, so that I may breathe forth my spirit with thine own sweet name and that of thy most holy Son upon any lips. This grace thou hast granted to many of thy servants; this, too, is my hope and my desire.

The three Ave Maria's *as before.*

PRAYER FOR WEDNESDAY.

Mother of God, most holy Mary, how often by my sins have I merited hell! Long ago, perhaps, judgment would have gone forth against my first mortal sin, hadst not thou in thy tender pity delayed the justice of God, and afterwards attracted me by thy sweetness to have confidence in thy prayers. And O, how very often should I have fallen in the dangers which beset my steps, hadst not thou, loving Mother that thou art, preserved me by the graces thou by thy prayers didst obtain for me. But O, my Queen, what will thy pity and thy favours avail me, if after all I perish in the flames of hell? If there was once a time when I loved thee not, yet now, next to God, I love thee before all. Wherefore, henceforth and for ever, suffer me not to turn my back upon thee and upon my God, who through thee has granted me so many mercies. O Lady, most worthy of all love, let it not be that I thy child shall have to hate and to utter maledictions for ever in hell. Thou wilt surely never endure to see thy servant lost who loves thee. O Mary, say not that I ever can be lost! Yet I shall assuredly be lost if I abandon thee. But who could ever have the heart to leave thee? Who can ever forget thy love? No; it is impossible for that man to perish who faithfully recommends himself to thee, and has recourse to thee. Only leave me not, my Mother, in my own hands, or I am lost! Let me but cling to thee! Save me, my Hope! save me from hell; or rather, save me from sin, which alone can condemn me to hell.

The three Ave Maria's *as before.*

PRAYER FOR THURSDAY.

Queen of Heaven, who sittest enthroned above all the choirs of the angels nighest to God, from this vale of miseries I, a poor sinner, salute thee, praying thee in thy love to turn upon me those gracious eyes of thine. See, Mary, the dangers among which I dwell, and shall ever have to dwell whilst I live upon this earth. I may yet lose my soul, Paradise, and God. In thee, Lady, is my hope. I love thee; and I sigh after the time when I shall see thee and praise thee in Paradise. O Mary, when will that blessed day come that I shall see myself safe at thy feet? When shall I kiss that hand, which has dispensed to me so many graces? Alas, it is too true, O my Mother, that I have ever been very ungrateful during my whole life; but if I go to Heaven, then I will love thee there every moment of a whole eternity, and make thee reparation in some sort for my ingratitude by ever blessing and praising thee. Thanks be to God, for that He hath vouchsafed me this hope through the Precious Blood of Jesus, and through thy powerful intercession. This has been the hope of all thy true lovers; and no one of them has been defrauded of his hope. No: neither shall I be deceived of mine. O Mary, pray to thine own Son Jesus, as I also will pray to Him, by the merits of His Passion, to strengthen and increase this my hope.

The three Ave Maria's *as before.*

PRAYER FOR FRIDAY.

O Mary, thou art the noblest, highest, purest, fairest creation of Coil, the holiest of all creatures! O, that all men knew thee, loved thee, my Queen, as thou deservest to be loved! Yet great is my consolation, Mary, that there are blessed souls in the courts of Heaven, and just souls still on earth, whose hearts thou leadest captive with thy beauty and thy goodness. But above all I rejoice in this, that our God himself loves thee alone more than all men and angels together. I too, O Queen most loveable, I, miserable sinner, dare to love thee, though my love is too little; I would I had a greater love, a more tender love: this thou must gain for me, since to love thee is a great mark of predestination, and a grace which God grants to those who shall be saved. Moreover, O my Mother, when I reflect upon the debt I owe thy Son, I see He deserves of me an immeasurable love. Do thou, then, who desirest nothing so much as to see Him loved, pray that I may have this grace - a great love for Jesus Christ. Obtain it, thou who obtainest what thou wilt. I covet not goods of earth, nor honours, nor riches, but I desire that which thine own heart desires most, - to love my God alone. O, can it be that thou wilt not aid me in a desire so acceptable to thee? No: it is impossible! even now I feel thy help, even now thou prayest for me. Pray for me, Mary, pray; nor ever cease to pray, till thou dost see me safe in Paradise, where I shall be certain of possessing and of loving my God and thee, my dearest Mother, for ever and for ever. Amen.

The three Ave Maria's *as before.*

PRAYER FOR SATURDAY.

Most holy Mary, I know the graces which thou hast obtained for me, and I know the ingratitude which I have shown thee. The ungrateful man is unworthy of favours; and yet for all this I will not distrust thy mercy. O my great Advocate, have pity on me. Thou, Mary, dost dispense the graces which God vouchsafes to give us sinners, and therefore did He make thee so mighty, rich, and kind, that thou mightest succour us. I will that I may be saved: in thy hands I place my eternal salvation, to thee I consign my soul. I will to be associated with those who are thy special servants; reject me not. Thou goest up and down seeking the wretched, to console them. Cast not away, then, a wretched sinner who has recourse to thee. Speak for me, Mary; thy Son grants what thou askest. Take me beneath thy shelter, and it is enough for me; for with thee to guard me I fear no ill; no, not even my sins; because thou wilt obtain God's pardon for them: no, nor yet devils; because thou art far mightier than all hell: no, nor my Judge Jesus Christ; for at thy prayer He will lay aside His wrath. Protect me, then, my Mother; obtain for me pardon of my sins, love of Jesus, holy perseverance, a good death, and Heaven. It is too true, I merit not these graces; yet do thou only ask them of our God, and I shall obtain them.

Pray, then, to Jesus for me. O Mary, my Queen, in thee I trust; in this trust I rest, I live; and with this trust I will that I may die. Amen.

The three Ave Maria's *as before; then the Litanies, it being Saturday, for which there is the indulgence, as* above.

---

85. PRAYER, "MOTHER OF GOD," ETC., WITH THE "SALVE REGINA" THREE TIMES, ETC.

The same Pope Pius VII., desirous that all the faithful should have recourse with confidence to most holy Mary, by means of various devotional exercises, praying her to obtain for all men grace that they may live as becometh good Christians, and so obtain everlasting salvation, granted by a decree of the S. Congr. of Indulgences of May 15, 1821 -

i. An indulgence of 300 days, once a day, to all who, with contrite heart and with devotion, say the prayer " Mother of God,"&c. with the *Salve Regina* three times.

ii. A plenary indulgence to all who practise this pious exercise once a day for a month, on any one day in that month when, after Confession and Communion, they visit some church or public oratory, and pray to God according to the intention of the Sovereign Pontiff.

The prayer prescribed, " Mother of God," &c., is the same as that above for Wednesday. The *Salve Regin*a three times is added at the end of this prayer to gain the aforesaid Indulgence.

---

86. PRAYER, "VIRGIN MOST HOLY," WITH THREE "AVE MARIA'S"

Pope Leo XII., by a decree of the S. Congr. of Indulgences of Aug. 11, 1824, besides confirming -

i. An indulgence of 100 days already granted in the year 1804 by Pope Pius VII., to all the faithful who say with contrite hearts, in honour of most holy Mary, the following prayer with three *Ave Maria's* -

Added by a fresh Rescript of the same S. Congr. of May 10, 1828 -

ii. A further indulgence of 100 days to the said devotion.

THE PRAYER.

Virgin most holy, Mother of the Word Incarnate, Who dost dispense graces, Refuge of us poor sinners; we fly to thy maternal love with lively faith, and we ask thee to obtain for us grace ever to do the will of God and thine own. Into

thy most holy hands we commit the keeping of our hearts; beseeching thee for health of soul amid body, in the certain hope that thou, our most loving Mother, wilt hear our prayer. Wherefore with lively faith we say
Ave Maria *three times.*

Oremus.
Defende, quaesumus Domine, ab omni infirmitate, Beata Maria semper Virgine intercedente, famulos tuos: et toto corde tibi prostratos ab hostium propitius tuere clementer insidiis. Per Christum Dominum nostrum. R. Amen.

Let us pray.
Defend, O Lord, we beseech Thee, us Thy servants from all infirmity, through the intercession of the Blessed Mary ever-Virgin; and mercifully protect its from the snares of the enemy, who prostrate ourselves before Thee with our whole heart. Through Christ our Lord. Amen.

87. THREE PRAYERS WITH THREE "AVE MARIA'S"

Pope Leo XII., by an autograph Rescript of October 21, 1823 (kept in the Archivium of the FF. Minor Observants here in Rome), granted to all the faithful -
i. The Indulgence of 100 days, every time they say the following three short prayers, with three *Ave Maria's*, to the Blessed Virgin, to ask her protection in the practice of every Christian virtue, and specially the virtue of chastity.
To all who shall say them daily for a month together, he granted at the end of the month -
ii. The plenary indulgence, on any one day when, after Confession and Communion, they pray according to the intention of the Sovereign Pontiff.

THE THREE PRAYERS.

i. Most Holy Virgin, I venerate thee with my whole heart above all angels and saints in Paradise, as the Daughter of the Eternal Father, and I consecrate to thee my soul with all its powers.
Ave Maria.

ii. Most holy Virgin, I venerate thee with my whole heart above all angels and saints in Paradise, as the Mother of the Only-begotten Son, and I consecrate to thee my body with all its senses.
Ave Maria.

iii. Most Holy Virgin, I venerate thee with my whole heart above all angels and saints in Paradise, as the Spouse of the Holy Ghost, and I consecrate to thee my heart and all its affections, praying thee to obtain for me from the ever-blessed

Trinity all that is necessary for my salvation.
Ave Maria.

88. CHAPLET OF TWELVE STARS

Pope Gregory XVI., of holy memory, by a Rescript of Jan. 8, 1838, kept in the Archivium of the Fathers of the Pious Schools at St. Pantaleon in Rome, granted to all the faithful -

An indulgence of 100 days, every time they devoutly say the following Chaplet of the Twelve Stars of the Blessed Virgin, composed by St. Joseph Calasantius, founder of these schools, who used always to make his scholars say it.

THE CHAPLET.

All praise and thanksgiving be to the ever-blessed Trinity, who hath shown unto us Mary, ever-Virgin, clothed with the sun, with the moon beneath her feet, and on her head a mystic crown of twelve stars.
R. For ever and ever, Amen.

Let us praise and give thanks to God the Father, who elected her for His Daughter.
R. Amen.
Pater noster.

Praise be to God the Father, who predestined her to be the Mother of His Son..
R. Amen.
Ave Maria.

Praise be to God the Father, who preserved her from all stain in her conception.
R. Amen.
Ave Maria.

Praise be to God the Father, who on her birthday adorned her with His choicest gifts.
R. Amen.
Ave Maria.

Praise be to God the Father, who gave her Joseph for her pure spouse and companion.
R. Amen.
Ave Maria and *Gloria Patri.*

Let us praise and give thanks to God the Son, who chose her for His Mother.
R. Amen.
Pater noster.

Praise be to God the Son, who became Incarnate in her womb, and abode there nine months.
R. Amen.
Ave Maria.

Praise be to God the Son, who was born of her, and gave to her her milk wherewith to nourish Him.
R. Amen.
Ave Maria.

Praise be to God the Son, who in His childhood willed that Mary should teach Him.
R. Amen.
Ave Maria.

Praise be to God the Son, who revealed to her the mysteries of the redemption of the world.
R. Amen.
Ave Maria and *Gloria Patri.*

Let us praise and give thanks to God the Holy Ghost, who made her His Spouse.
R. Amen.
Pater noster.

Praise be to God the Holy Ghost, who revealed to her first His name of Holy Ghost.
R. Amen.
Ave Maria.

Praise be to God the Holy Ghost, through whose operation she became at once Virgin and Mother.
R. Amen.
Ave Maria.

Praise be to God the Holy Ghost, through whom she became the living temple of the Most Holy Trinity.
R. Amen.
Ave Maria.

Praise be to God the Holy Ghost, by whom she was exalted in heaven high above all creatures.
R. Amen.
Ave Maria and *Gloria Patri.*

For the Holy Catholic Church, for the propagation of the faith, for peace among Christian princes, and for the uprooting of heresies, let us say, *Salve Regina,* &c.

89. PRAYER TO THE BLESSED VIRGIN AND TO ST. ANNE

Pope Pius VII., by a Rescript of the S. Congr. of Indulgences of Jan. 10, 1815, granted to the faithful -
i. An indulgence of 100 days, every time that, with contrite heart and devotion, they say the following prayer in honour of the most holy Virgin and her mother, St. Anne.
ii. A plenary indulgence to those who shall say this prayer at least ten times every month, on the Feast of St. Anne, July 26, provided that, being truly penitent, they do on that day, alter Confession and Communion, devoutly visit a church and pray according to the intention of the Sovereign Pontiff.

Ave gratia plena, Dominus tecum, tua gratia sit mecum; benedicta tu in mulieribus, et benedicta sit S. Anna mater tua, ex qua sine macula et peccato processisti, Virgo Maria; ex te autem natus est Jesus Christus Filius Dei vivi. Amen.

TRANSLATION.

Hail, Mary, full of grace, the Lord is with thee; may thy grace be with me. Blessed art thou amongst women, and blessed is holy Anne thy mother, from whom, O Virgin Mary, thou didst come forth free from all stain of sin; then of thee was born Jesus Christ, Son of the living God. Amen.

90. MONTH OF MAY

It is a well-known devotion, to consecrate to most holy Mary the month of May, as the most beautiful and florescent month of the whole year. This devotion has long prevailed throughout Christendom; and it is common here in Rome, not only in private families, but as a public devotion in very many churches.
Pope Pius VII., in order to animate all Christian people to the practice of a devotion so tender and agreeable to the most blessed Virgin, and calculated to be of such great spiritual benefit to themselves, granted, by a Rescript of the *Segretaria* of the Memorials, March 21, 1815 (kept in the *Segretaria* of his Eminence the Cardinal-Vicar), to all the faithful of the Catholic world, who either in public or in private should honour the Blessed Virgin with some

special homage or devout prayers, or other virtuous practices -
i. An indulgence of 300 days for each day.
ii A plenary indulgence once in this month; to be gained on that day when, after Confession and Communion, they shall pray to God for the Holy Church, &c.
These Indulgences were confirmed for ever by the same holy Pontiff, by means of a decree of the S. Congr. of Indulgences, June 18, 1822.

91. PRAYER, "AVE AUGUSTISSIMA," TO OUR LADY FOR PEACE

In order to encourage the faithful to have frequent recourse to the most holy Virgin, imploring her most efficacious aid, our Sovereign Pontiff his Holiness Pope Pius IX., by a decree of the S. Congr. of Indulgences, of Sept. 23, 1846, grants -
i. An indulgence of 300 days to all the faithful, as often as they say the following prayer, with contrite hearts and devotion.
ii. A plenary indulgence to all who say it at least once a day for a month, on any one day in the said month when, after Confession and Communion, they visit some church or public oratory, and pray there according to the mind of the Sovereign Pontiff.

Ave Augustissima, Regina pacis, sanctissima Mater Dei, per Sacratissimum Cor Jesu Filii tui Principis Pacis, fac ut quiescat ira ipsius et regnet super nos in pace. Memorare, O piissima Virgo Maria, non esse auditum a saeculo quemquam tua petentem suffragia esse derelictum. Ego tali animatus confidentia ad te venio. Noli, Mater Verbi, verba mea despicere; sed audi propitia, et exaudi, O clemens, O pia, O dulcis Virgo Maria.

TRANSLATION.

Hail, thou that art most Venerable, Queen of Peace, most holy Mother of God; through the Sacred Heart of Jesus thy Son, the Prince of Peace, cause His anger to cease from us, that so He may reign over us in peace. Remember, O most gracious Virgin Mary, that never was it known that any one who sought thy prayers was forsaken by God. Inspired with this confidence, I come unto thee. Despise not my petitions, O Mother of the Incarnate Word; but in thy loving kindness hear and answer me, O merciful, O kind, O sweet Virgin Mary.

92. THE PRAYER, "MEMORARE," ETC.

The same Sovereign Pontiff Pius IX., in order to satisfy the earnest wish of his Eminence Cardinal Louis James Maurice de Bonald, Archbishop of Lyons, by a Rescript of the S. Congr. of Indulgences of July 25, 1846, granted to all the faithful in the kingdom of France -
i. An indulgence or 300 days every time the most efficacious and devout prayer of St. Bernard to the Blessed Virgin, called the "Memorare," is said with contrition.
ii. A plenary indulgence, to all those who have the devout habit of saying this prayer at least once a day every month, on any one day in the month, provided that, after Confession and Communion, they visit a church or public oratory, and pray there according to the mind of the Sovereign Pontiff.
Afterwards his Holiness, at the prayer of several ecclesiastics and persons of consideration in Rome, vouchsafed, by a decree of the S. Congregation of Indulgences of Dec. 11, 1846, to extend these Indulgences to all the faithful in the whole Catholic world for over, under the aforesaid conditions.

THE PRAYER.

Memorare, O piissima Virgo Maria, non esse auditum a saeculo quemquam ad tua currentem praesidia, tua implorantem auxilia, tua petentem suffragia, ease derelictum. Ego tali animatus confidentia, ad te, Virgo virginum, Mater, curro, ad te venio, coram te gemens peceator assisto; noli, Mater Verbi, verba men despicere; sed audi propitia, et exaudi. Amen.

TRANSLATION.

Remember, O most gracious Virgin Mary, that never was it known that any one who fled to thy protection, implored thy help, and sought thy intercession was left unaided. Inspired with this confidence, I fly unto thee, Virgin of virgins, my Mother; to thee I come, before thee I stand sinful and sorrowful. O Mother of the Word Incarnate, despise not my petitions; but in thy clemency hear and answer me, Amen.

93. PRAYER, "O DOMINA MEA!"

Our Sovereign Pontiff Pius IX., at the prayer of the Father- General of the Society of Jesus, granted, by a decree of the S. Congr. of Indulgences, of Aug. 5, 1851 -
i. An indulgence of 100 days, to be gained once a day by saying, morning and evening, with contrite heart, one *Ave Maria,* with the accompanying Prayer and Ejaculation, *O Domina mea!* &c., for the purpose of imploring the aid of the most holy Virgin in temptations, especially in those against chastity.

ii. A plenary indulgence, once a month, to all who practise this devotion for a month together, on any one day in the month, provided that, after Confession and Communion, they visit a church or public oratory, and pray there according to the mind of his Holiness, he granted also -

iii. An indulgence of forty days, every time any one, when assaulted by any temptation, shall have recourse to the most holy Virgin with nothing more than the ejaculation, *O Domina mea! O Mater mea! Memento,* &c.

PRAYER.

O Domina mea! O Mater mea! tibi me totum offero, atque ut me tibi probem devotum, consecro tibi hodie oculos meos, aures meas, os meum, cor meum, plane me totum. Quoniam itaque tuus sum, O bona Mater, serva me, defende me, ut rem et possessionem tuam.

EJACULATION IN ANY TEMPTATION.

O Domina mea! O Mater mea! memento me esse tuum.
Serva me, defende me, ut rem et possessionem

TRANSLATION.

My Queen! my Mother! I give thee all myself; and to show my devotion to thee, I consecrate to thee this day my eyes, ears, mouth, heart, myself wholly and without reserve. Wherefore, O loving Mother, as I am thine own, keep me, defend me, as thy property and thy own possession.

EJACULATION.

My Queen! my Mother! remember I am thine own.
Keep me, defend mc, as thy property, thy own possession.

Three Ejaculations, Jesus, Mary, Joseph, &c. *as above.*

94. PRAYER, "O BEATA VIRGO," ETC.

Our Sovereign Pontiff Pius IX., at the prayer of several devout persons, vouchsafed to grant, by a Rescript of the *Segretaria* of the Memorials, dated May 19, 1854 -

The indulgence of fifty days, every time that, with contrite heart, the following prayer is said to the most holy Virgin, extracted from the eighteenth Sermon of St. Augustine, *De Sanctis.*

PRAYER.

O Beata Virgo Maria! quis tibi digne valeat jam gratiarum, ac laudum praeconia rependere, quae singulari tuo assensu mundo succurristi perdito?

155

Quas tibi laudes fragilitas humani generis persolvat, quae solo tuo commmercio recuperandi aditum invenit? Accipe itaque quascumque exiles, quascunque meritis tuis impares, gratiarum actiones, et cum susceperis vota, culpas nostras orando excusa. Admitte nostras preces intra sacrarium exauditionis, et reporta nobis antidotum reconciliationis. Sit per te excusabile, quod per te ingerimus, fiat impetrabile quod fida mente poscimus. Accipe quod offerimus, redona quod rogamus, excusa quod timemus, quia tu es spes unica peccatorum. Per te speramus veniam delictorum, et in te, beatissima, nostrorum est expectatio praemiorum. Sancta Maria, succurre miseris, juva pusillanimes, refove flebiles, ora pro populo, interveni pro clero, intercede pro devoto femineo sexu; sentiant omnes tuum juvamen quicumque celebrant tuam sanctam Commemorationem. Assiste parata votis poscentium, et reporta nobis optatum effectum. Sint tibi studia assidua orare pro populo Dei, quae meruisti, benedicta, Redemptorem ferre mundi, qui vivit et regnat in saecula saeculomum. Amen.

TRANSLATION.

Mary, Virgin ever-blessed! who can worthily praise thee or give thanks to thee, who, by the assent of thy will alone hast rescued a fallen world? What honours can the weakness of our human nature pay to thee, which by thy intervention alone hath found the way to restoration? Accept, then, such poor thanks as we have here to offer, though they are unequal to thy merits, and receiving our vows, obtain by thy prayers the remission of our offences. Admit thou our prayers into the sanctuary of the heavenly audience, and bring back to us the medicine of our reconciliation. Through thee may that be pardonable which through thee we bring before God; and that be admissible which we ask with faithful heart. Accept what we offer, grant us what we ask, pardon us what we fear; for thou art the sole hope of sinners. Through thee we hope for the forgiveness of our faults; and in thee, most blessed one, is the hope of our reward. Holy Mary, succour the wretched, help the faint-hearted, comfort the sorrowful, pray for the people, shield the clergy, intercede for the devout female sex, let all feel thy help who celebrate thy holy commemoration. Be thou at hand, ready to aid our prayers, when we pray; and bring back to us their desired result. Make it thy care, blessed one, to intercede ever for the people of God - thou who didst deserve to bear the Redeemer of the world, who liveth and reigneth for ever and ever. Amen.

95. LITTLE CHAPLET IN HONOUR OF THE IMMACULATE HEART OF MARY

His Holiness Pope Pius IX., in order that the fervour of the devotion of the faithful might be the more inflamed towards the Sacred and Immaculate Heart of Mary, granted at the prayer of the Bishop of Verona -

i. An Indulgence of 300 days, once a day, to every one who should say with contrite heart the following little chaplet.

ii. A plenary indulgence to all who have the devout custom of saying it once a day; to be gained once a month, on the day when, after Confession and Communion, they shall visit a church or public oratory, and play there for a while according to the mind of his Holiness. See decree of the S. Congr. of Indulgences, Dec. 11, 1854.

THE LITTLE CHAPLET.

V. Deus in adjutorium meum intendo.
R. Domine ad adjuvandum me festina.
V. Gloria Patri, &c.
R. Sicut erat, &c.

i. Immaculate Virgin, who, being conceived without sin, didst direct every movement of thy pure heart to God, ever the object of thy love, and who wast ever most submissive to His will; obtain for me the grace to hate sin with my whole heart, and to learn of thee to live in perfect resignation to the will of God.
One Pater noster, *seven* Ave Maria's.

Heart of Mary, pierced with grief, set my heart on fire with the love of God.
Or else,
My heart, O heart of Mary,
Sore pierced for me with pain,
With burning fire of charity,
Cleanse thou from sinful stain.

ii. Mary, I wonder at thy deep humility, troubling thy blessed heart at the gracious message brought thee by Gabriel the Archangel, how that thou wast chosen to be Mother of the Son of God Most High, and making thee proclaim thyself His humble handmaid; and, in great confusion at my pride, I ask thee for the grace of a contrite humbled heart, that, knowing my own misery, I may obtain that crown of glory promised to those who are truly humble of heart.
One Pater, *&c.*; Heart of Mary, *&c.*

iii. Sweetest Heart of Mary, precious treasury, wherein the Blessed Virgin kept the words of Jesus whilst she thought upon the high mysteries which she had heard from the lips of her Son, and whereby she learned to live for God alone;

157

how does the coldness of my heart confound me! Dearest Mother, obtain for me grace so to meditate within my heart upon the holy law of God, that I may strive to follow thee in the fervent practice of every Christian virtue.
One Pater, *&c.*; Heart of Mary, *&c.*

iv. Glorious Queen of Martyrs, whose sacred heart was cruelly transfixed in the bitter Passion of thy Son by the sword foretold by the holy old man Simeon, obtain for my heart true courage and a holy patience to bear well the troubles and adversities of this miserable life, and, by crucifying my flesh with its desires in following the mortification of the cross, to show myself truly thy son.
One Pater, *&c.*; Heart of Mary, *&c.*

v. O Mary, Mystic Rose, whose loving heart, burning with the living fire of charity, accepted us for thy sons at the foot of the cross, whereby thou didst become our most tender Mother; make me feel the sweetness of thy maternal heart, and thy power with Jesus in all the perils of this mortal life, and especially in the terrible hour of death, that so my heart, united with thine, may love Jesus now and throughout all ages. Amen.
One Pater, *&c.*; Heart of Mary, *&c.*

Let us entreat the Most Sacred Heart of Jesus to inflame us with His holy love. O Divine Heart of Jesus, I consecrate myself to Thee, full of deep gratitude for the many blessings I have received, and daily receive, from Thy infinite charity. I thank Thee with my whole heart for having also vouchsafed to give me thine own Mother to be my Mother, consigning me to her as son in the person of the beloved disciple. Grant unto me that my heart may be ever ardently inflamed with this love of Thee, and that it may ever find in Thy most sweet Heart its peace, its refuge, and its happiness.

APPENDIX

174. LIVING ROSARY.

This pious practice consists in an association of fifteen persons, who distribute amongst themselves the fifteen Mysteries of the Rosary, obliging themselves to say daily, for the space of one month, one Decade of the Rosary, meditating on the Mystery which has fallen to them by lot.
Gregory XVI., in two Briefs of January 27 and February 2 1832, approved this pious exercise, and granted to the faithful who practise it the following Indulgences -
i. Plenary indulgence the first feast-day after they have been enrolled, provided they Confess and Communicate.

ii. The indulgences granted by Sovereign Pontiffs for saying the Rosary.

iii. The indulgences of 100 years every time the portion of the Rosary assigned to each member is said.

iv. The indulgence of seven years and seven quarantines to those who say it on the Sundays throughout the year, and on festival days, including those feasts on which the hearing of Mass is not of obligation, and on the Octaves of Christmas, Easter, Corpus Christi, Whitsuntide, the Assumption, the Nativity, and Conception of the Blessed Virgin.

v. Plenary indulgence on the solemn festivals of the Nativity, Circumcision, Epiphany, Easter, Ascension, Corpus Christi, Whitsunday, the Most Holy Trinity, as well as on all feasts of the Blessed Virgin Mary (including even the smaller feasts), on the Feast of the holy Apostles SS. Peter and Paul, on All Saints, and on the third Sunday in every month. In order to gain these Indulgences, the members of the associations (except in the case of some legitimate impediment) ought to have said every day, at least for the space of one month, the part of the Rosary which has been assigned to them; and moreover they ought to Confess, Communicate, and visit a church.

175. LITTLE CHAPLET IN HONOUR OF THE IMMACULATE CONCEPTION OF MARY EVER-VIRGIN.

By a Brief of June 22, 1855, his Holiness Pope Pius IX. vouchsafed to grant to all the faithful who with contrite heart shall say the following little Chaplet - 300 days indulgence; and to every one who shall have said it every day for a month he granted -

The plenary indulgence on any one day at pleasure when, after Confession and Communion, he shall pray according to the intention of his Holiness.

THE LITTLE CHAPLET

In the name of the Father, of the Son, and of the Holy Ghost. Amen.

First Set of Beads

Blessed be the Holy and Immaculate Conception of the most Blessed Virgin Mary.

Then say one Pater noster, *four* Ave Maria's, *and one* Gloria Patri.

Second Set.

Blessed, &c. *as before*

One Pater, &c. *as before.*

Third Set.

Blessed, &c. *as before*

One Pater, *&c. as before.*

176. PSALMS AND PRAYERS OF ST. BONAVENTURE IN HONOUR OF THE MOST HOLY VIRGIN, FOR EVERY DAY IN THE WEEK.

By a Brief of December 9, 1856, his Holiness Pope Pius IX. granted to the recital of the psalms and prayers of St. Bonaventure in honour of the most holy Virgin - this devotion being entitled "Daily Tribute of loving Prayers and Praises for every day of the week to the Immaculate Mother of God" - the following Indulgences -

i. Indulgence of seven years and seven quarantines by reciting in any language, provided the translation be correct, these psalms and prayers for each day, according to the order of the days of the week.

ii. Plenary indulgence, on the accustomed conditions of Confession and Communion and a visit to a church, on the Feast of the Immaculate Conception and during its Octave, on the Feast of St. Joseph, of St. Bonaventure (July 14), and on any one day at pleasure during the mouth of May, to those of the faithful who for one month previous to these days shall have said the above-named psalms and prayers.

The little book which contains these psalms and prayers is on sale at the printer's in the Piazza di. S. Ignazio, No. 153, and it is called "Daily Tribute of loving Prayers and Praises for each day in the week to the Immaculate Mother of God, &c. extracted from the works of the Seraphic Doctor St. Bonaventure."

177. LITTLE CHAPLET OF THE TWELVE PRIVILEGES OF THE MOST BLESSED VIRGIN MARY, COMPOSED BY ST. ANDREW AVELLINO.

By a Brief of June 26, 1860, the Sovereign Pontiff Pope Pius IX. granted to all the faithful of both sexes -

The indulgence of 300 days, who, once a day, devoutly and with contrite heart, say the following little Chaplet; and

The plenary indulgence once a month, to be gained by saying it every day for the space of one month, provided that on any one day at pleasure in the same month, being truly penitent, having Confessed and Communicated, they shall visit some one church or public oratory, and there pray to God for concord amongst Christians princes, for the extirpation of heresies, and for the exaltation of our holy Mother the Church.

THE CHAPLET.

In nomine Patris et Filii et Spiritus Sancti. Amen.
In the name of tine Father, and of the Son, and of the Holy Ghost. Amen.

V. Deus in adjutorium meum intende.
R. Domine ad adjuvandum me festina.
V. Incline unto my aid, O God.
R. O Lord, make speed to help nine

i. Hail to thee, purest, holiest Mother of Jesus. We humbly pray thee, by thy Predestination, whereby thou wast even from all eternity elected Mother of God; by thy Immaculate Conception, whereby thou wast Conceived without stain of original sin; by thy most perfect resignation, whereby thou wast ever conformed to the will of God; and lastly by thy consummate holiness, whereby throughout thy whole life thou didst never commit one single fault: we pray thee to become our advocate with our Lord, that He may pardon so many sins of ours, which are the cause of His wrath. And Thou, O Father Almighty, by the merits of these privileges vouchsafed to this Thy well-beloved Daughter, hear her supplications for us, and pardon us her clients.

Parce, Domine, parce populo tuo.
Spare, O Lord, spare Thy people.

One Pater, *four* Ave's, *and one* Gloria. *Then -*

V. Per Sanctam Conceptionem tuam libera nos, gloriosa Virgo Maria.
By thy holy Conception deliver us, glorious Virgin Mary.

ii. Hail to thee, purest, holiest Mother of Jesus. We humbly pray thee, by thy most holy Annunciation, when thou didst conceive the Divine Word in thy womb; by thy most happy delivery, in which thou didst experience no pain; by thy perpetual virginity, which thou didst unite with the fruitfulness of a mother; and lastly, by the bitter martyrdom when thou didst undergo in our Saviour's death: we pray thee to become our mediatrix, that we may reap the fruit of the precious death of thy Son. And Thou, O divine Son, by the merits of these privileges granted to Thy well-beloved Mother, hear our supplications, and pardon us her clients.

Parce, Domine, parce populo tuo.
Spare, O Lord, spare Thy people.

One Pater, *four* Ave's, *and one* Gloria.

V. Per Sanctam Conceptionem tuam libera nos, gloriosa Virgo Maria.
By thy holy Conception deliver us, glorious Virgin Mary.

iii. Hail to thee, purest, holiest Mother of Jesus. We humbly pray thee by the joys which thou didst feel in thy heart at the Resurrection and Ascension of Jesus Christ; by thy Assumption into Heaven, whereby thou wast exalted above all the choirs of the angels; by the glory which God has given thee to be Queen of all saints; and lastly, by that most powerful intercession, whereby thou art able to obtain all that thou dost desire: we pray thee obtain for us true love of God. And Thou, O Holy Spirit, by the merits of these privileges of Thy well-beloved Spouse, hear her supplications, and pardon us her clients. Amen.

Parce, Domine, parce populo tuo.
Spare, O Lord, spare Thy people.

One Pater, *four* Ave's, *and one* Gloria. *Then -*

V. Per Sanctam Conceptionem tuam libera nos, gloriosa Virgo Maria.
By thy holy Conception deliver us, glorious Virgin Mary.

*Here, at pleasure, th*e Litany of Loretto *may be said, to gain another Indulgence of 300 days. See* above*. Afterwards add:*

Ant. Conceptio tua, Dei Genitrix Virgo, gaudium annuntiavit universo mundo: ex te enim ortus est Sol Justitiae, Christus Deus noster; qui solvens maledictionem, dedit benedictionem et confundens mortem, donavit nobis vitam sempiternam.

V. In conceptione tua, Virgo Maria, Immaculata fuisti.
R. Ora pro nobis Patrem, cujus Filium Jesum de Spiritu Sancto conceptum peperisti.

Oremus.
Deus misericordiae, Deus pietatis, Deus indulgentiae, qui misertus es super afflictionem populi tui, et dixisti Angelo percutienti populum tuum, "Contine manum tuam;" ob amorem illius Matris gloriosae, cujus ubera pretiosa contra venena nostrorum delictorum dulciter suxisti: praesta auxilium gratiae tuae, ut ab omni malo secure liberemur, et a totius perditionis incursu misericorditer salvemur. Qui vivis et regnas in saecula saeculorum. Amen.

Ant. Thy Conception, Virgin Mother of God, brought tidings of joy to the whole world, for from thee arose the Son of Justice, Christ our God; who, loosing the Curse, gave the blessing, and confounding death, granted unto us eternal life.

V. In thy Conception, O Mary the Virgin, thou wast Immaculate.
R. Pray for as to the Father, whose Son Jesus, conceived of the Holy Spirit, thou didst bring forth.

Let us pray.
God of mercy, God of pity, God of tenderness, who hast compassion upon the affliction of Thy people, and didst say to the angel smiting Thy people, "Stay thy hand;" for the love of that glorious Mother, whose precious breasts Thou didst sweetly suck, as the antidote of our sins, grant us the help of Thy grace, that we may be safely freed from every evil, and mercifully preserved from the attack of all destruction. Who livest and reignest for ever and ever. Amen.

MARY SORROWING

96. THE HYMN "STABAT MATER."

The "venerable" Pope Innocent XI., desirous that all faithful Christians should often call to mind the bitter sorrow endured by most holy Mary whilst she stood beneath the cross of her divine Son Jesus, entreating her through that great sorrow of hers to obtain for them spiritual favours in their life and in their death, - granted, by his Brief, *Commissae nobis,* of Sept. 1, 1681 -
An indulgence of 100 days to all the faithful every time that, in honour of the sorrow of the B. V. Mary, they devoutly say the sequence or hymn *Stabat Mater*; a hymn which, * though not composed by St. Gregory the Great or St. Bonaventure, as some suppose, yet acknowledges for its author the learned Pope Innocent III., as attested by many writers of great authority.

* Benedict XIV. on the Feasts of our Lord and B.V.M. Part ii. cap. iv. § 1, at the end.

Stabat Mater dolorosa
Juxta crucem lacrymosa
Dum pendebat Filius.

Cujus animam gementem,
Contristatam et dolentem,
Pertransivit gladius.

O quam tristis et afflicta
Fuit illa benedicta
Mater Unigeniti!

Quae moerebat, et dolebat,
Illa Mater dum videbat
Nati poenas incliti.

Quis est homo qui non fleret,
Matrem Christi si videret
In tanto supplicio?

Quis non posset contristari
Christi Matrem contemplari
Dolentem cum Filio.

Pro peccatis suae gentis
Vidit Jesum in tormentis,
Et flagellis subditum.

Visit suum dulcem Natum
Moriendo desolatum,
Dum emisit Spiritum.

Eja Mater, fons amoris,
Me sentire vim doloris
Fac, ut tecum lugeam.

Fac, ut ardeat cor meum
In amando Christum Deum,
Ut sibi complaceam.

Sancta Mater istud agas,
Crucifixi fige plagas
Cordi meo valide.

Tui Nati vulnerati,
Tam dignati pro me pati,
Poenas mecum divide.

Fac me tecum pie flere,
Crucifixo condolere,
Donec ego vixero.

Juxta crucem tecum stare,
Et me tibi sociare
In planctu desidero.

Virgo virginum praeclara
Mihi jam non sis amara,
Fac me tecum plangere.

Fac, ut portem Christi mortem,
Passionis fac consortem,
Et plagas recolere.

Fac me plagis vulnerari,
Fac me cruce inebriari,
Et cruore Filii.

Flammis ne urar succensus,
Per te, Virgo, sim defensus,
In die judicii.

Christe, cum sit hinc exire,
Da per Matrem me venire
Ad patrem victoriae.

Quando corpus morietur,
Fac ut animae donetur
Paradisi gloria. Amen.

TRANSLATION.

At the cross her station keeping,
Stood the mournful Mother weeping,
Close to Jesus to the last;

Through her heart, His sorrow sharing,
All His bitter anguish bearing,
Now at length the sword had passed.

O, how sad and sore distressed
Was that Mother, highly blest,
Of the sole-begotten One!

Christ above in torment hangs;
She beneath beholds the pangs
Of her dying glorious Son.

Is there one who would not weep,
'Whelmed in miseries so deep
Christ's dear Mother to behold?

Can the human heart refrain
From partaking in her pain,
In that Mother's pain untold.

Bruised, derided, cursed, defiled,
She beheld her tender child,
All with bloody scourges rent;

For the sins of His own nation
Saw Him hang in desolation
Till His Spirit forth He sent.

O thou Mother! Fount of love!
Touch my spirit from above,
Make my heart with thine accord;

Make me feel as thou hast felt;
Make my soul to glow and melt
With the love of Christ my Lord.

Holy Mother! pierce me through;
In my heart each wound renew
Of my Saviour crucified;

Let me share with thee His pain,
Who for all my sins was slain,
Who for me in torment died.

Let me mingle tears with thee,
Mourning Him who mourned for me,
All the days that I may live:

By the cross with thee to stay;
There with thee to weep and pray,
Is all I ask of thee to give.

Virgin of all virgins best!
Listen to my fond request:
Let me share thy grief divine;

Let me to my latest breath
In my body bear the death
Of that dying Son of thine.

Wounded with His every wound,
Steep my soul till it hath swooned
In His very Blood away;

Be to me, O Virgin, nigh,
Lest in flames I burn and die
In His awful judgment-day.

Christ, when Thou shalt call me hence,
Be Thy Mother my defence,
Be Thy cross my victory.

While my body here decays,
May my soul Thy goodness praise
Safe in Paradise with Thee.

97. CHAPLET OF THE SEVEN DOLOURS.

It was about the year 1233 that seven holy men of noble birth, by name Bonfiglio, Monaldio, Bonagiunta, Manetto, Amadeo, Uguccio, and Alessio Falconieri, withdrew from the city of Florence into the solitude of Mount Senario, receiving afterwards from the Church the appellation of the "Seven Blessed Founders." For it was in that solitude that, passing their days in the constant exercise of prayer, penitence, and other virtues, they, by a special revelation from the Blessed Virgin, instituted the Order called "Servants of Mary," taking for the object of their institution, meditation on the bitter pains she suffered in the Life, Passion, and Death of her Son Jesus, and, undertaking to promulgate this devotion amongst Christian people. One of the devout practices which they made use of for their purpose was a Chaplet or Rosary of Seven Divisions, in remembrance of the seven principal Dolours of the Blessed Virgin, which were to form the subject of the reciter's meditation according to his ability; the prayers to be said during such meditation being one *Pater noster* and seven *Ave Maria's* for each division, with three more *Ave Maria's* at the end of all, in honour of the tears shed by the same most holy Virgin in her Dolours.

This devout prayer, so acceptable to our most holy Sorrowful Mother, and so useful to Christian souls, was propagated throughout the Christian world by these Servants of Mary and it afterwards received much encouragement from Pope Benedict XIII., who, in order to induce the faithful to adopt it more and more, granted by his Brief *Redemptoris*, of Sept. 26, 1724 -
i. An indulgence of DAYS for every *Pater noster*, and the same for every *Ave Maria*, to every one who, having Confessed and Communicated, or at least

made a firm resolution to Confess, should say this Chaplet in the churches of the Order of the Servants of Mary.

ii. The same indulgence of 200 days to be gained by all who shall say it any where on Fridays, during Lent, and on the Feast and Octave of the Seven Dolours of our Blessed Lady, and -

iii. An indulgence of 100 days, on any other day.

Lastly, the same Pope added -

iv. An indulgence of seven years and seven quarantines to any one who says this Chaplet either alone or in company with others.

Afterwards Pope Clement XII., " that the faithful might often recollect and sympathise with the Dolours of Mary," confirmed by his Bull of *Unigeniti*, Dec. 12, 1734, the before-named Indulgences, adding also the following:

v. A plenary indulgence and remission of all sins to every one who shall say this Chaplet daily for a month together, and shall then, after Confession and Communion, pray for holy Church, &c.

vi. An indulgence of 100 years, every time it is said, to all who say this chaplet, being truly penitent and having confessed, or having at least made a firm resolution to confess their sins.

vii. An indulgence of 150 years, every Monday, Wednesday, Friday, and Feast of Obligation of the Holy Church, after Confession and Communion.

viii. A plenary indulgence all who say it four times a week, on any one day in the year when, after Confession and Communion, they shall say the said Chaplet of Seven Dolours.

ix. An indulgence of 200 years * also to those who shall say it devoutly after their Confession.

x. An indulgence of ten years to those who keep one of these Chaplets about them, and are in the habit of saying it frequently, every time that, after Confession and Communion, they shall hear Mass, be present at a sermon, accompany the Blessed Sacrament to the sick, make peace between enemies, bring sinners to Confession, &c. &c.; or whenever, saying at the same time seven *Pater noster's* and seven *Ave Maria's*, they shall do any spiritual or temporal good work in honour of our Lord Jesus Christ, the Blessed Virgin, or their Patron Saint.

All these Indulgences Mere confirmed by decrees of the S. Congr. of Indulgences issued at the command of Pope Benedict XIV. on January 10, 1711. and Clement XIII.. March 13, 1763. It is, however, requisite, in order to gain these Indulgences, that these Chaplets should be blessed by the Superiors of the Order of the Servants of Mary, or by other priests of the Order deputed by them; and when blessed, they cannot be sold or lent for the purpose of communicating these Indulgences to others, as in that case they would lose the Indulgences. See the above-named Brief of Benedict XIII.

* In some summaries of these Indulgences, and more particularly in that reprinted in Rome in 1518, we find 150 *days* and a few lines after, 200 *days*; but in the Bull above named published at the Office of the Reverend Apostolic Chamber in 1135, we find in both places not days but years.

WAY OF SAYING THE CHAPLET.

Act of Contrition.

O my Lord, Thou who alone art most worthy of my love, behold me standing before Thy Divine Presence all in confusion at the thought of the many grievous injuries I have done Thee. I ask Thy pardon for them with my whole heart, repenting of them purely for love of Thee, and hating and loathing them above every other evil of this life, when I think of Thy infinite goodness. As I would rather have died a thousand times than have offended Thee, so now I am most firmly resolved to lose my life rather than offend Thee again. My crucified Jesus, I firmly purpose to cleanse my soul as soon as possible by Thy most Precious Blood in the Sacrament of Penance. And thou, most tender Virgin, Mother of Mercy and Refuge of sinners, do thou obtain for me the pardon of sin by virtue of thy bitter pains; whilst praying according to the mind of so many holy Pontiffs in order to obtain the indulgences granted to this thy holy Rosary, I hope thereby to obtain remission of all pains due to my sins.

1. With this confidence in my heart, I meditate on the *First* Sorrow, when Mary, Virgin Mother of my God, presented Jesus, her only Son, in the Temple, laid Him in the arms of holy aged Simeon, and heard his prophetic word, "This One shall be a sword of pain to pierce thine own heart," foretelling thereby the Passion and Death of her Son Jesus.

One Pater noster *and seven* Ave Maria's.

ii. The *Second* Sorrow of the Blessed Virgin was when she was obliged to fly into Egypt by reason of the persecution of cruel Herod, who impiously sought to slay her well-beloved Son.

One Pater noster *and seven* Ave Maria's.

iii. The *Third* Sorrow of the Blessed Virgin was when, after having gone up to Jerusalem at the Paschal Feast with Joseph her spouse and Jesus her dear Son, she lost Him on her return to her poor house, and for three days bewailed the loss of her beloved only Son.

One Pater noster *and seven* Ave Maria's.

iv. The *Fourth* Sorrow of the Blessed Virgin was when she met her dear Son Jesus carrying on His tender shoulders the heavy cross whereon He was to be crucified for our salvation.

One Pater noster *and seven* Ave Maria's.

v. The *Fifth* Sorrow of the Blessed Virgin was when she saw her Son Jesus raised upon the tree of the cross, and Blood pouring forth from every part of His Sacred Body ; and when then, after three long hours' agony, she beheld Him die.

One Pater noster *and seven* Ave Maria's.

vi. The *Sixth* Sorrow of the Blessed Virgin was when she saw the lance cleave the Sacred Side of Jesus, her beloved Son, and when taken down from the cross, His Holy Body was laid in her purest bosom.

One Pater noster *and seven* Ave Maria's.

vii. The *Seventh* and last sorrow of the Blessed Virgin, Queen and Advocate of us her servants, miserable sinners, was when she saw the Holy Body of her Son buried in the grave.

One Pater noster *and seven* Ave Maria's.

Then say three Ave Maria's *in veneration of the tears which Mary shed in her sorrows, to obtain thereby true sorrow for sins and the holy Indulgences attached to this pious exercise.*

V. Ora pro nobis, Virgo dolorosissima.
R. Ut digni efficiamur promissionibus Christi.

Oremus.
Interveniat pro nobis, quaesumus, Domine Jesu Christe, nunc et in hora mortis nostrae, apud tuam clementiam beata Virgo Maria Mater tua, cujus sacratissimam animam in hora tuae Passionis deloris gladius pertransivit. Per te, Jesu Christe, Salvator mundi, qui cum Patre et Spiritu Sancto vivis et regnas, &c. R. Amen.

V. Pray for us, Virgin most sorrowful.
R. That we may be made worthy of the promises of Christ.

Let us pray.
Grant, we beseech Thee, O Lord Jesus Christ, that the most blessed Virgin Mary, Thy Mother, may intercede for us before the throne of Thy mercy, now and at the hour of our death, whose most holy soul was transfixed with the sword of sorrow in the hour of Thine own Passion. Through Thee, Jesus Christ, Saviour of the world, who livest and reignest with the Father and the Holy Ghost for ever and ever. Amen.

98. ONE HOUR'S PRAYER IN THE YEAR.

Pope Clement XII., by a decree of the S. Congr. of Indulgences, Feb. 4, 1736, and Benedict XIV., by another decree of July 14, 1757, granted -
A plenary indulgence once in the year to all the faithful who on any one day should, after Confession and Communion, make one hour's prayer in honour of the sorrows of most holy Mary, calling them to mind by saying the Chaplet of them, or other prayers adapted to this devotion. Pope Pius VI., of blessed memory, renewed this Indulgence and confirmed it for ever, July 8, 1785.

99. EXERCISE IN HONOUR OF HER SORROWFUL HEART.

Pope Pius VII., at the prayer of the priests of the Pious Union of the Sacred Heart of Jesus, sometimes called "Pious Union of St. Paul" (already several times referred to above), granted, by a Rescript of Jan. 14, 1815, issued through the Archbishop of Philippi, at that time vicegerent here in Rome, and kept in the *Segretaria* of his Eminence the Cardinal-Vicar -
An indulgence of 300 days to all Christians every time they say with devotion the following pious exercise in honour of the sorrowing heart of most Holy Mary.

THE EXERCISE.

V. Deus in adjutorium meum intende.
R. Domine ad adjuvandum me festina.
Gloria Patri et Filio, &c.

i. I compassionate thee, sorrowing Mary, in the affliction of thy tender heart when the holy old man Simeon prophesied to thee. Dear Mother, by thy heart then so afflicted, obtain for me the virtue of humility and the gift of holy fear of God.
Ave Maria.

ii. I compassionate thee, sorrowing Mary, in the anxiety which thy sensitive heart underwent in the flight to and sojourn in Egypt. Dear Mother, by thy heart which was then made so anxious, obtain for me the virtue of liberality, specially towards the poor, and the gift of piety.
Ave Maria.

iii. I compassionate thee, sorrowing Mary, in the trouble of thy careful heart when thou didst lose thy dear Son Jesus. Dear Mother, by thy heart then so troubled, obtain for me the virtue of holy chastity and the gift of knowledge.
Ave Maria.

iv. I compassionate thee, sorrowing Mary, in the shock thy maternal heart underwent when Jesus met thee as He carried His cross. Dear Mother, by thy loving heart then so overwhelmed, obtain for me the virtue of patience and the gift of fortitude.
Ave Maria.

v. I compassionate thee, sorrowing Mary, in the martyrdom thy generous heart bore so nobly whilst thou didst stand by Jesus in His agony. Dear Mother, by thy heart then so martyred, obtain for me the virtue of temperance and the gift of counsel.
Ave Maria.

vi. I Compassionate thee, sorrowing Mary, in the wound of thy tender heart when the sacred Side of Jesus was pierced with the lance. Dear Mother, by thy heart then so transfixed, obtain for me the virtue of fraternal charity and the gift of understanding.
Ave Maria.

vii. I compassionate thee, sorrowing Mary, in the pang felt by thy loving heart when the Body of Jesus was buried in the grave. Dear Mother, by all the bitterness of desolation thou didst then experience, obtain for me the virtue of diligence and the gift of wisdom.
Ave Maria.

V. Ora pro nobis, Virgo dolorosissima.
R. Ut digni efficiamur promissienibus Christi.

Oremus.
Interveniat pro nobis, &c. as above.

---

100. SEVEN "AVE MARIA'S" AND SEVEN "SANCTA MATER'S" ETC.

Pope Pius VII., by a Brief of Dec. 1, 1815, in order to augment in all the faithful devotion towards the sorrows of most holy Mary, and the more to excite in them grateful recollections of the Passion of her Son, Jesus, granted -
i. A 300 days indulgence, once a day, to all who, contrite in heart, shall say seven *Ave Maria's*, with the versicle to each,

Sancta Mater istud agas,
Crucifixi fige plagas
Cordi meo valide.

Or in English,
Holy Mother, pierce me through;

172

In my heart each wound renew
Of thy Saviour crucified.

ii. A plenary indulgence, once every month, and remission of all sins, to all who should have devoutly practised this pious exercise for a month together, on any one day when, after Confession and Communion, they shall pray for the Holy Church, &c.
This Brief is kept in the Capitular Archivium of the cathedral of Arezze, whose bishop made prayer to the Holy Father for the Indulgence.

---

101. PIOUS PRACTICE ON THE LAST DAYS OF THE CARNIVAL.

Pope Pius VII., in order to augment the devotion of the faithful towards the Sacred Heart of Mary Sorrowing, and at the same time to make some compensations for the many offences which are committed against God on the days of the carnival, granted by a Rescript given through the *Segretaria* of the Memorials, Dec. 9, 1815, and kept in the *Segretaria* of his Eminence the Cardinal-Vicar -
i. A 300 days' indulgence, to all the faithful of the Catholic world, every time they shall assist at any devout exercise in honour of the Sorrows of most holy Mary, on the ten last days of the carnival, in any church or public oratory, or in any church of regulars of either sex, or in any oratory or chapel in monasteries, seminaries, or other pious places where prayer is wont to be made.
ii. A plenary indulgence, to those who shall assist at this pious exercise for at least five out of the ten days; provided that on one of the ten days, they, after Confession and Communion, pray to God for the Holy Church, &c.
These Indulgences were confirmed for ever by the same Pius VII., through the S. Congr. of Indulgences, June 18, 1822.

---

102. THE HOUR OR HALF-HOUR OF PRAYER ON GOOD FRIDAY AND OTHER FRIDAYS.

In order to engage the faithful to endeavour to give an increase of consolation to most holy Mary in her desolation, Pius VII., by two Rescripts given through the *Segretaria* of the Memorials, Feb. 25 and March 21, 1815, kept in the *Segretaria* of his Eminence the Cardinal-Vicar, granted -
i. A plenary indulgence to all those who, from three o'clock en Good Friday until midday an Holy Saturday (the hour on that day when the Holy Church invites the faithful to rejoice in the Resurrection of Jesus Christ), shall, either in public or in private, keep one hour, or at least half an hour, in honour of

most holy Mary in desolation, by meditating on her seven dolours, saying the Chaplet of her Dolours, or any other prayers having reference to her desolation. This Indulgence is gained when, by Confessions and Communions, they satisfy the precept of Paschal Communion.

ii. An indulgence of 300 days, on other Fridays when ever between three o'clock on that day and the dawn of Sunday, they practise this devotion.

iii. A plenary indulgence each month to all who have practised it every week in the month, provided that they go to Confession and Communion on one of the last days of the devotion.

All these Indulgences were Confirmed by the same Pope Pius VII. for ever, through the S. Congr. of Indulgences, June 18, 1822.

103. SHORT PRAYER TO THE MOST HOLY VIRGIN IN HER DESOLATION.

His Holiness Pope Pius IX., by a decree of the S. Congr. of Indulgences, of Dec. 23, 1847, deigned to grant -

An indulgence of 100 days to all the faithful, every time they say with contrite heart the following prayer in honour of the most holy Virgin in her desolation.

Ave Maria doloribus plena, Crucifixus tecum: lacrymabilis te in mulieribus, et lacrymabilis fructus ventris tui, Jesus. Sancta Maria, Mater Crucifixi: lacrymas impertire nobis crucifixoribus Filii tui, nunc et in hora mortis nostrae. Amen.

TRANSLATION.

Hail Mary, full of sorrows, the Crucified is with thee: tearful art thou amongst women, and tearful is the fruit of thy womb, Jesus. Holy Mary, Mother of the Crucified, grant tears to us crucifiers of thy Son, now and at the hour of our death. Amen.

APPENDIX

178. THE MONTH OF SEPTEMBER; OR CONSIDERATIONS AND DEVOUT AFFECTIONS UPON THE DOLOURS OF MOST HOLY MARY

By a Brief of April 3, 1857, his Holiness Pope Pius IX. granted -

300 days indulgence, to be gained on any day in the month of September by all the faithful who, with contrition of heart, shall practise this devout exercise for the month of September, dedicated to the Dolours of most holy Mary, on

condition of their making use of the following little book, entitled *The Month of September; or Considerations and Devout Affections upon the Dolours of most holy Mary; adapted to the use of every one who is devoted to this same Mother of God, &c.* It is reprinted at the press of Baldassari, at Rome, under the date of the year 1857, and is on sale at the shop of Joseph Ossani, No. 21A, in the street of the Pie di Marmo.

NOVENAS OF MOST HOLY MARY

To all faithful Christians who, in private or public, in church or in their own houses, shall keep any of the following Novenas, in preparation for the principal feasts of most holy Mary, Pope Pius VII., at the prayer of several holy persons, granted, by Rescripts issued through his Eminence the Cardinal-Vicar, Aug. 4 and Nov. 24, 1808, and Jan. 11, 1800 (all of which are kept in the *Segretaria* of the Vicariate) -
i. An indulgence of 300 days, daily.
ii. A plenary indulgence to all who shall assist at these Novenas every day, and who shall afterwards, either on the Feast-day itself, to which each Novena respectively has reference, or on some one day in its Octave, after Confession and Communion, pray to our Lord and to the Blessed Virgin ac cording to the pious intention of the Sovereign Pontiff.

104. FIRST NOVENA.

FOR THE FEAST OF THE IMMACULATE CONCEPTION.

Veni Sancte Spiritus, reple tuorum corda fidelium, et tui amoris in eis ignem accende.
V. Emitte Spiritum tuum, et creabuntur.
R. Et renovabis faciem terrae.

Oremus.
Deus, qui corda fidelium Sancti Spiritus illustratione docuisti: da nobis in

eodem Spiritu recta sapere, et de ejus semper consolatione gaudere. Per Christum Dominum nostrum. R. Amen.

TRANSLATION.

Come, Holy Spirit, fill the hearts of Thy faithful, and kindle in them the fire of Thy love.

V. Send forth Thy Spirit, and they shall be created.
R. And Thou shalt renew the face of the earth.

Let us pray.
O God, who hast taught the hearts of Thy faithful people by the light of the Holy Spirit; grant us in the same Spirit to relish what is right, and evermore to rejoice in his holy comfort. Through Christ our Lord. R. Amen.

PREPARATORY PRAYER FOR EVERY DAY OF THE NOVENA.

Virgin most pure, conceived without sin, all fair and stainless from thy Conception; glorious Mary, full of grace, Mother of my God, Queen of angels and of men, - I humbly venerate thee as Mother of my Saviour, who, though He was God, taught me by His own veneration, reverence, and obedience to thee, the honour and homage which are due to thee. Vouchsafe, I pray thee, to accept this Novena, which I dedicate to thee. Thou art the safe refuge of the penitent sinner; it is very fitting, then, that I should have recourse to thee. Thou art the Mother of compassion; then wilt thou surely be moved with pity for my many miseries. Thou art my best hope after Jesus; thou canst not but accept the loving confidence that I have in thee. Make me worthy to be called thy son, that so I may dare to cry unto thee,
Monstra te esse matrem.
Show thyself a mother.

Nine Ave Maria's, *one* Gloria Patri, *and the following Prayer.*

PRAYER FOR THE FIRST DAY. Nov. 29.

Behold me at thy sacred feet, O Immaculate Virgin. I rejoice with thee, because from all eternity thou wast elected to be the Mother of the Eternal Word, and wast preserved stainless from the taint of original sin. I praise and bless the Most Holy Trinity, who poured out upon thy soul in thy Conception the riches of that privilege. I humbly pray thee to obtain for me grace effectually to overcome the sad effects produced in my soul by original sin; make me wholly victorious over them, that I may never cease to love my God.

Then say the Litanies of the Blessed Virgin, or else:

V. Tota pulchra es, Maria.
R. Tota pulchra es, Maria.

V. Et macula originalis non est in te.
R. Et macula originalis non est in te.
V. Tu gloria Jerusalem.
R. Tu laetitia Israel.
V. Tu honorificentia populi nostri.
R. Tu advocata peccatorum.
V. O Maria.
R. O Maria.
V. Virgo prudentissima.
R. Mater clementissima.
V. Ora pro nobis.
R. Intercede pro nobis ad Dominum Jesum Christum.

After the Litanies, or Hymn as above, say as follows:

V. In Conceptione tua, Virgo, immaculata fuisti.
R. Ora pro nobis Patrem, cujus Filium peperisti.

Oremus.
Deus, qui per Immaculatam Virginis Conceptionem dignum Filii tui habitaculum preparasti: quaesumus, ut qui ex morte ejusdem Filii sui praevisa eam ab omni labe praeservasti, nos quoque mundos ejus intercessione ad te pervenire concedas.

Dens omnium fidelium pastor et rector, famulum tuum N., quem pastorem Ecelesiae tuae praesse voluisti, propitius respice: da ei quaesumus, verbo et exemplo, quibus praeest, proficere, ut ad vitam una cum grege sibi credito perveniat sempiternam.

Deus refugium nostrum et virtus, adesto piis Ecclesiae tuae precibus, auctor ipse pietatis; et praesta, ut quod fideliter petimus, efficaciter consequamur. Per Christum Dominum nostrum. R. Amen.

TRANSLATION.

V. All fair art thou, O Mary.
R. All fair art thou, O Mary.
V. The original stain is not in thee.
R. The original stain is not in thee.
V. Thou art the glory of Jerusalem.
R. Thou art the joy of Israel.
V. Thou art the honour of our people.
R. Thou art the advocate of sinners.
V. O Mary.
R. O Mary.
V. Virgin most prudent.

177

R. Mother most clement.

V. Pray for us.

B. Intercede for us to our Lord Jesus Christ.

V. In thy Conception, O Virgin, thou wast immaculate.

R. Pray for us to the Father, whose Son was born of thee.

Let us pray.

O God, who through the Immaculate Conception of a Virgin didst prepare a worthy dwelling-place for Thy Son, we beseech Thee, who by the death of that Son, foreseen by Thee, didst preserve her from every stain of sin, to grant that by her intercession we also may be purified, and so may come to Thee.

O God, the Shepherd and Ruler of all the faithful, graciously look down upon Thy servant N., whom Thou host chosen to be the pastor of Thy Church; and grant him, we beseech Thee, both by word and example, so to direct those over whom Thou hast placed him, that, together with the flock entrusted to his care, he may attain eternal life.

O God, our refuge and strength, who art the author of all holiness, listen to the pious prayers of thy Church, and grant that what we ask in faith we may effectually obtain. Through Christ our Lord. Amen.

The same order is to be observed en all the other days of the Novena, the Prayers for the Day alone being changed.

PRAYER FOR THE SECOND DAY. Nov. 30.

Mary, unsullied Lily of purity, I rejoice with thee, because from the first moment of thy Conception thou wast filled with grace, and hadst given unto thee the perfect use of reason. I thank and I adore the Ever-blessed Trinity, who gave thee these high gifts. Behold me at thy feet overwhelmed with shame to see myself so poor in grace. O thou who wast filled full of heavenly grace, grant me a portion of that same grace, and make me a partaker in the treasures of thy Immaculate Conception.

Litanies, &c., as before.

PRAYER FOR THE THIRD DAY. Dec. 1.

Mary, mystic Rose of purity, I rejoice with thee at the glorious triumph thou didst gain over the serpent by thy Immaculate Conception, in that then wast conceived without original sin. I thank and praise with my whole heart the Ever-blessed Trinity, who granted thee that glorious privilege and I pray thee to obtain for me courage to overcome every snare of the great enemy, and never to stain my soul with mortal sin. Be thou always mine aid, and enable me with thy protection to obtain the victory over all the enemies of man's eternal

welfare.
Litanies, &c., as before.

PRAYER FOR THE FOURTH DAY. Dec. 2.

Mary, Immaculate Virgin, Mirror of holy purity, I rejoice exceedingly to see how from thy Immaculate Conception there were infused into thy soul the most sublime and perfect virtues, with all the gifts of the Most Holy Spirit. I thank and praise the Ever-Blessed Trinity, who bestowed upon thee these high privileges, and I beseech thee, gracious Mother, obtain for me grace to practise every Christian virtue, and so to become worthy to receive the gifts and graces of the Holy Ghost.
Litanies, &c., as before.

PRAYER FOR THE FIFTH DAY. Dec. 3.

Mary, bright Moon of purity, I congratulate thee in that the mystery of thy Immaculate Conception was the beginning of salvation to the human race, and was the joy of the whole world. I thank and bless the Ever-blessed Trinity, who did so magnify and glorify thy Person. I entreat thee to obtain for me the grace so to profit by the Death and Passion of thy dear Son, that His Precious Blood may not have been shed upon the cross for me in vain, but that after a holy life I may be saved.
Litanies, &c., as before.

PRAYER FOR THE SIXTH DAY. Dec. 4.

Mary Immaculate, brilliant Star of purity, I rejoice with thee, because thy Immaculate Conception brought exceeding joy to all the angels in Paradise. I thank and bless the Ever-blessed Trinity, who enriched thee with this privilege. Enable me also one day to take part in this heavenly joy, praising and blessing thee in the company of angels world without end. Amen.
Litanies, &c., as before.

PRAYER FOR THE SEVENTH DAY. Dec. 5.

Mary immaculate, rising Morn of purity, I rejoice with thee, and I am filled with admiration at beholding thee confirmed in grace and rendered sinless from the first moment of thy Conception. I thank and praise the Ever-blessed Trinity, who elected thee alone from all mankind for this especial privilege. Holiest Virgin, obtain for me an entire and lasting hatred of sin, as the worst of all evils, that I may rather die than ever again commit a mortal sin.
Litanies, &c., as before.

PRAYER FOR THE EIGHTH DAY. Dec. 6.

Mary, Virgin, Sun without stain, I congratulate thee, and I rejoice with thee, because God gave unto thee in thy Conception a greater and a more abundant grace than He gave to all His angels and His saints together, even when their merits were most exalted. I thank and admire the immense beneficence of the Ever-blessed Trinity, who hath dispensed to thee alone this privilege. O, enable me too to correspond with the grace of God, and never more to receive it in vain; change my heart, and help me to begin in earnest a new life.
Litanies, &c., as before.

PRAYER FOR THE NINTH DAY. Dec. 7.

Immaculate Mary, living Light of holiness, Model of purity, Virgin and Mother, as soon as thou wast conceived thou didst profoundly adore thy God, giving Him thanks, because by means of thee the ancient curse was blotted out, and blessing was again come upon the sinful sons of Adam. Let this blessing kindle in my heart love towards God; and do thou inflame my heart still more and more, that I may ever love Him more constantly, and afterwards eternally enjoy Him in heaven, there to thank and praise Him more and more fervently for all the wondrous privileges conferred on thee, and to rejoice with thee for thy high crown of glory.
Litanies, &c., as before.

105. SECOND NOVENA.

IN PREPARATION FOR THE FEAST OF OUR LADY'S NATIVITY.

(Beginning Aug. 30.)

Veni Sancte Spiritus, as above.

Most holy Mary, Elect One, predestined from all eternity by the Most Holy Trinity to be Mother of the only-begotten Son of the Eternal Father, foretold by the Prophets, expected by the Patriarchs, desired by all nations, Sanctuary and living Temple of the Holy Ghost, Sun without stain, conceived free from original sin, Mistress of Heaven and of Earth, Queen of angels:- humbly prostrate at thy feet we give thee our homage, rejoicing that the year has brought round again the memory of thy most happy Nativity; and we pray thee with all our hearts to vouchsafe in thy goodness now to come down again and be reborn spiritually in our souls, that, led captive by thy loveliness and sweetness, they may ever live united to thy most sweet and loving heart.

i. So now whilst we say nine angelic salutations, we will direct our thoughts to the nine months which thou didst pass enclosed in thy mother's womb; celebrating at the same time thy descent from the royal house of David, and

how thou didst come forth to the light of heaven with high honour from the womb of holy Anna, thy most happy mother.
Ave Maria.

ii. We hail thee, heavenly Babe, white Dove of purity; who in spite of the serpent wast conceived free from original sin.
Ave Maria.

iii. We hail thee, bright Morn; who, forerunner of the Heavenly Sun of Justice, didst bring the first light to earth.
Ave Maria.

iv. We hail thee, Elect; who, like the untarnished Sun, didst burst forth in the dark night of sin.
Ave Maria.

v. We hail thee, beauteous Moon; who didst shed light upon a world wrapt in the darkness of idolatry.
Ave Maria.

vi. We hail thee, dread Warrior-Queen; who, in thyself a host, didst put to flight all hell.
Ave Maria.

vii. We hail thee, fair Soul of Mary; who from eternity wast possessed by God and God alone.
Ave Maria.

viii. We hail thee, dear Child, and we humbly venerate thy most holy infant body, the sacred swaddling-clothes wherewith they bound thee, the sacred crib wherein they laid thee, and we bless the hour and the day when thou wast born.
Ave Maria.

ix. We hail thee, much-loved Infant, adorned with every virtue immeasurably above all saints, and therefore worthy Mother of the Saviour of the world; who, having been made fruitful by the Holy Spirit, didst bring forth the Word Incarnate.
Ave Maria.

PRAYER

O most lovely Infant, who by thy holy birth hast comforted the world, made glad the heavens, struck terror into hell, brought help to the fallen, consolation to the sad, salvation to the weak, joy to all men living; we entreat thee, with the most fervent love and gratitude, to be spiritually reborn in our souls by means of thy most holy love; renew our spirits to thy service, rekindle in our hearts the fire of charity, bid all the virtues blossom there, that so we may find more

181

and more favour in thy gracious eyes. Mary! be thou our Mary, and may we feel the saving power of thy sweetest name; may it ever be our comfort to call on that name in all our troubles; may it be our hope in dangers, our shield in temptation, and our last utterance in death. *Sit nomen Mariae mel in ore, melos in aure, et jubilus in corde. Amen.* Let the name of Mary be honey in the mouth, melody in the ear, joy in the heart. Amen.

V. Nativitas tua, Dei Genitrix Virgo.
R. Gaudium annuntiavit universo mundo.

Oremus.
Famulis tuis, quaesumus Domine, coelestis gratiae munus impertire: ut quibus Beata Virginis partus extitit salutis exordium, nativitatis ejus votiva solemnitas pacis tribuat incrementum.

Deus omnium fidelium, *&c., with the other Prayers* as above.

TRANSLATION.

V. Thy Nativity, O Virgin Mother of God.
R. Hath brought joy to the whole world.

Let us pray.
Grant to us Thy servants, we beseech Thee, O Lord, the gift of heavenly grace; that to all those for whom the delivery of the Blessed Virgin was the beginning of salvation, this her votive festival may give increase of peace. Through, &c.

O God, &c., as above.

---

106. THIRD NOVENA.

IN PREPARATION FOR THE FEAST OF THE ANNUNCIATION.

(Beginning March 16.)

Veni Sancte Spiritus, &c., as above.

i. I venerate and I admire thee, most holy Virgin Mary, as the humblest of all the creatures of God in the very day of thy Annunciation, when God himself exalted thee to the most sublime dignity of His own Mother. O mighty Virgin, enable me, wretched sinner that I am, to know the depths of my own nothingness, and at once with all my heart to humble myself before all men. *Ave Maria.*

ii. Mary, most holy Virgin, when thou wast saluted by Gabriel the archangel, and the message from God was conveyed to thee, and thou wast exalted by

God above all the choirs of the angels, then thou didst confess thyself the handmaid of the Lord. O, obtain for me true humility and angelic purity, enabling me so to live on earth that I may ever be worthy of the blessing of God.
Ave Maria.

iii. O Virgin ever blest, I rejoice with thee because by thy sole *fiat*, uttered by thee so lowlily, thou didst draw down from the bosom of the Eternal Father the Divine Word into thine own pure bosom. Draw, then, ever my heart to God; and with God draw grace into my heart, that I may ever bless thy *Fiat* (Be it done), and cry with devotion, "O mighty *Fiat*! O efficacious *Fiat*! O *Fiat* be venerated above all *Fiats*." (St. Thom. de Villan.)
Ave Maria.

iv. O Virgin Mary, on the day of thy Annunciation thou wast found by Gabriel the archangel on the watch, quick to do God's will, and correspond with the desires of the Most holy Trinity for the redemption of man, waiting thy assent in order to redeem the world. Enable me in every good and bad fortune to turn to God with resignation and say, Be it unto me according to Thy word.
Ave Maria.

v. Most holy Mary, I well understand that thy obedience made the union between thy God and thee more intimate than shall ever again be possible for any other creature. * I am confounded to see how sin hath separated me from God. Help me, then, kind Mother, truly to do penance for my sins, that thy own loving Jesus may yet once more live in me and I in Him.
Ave Maria.

* Magis Deo conjungi, nisi fieret Deus, non potuit: "She could not have been more united to God except by becoming God herself." - B. Albert. Magnus.

vi. Most holy Mary, thou wast troubled by reason of thy modesty when Gabriel the archangel stood be fore thee in thy house; but I, when I come before thee, am troubled because of my great pride; wherefore do thou, in thy incomparable humility, "which brought forth God for men, reopened Paradise, and let the captive souls go free from hell beneath," * draw me, I pray thee, out of the deep pit of my sins, and enable me to save my soul.
Ave Maria.

* *Quae Deum hominibus peperit, paradisum aperuit et animas ab inferno liberavit.* - St. Augus., Serm. de Sanct.

vii. Most holy Virgin, though I have an unhallowed tongue, 1 have the boldness to salute thee all hours of the day: "Hail, hail, Mary, full of grace." I pray thee, from my heart, to replenish my soul with a little of that grace

wherewith the Holy Spirit, when he overshadowed thee, filled thee to the full.
Ave Maria.

viii. Most holy Mary, I know by faith that the great God who has been ever with thee from thy Conception, is, by his Incarnation in thy purest womb, made still more closely one with thee; make it thy care, I pray thee, that I may ever be one heart and soul with that same dear Lord Jesus, by means of His sanctifying grace.
Ave Maria.

ix. Most holy Mary, pour out upon my heart and soul the heavenly blessing, as thou thyself wast ever blest of God among all women; for I have this sure hope, that if, my dear Mother, thou shalt bless me while I live, then when I die I shall be blest of God in the everlasting glory of heaven.
Ave Maria.

Then the Litanies, &c.

V. Angelus Domini nuntiavit Mariae.
R. Et concepit de Spiritu Sancto.

Oremus.
Deus, qui de Beatae Mariae Virginis utero Verbum tuum, Angelo nuntiante, carnem suscipere voluisti: praesta supplicibus tuis, ut qui vere eam Genitricem Dei credimus, ejus apud te intercessionibus adjuvemur.

Dens omnium fidelium pastor, &c., as above.

TRANSLATION.

V. The angel of the Lord declared unto Mary.
R. And she conceived of the Holy Ghost.

Let us pray.
O God, who by the message of an angel didst will that Thy Divine Word should take flesh of the blessed Virgin Mary; grant unto us Thy suppliants, that we, who believe her to be truly the Mother of God, may be helped by her intercession with Thee. Through, &c.

O God, the Shepherd, &c., as above.

107. FOURTH NOVENA.

IN PREPARATION FOR THE FEAST OF THE PURIFICATION.

(Beginning Jan. 24.)

Veni Sancte Spiritus, &c., <u>as above</u>.

i. Most holy Mary, bright Mirror of all virtue, the forty days after thy delivery were no sooner past than thou, though the purest of all virgins, didst will to be presented in the Temple to be purified; O, help us, then, by imitating thee, to keep our hearts unstained by sin, that so we too may be made worthy one day to be presented to our God in Heaven.
Ave Maria.

ii. Virgin most obedient, at thy Presentation in the Temple, thou didst willingly offer the accustomed sacrifice of women; enable us so to follow thy example, that we may make ourselves a living sacrifice to God, by practising every virtue.
Ave Maria.

iii. Virgin most pure, thou didst despise the reproach of men whilst observing the precept of the Law; ask for his grace always to keep our hearts pure, what ever the world may think of us.
Ave Maria.

iv. Virgin most holy, by offering thy Son, the Divine Word, to His Eternal Father, thou didst makeHeaven glad; present our poor hearts to God, that by His grace they may be kept free from mortal sin.
Ave Maria.

v. Virgin most humble, in consigning Jesus into the arms of the holy old man Simeon, thou didst fill His spirit full of heavenly joy; consign our hearts to God, that He may fill them full of His Holy Spirit.
Ave Maria.

vi. Virgin most diligent, in ransoming thy Son Jesus according the Law, thou didst cooperate in the salvation of the world; ransom our pour hearts from the slavery of sin, that they may be ever pure in the sight of God.
Ave Maria.

vii. Virgin most meek, on hearing the prophecy of Simeon foretelling thy woes, thou didst humbly resign thyself to the good pleasure of thy God; make us always resigned to the dispositions of His Providence, and enable us to bear all troubles with patience.
Ave Maria.

viii. Virgin most compassionate, when thou didst fill the soul of Anna the prophetess with light, by means of thy divine Son, thou didst make her magnify the mercies of God by recognising Jesus for the Redeemer of the world; enrich our spirit too with heavenly grace, that we may joyfully reap in

full measure the fruits of our Lord's Redemption.
Ave Maria.

ix. Virgin most resigned, although thou didst feel thine own soul transfixed with sorrow, foreseeing all the bitter Passion of thy Son, yet knowing the grief of Joseph thy Spouse for all thy sufferings, thou didst console him with holy words; pierce through and through our souls with true sorrow for our sins, that we may one day come to rejoice with thee in everlasting bliss, partakers of thy glory.
Ave Maria.

Then the Litanies, and the following Responses, &c.

V. Responsum accepit Simeon a Spiritu Sancto.
R. Non visurum ei mortem nisi videret Christum Domini.

Oremus.
Omnipotens sempiterne Deus, majestatem tuam supplices exoramus, ut sicut unigenitus Filius tuus cum nostrae carnis substantia in Templo est Praesentatus, ita nos facias purificatis tibi mentibus praesentati.

Deus omnium fidelium pastor, &c. with the other Prayers, as above.

TRANSLATION.

V. Simeon received answer from the Holy Spirit.
R. That he should not see death till he had seen the Christ of God.

Let us pray.
Almighty, everlasting God, we humbly pray Thy Majesty, that as Thine only-begotten Son was presented in the Temple in the substance of our flesh, so Thou wouldst enable us to present ourselves before Thee with clean hearts. Through, &c.

O God, the Shepherd, &c., as above.

---

108. FIFTH NOVENA.

IN PREPARATION FOR THE FEAST OF THE ASSUMPTION.

(Beginning Aug. 6.)

FIRST DAY.

Veni Sancte Spiritus, &c., as above.

HYMN.

O gloriosa Virginum,
Sublimis inter sidera,
Qui te creavit, parvulum
Lactente nutris ubere.

Quod Heva tristis abstulit,
Tu reddis almo germine:
Intrent ut astra flebiles,
Coeli recludis cardines.

Tu regis alti janua,
Et aula lucis fulgida:
Vitam datam per Virginem,
Gentes redemptae plaudite.

Jesu, tibi sit gloria,
Qui natus es de Virgine,
Cum Patre, et almo Spiritu
In sempiterna saecula. Amen.

TRANSLATION.

O Queen of all the Virgin choir,
Enthroned above the starry sky;
Who with pure milk from thy own breast
Thy own Creator didst supply.

What man hath lost in hapless Eve,
Thy sacred womb to man restores;
Thou to the sorrowing here beneath
Hast open'd Heaven's eternal doors.

Hail, O refulgent Hall of light!
Hail, Gate sublime of Heaven's high King!
Through thee redeem'd to endless life,
Thy praise let all the nations sing.

O Jesu! born of Virgin bright,
Immortal glory be to Thee;
Praise to the Father infinite,
And Holy Ghost eternally.

GLORY OF MARY IN DEATH.

She was well prepared to die.

Let us meditate how glorious Mary was at the moment of her death, because in life she was so well prepared to die: first, by reason of her ardent longing to see her God and to be again united to her Son; and next, by the unapproachable merit of her consummate perfection. Then reflecting how different we are from Mary in our own practice of preparation for our death, let us say:

i. Most holy Virgin, who, in order to prepare thyself for a holy death, didst live in continual desire after the Beatific vision; O, take from us all vain desires for the frail things of earth.
Three Ave Marias.

ii. Most holy Virgin, who, in order to prepare thyself holily to die, didst in life ever sigh to be united to thy Son Jesus; obtain for us fidelity to Jesus, even unto death.
Three Ave Marias.

iii. Most holy Virgin, who, in order that thou mightest die holily, didst attain an unapproachable height of merit and of virtue; intercede for us, that we may know that virtue alone and the grace of God will lead us to salvation.
Three Ave Maria's.

Let us now give praise to Mary, so prudent in preparing for death; and whilst we exalt her glory, we will unite with the nine angel choirs who, on her Assumption into heaven, escorted her; singing with the first choir -

The Litanies; then -

V. Exaltata est Sancta Dei Genitrix.
R. Super choros angelorum ad coelestia regna.

Oremus.
Famulorum tuorum, quaesumus Domine, delictis ignosce: ut qui tibi placere de actibus nostris non valemus, Genitricis Filii tui Domini nostri intercessione salvemur.

Deus omnium fidelium pastor, &c., as above.

TRANSLATION.

V. The holy Mother of God is exalted.
R. Into the heavenly kingdom above the angel choirs.

Let us pray.
We beseech thee, Lord, pardon the shortcomings of Thy servants; that we who by our own works are not able to please Thee, may be saved by the intercession of the Mother of thy Son our Lord Jesus Christ.. Who, &c.

O God, &c., as above.

SECOND DAY. Aug. 7.

Veni Sancte Spiritus, &c., as above.

O gloriosa Virginum, &c. as above.

GLORY OF MARY IN DEATH.

She died in the midst of the Apostles, her Son Jesus assisting.

Let us meditate how glorious Mary was at her death, in that she was comforted not only by the apostles and saints, but also by her dear Son Jesus; and while we contemplate the unspeakable joy which filled her soul at this grace granted alone to her, let us entreat her for ourselves:

i. Glorious Virgin, who for thy consolation didst merit to die in the blessed company of apostles and of saints; obtain for us, that when we breathe forth our souls we may feel thy presence, and that of our holy patrons, assisting us. *Three* Ave Marias.

ii. Glorious Virgin, who at the moment of thy death wast comforted by the sight of thy dear Son Jesus; O, pray for us, that at that awful moment we too may be comforted by receiving Jesus in the most holy Viaticum. *Three* Ave Marias.

iii. Glorious Virgin, who didst deposit thy spirit into the arms of Jesus; assist us, that we may deposit our souls also into the arms of Jesus, always desirous that His most holy will be done. *Three* Ave Maria's.

Come, then, let us magnify the glory of Mary, assisted at her death by her Son Jesus and His apostles, and joining in jubilee at her triumph, say with the second choir of the Heavenly Host:

Litanies. Then V. and R. and Oremus as before.

THIRD DAY, Aug. 8.

Veni Sancte Spiritus, &c., as above.

O gloriosa Virginum, &c. as above.

GLORY OF MARY IN DEATH.

She died in an ecstasy of love.

Let us meditate how glorious the most holy Mary was in her death, because she died of a very ecstasy of the love of God; and desiring that we too may be strengthened by that holy fire of love, let us ask for her help:

i. Mary, most happy Virgin, who didst die of the vehemence of thy love of God; make it thy care that in our hearts, as God doth will, there be lit up this living fire of His love.
Three Ave Maria's.

ii. Mary, most happy Virgin, who dying of divine love didst teach us what our love of God ought to do; pray for us, that we may never leave our God in life or death.
Three Ave Marias.

iii. Mary, most happy Virgin, who in leaving this mortal life by virtue of an ecstasy of love didst make known the fire which ever burnt within thy heart; obtain for us at least a spark of that same fire, to give us true sorrow for our sins.
Three Ave Marias.

Let us with the third choir of angels now exalt the ineffable glory of Mary, inflamed with the love of her God, and say with her:

Litanies. Then V. and R. and Oremus as before.

FOURTH DAY. Aug. 9.

Veni Sancte Spiritus, &c., as above.

O gloriosa Virginum, &c. as above.

GLORY OF MAY AFTER DEATH

In her dead body.

Let us meditate how glorious Mary was in her (Dad body, because it was adorned with marvellous splendour and majesty, and spread around an odour of sanctity, which was the very fragrancy of Paradise, and because innumerable miracles were wrought at the sight of it. Then, thinking upon our own miseries, let us say:

i. O Lady most pure, who by reason of thy virginal purity didst merit the glory to be so bright and so majestic in thy body after death; obtain for us the strength to detach ourselves from every foul spirit of impurity.
Three Ave Marias.

ii. O Lady most pure, who by reason of thy rare virtue didst from thy dead body spread around the sweetnesses of Paradise; make it thy care that we may edify our neighbour by our life, and never more by our bad example become a stumbling-block to others.
Three Ave Maria's.

iii. O Lady most pure, at the sight of whose body numberless bodily maladies were cured; intercede for us, that by thy prayers all our spiritual ills may be healed.
Three Ave Marias.

Come, let us rejoice for the glory given to the dead body of Mary, magnifying her with the fourth choir of the angels:

Litanies. Then V. and R. and Oremus as before.

FIFTH DAY. Aug. 10.

Veni Sancte Spiritus, &c., as above.

O gloriosa Virginum, &c. as above.

GLORY OF MARY AFTER DEATH.

In the resurrection of her body.

Let us meditate how glorious Mary was after death, since by the power of the Highest her body, raised again to life, forthwith acquired the four gifts of brightness, subtlety, agility, and impassibility; and, filled with consolation at the excellency of her glory, let us thus invoke her:

i. O Lady exalted, who wast so gloriously raised again to life by thy God; help us so to live on earth, that we also may rise again like unto thee in the last judgment-day.
Three Ave Marias.

ii. O Lady exalted, to whose risen body were given the gifts of brightness and of subtlety, by reason of the bright example and the humility of thy life on earth; pray for us, that all contemptuous affectation may be taken from us; that so our souls, being freed from all self-love, may be adorned with humility.
Three Ave Maria's.

iii. O Lady exalted, by the gifts of agility and impassibility with which thy risen body was glorified, by reason of thy spiritual zeal and patience while on earth; obtain for us courage valiantly to mortify our bodies, and patiently to curb all our disordinate inclinations.
Three Ave Marias.

Then let us render due praise to Mary, and magnify the glory which adorned her risen body; while with the fifth choir we exalt her:

Litanies. Then V. and R. and Oremus as before.

SIXTH DAY. Aug. 11.

Veni Sancte Spiritus, &c., *as above*.

O gloriosa Virginum, &c. *as above*.

GLORY OF MARY AFTER DEATH.

In her Assumption into heaven.

Let us meditate how gloriously Mary was taken up to heaven, being escorted thither by many legions of the heavenly hosts and blessed souls drawn by her merits out of Purgatory; and rejoicing in that majestic triumph, let us with all humility offer to her our supplications:

i. Great Queen, who wast assumed so royally into the kingdom of eternal peace; obtain for us that all sordid earthly thoughts be taken away from us, and our hearts fixed upon the contemplation of the unchangeable happiness of heaven.
Three Ave Maria's.

ii. Great Queen, who wast assumed to heaven amidst a company of the Angelic Hierarchy; obtain for us strength to overcome the wiles of all our enemies, and that we may lend a docile ear to the counsels of that good Angel who continually assists and governs us.
Three Ave Marias.

iii. Great Queen, who wast assumed to heaven most gloriously, in the company of souls drawn by thy merits out of Purgatory; free us from the slavery of sin, and make us worthy to praise thee for all eternity.
Three Ave Marias.

Let us not cease to applaud at the royal triumph of Mary; and uniting our homage with the sixth choir of the angels, let us honour the singular glory of her Assumption into heaven, while we say:

Litanies. Then V. and R. and Oremus *as before*.

SEVENTH DAY. Aug. 12.

Veni Sancte Spiritus, &c., *as above*.

O gloriosa Virginum, &c. *as above*.

GLORY OF MARY AFTER DEATH.

In her Assumption into heaven.

Let us meditate how glorious Mary is in heaven, because she is enthroned there as Queen of the universe, and is ever receiving homage and veneration from countless hosts of angels and of saints; and assisting at her royal throne, let us implore her aid:

i. Sovereign Queen of the universe, who for thy incomparable merit art raised to such high glory in the heavens; in thy pity look upon our miseries, and rule us with the gentle sway of thy protection.
Three Ave Marias.

ii. Sovereign Queen of the universe, who art ever receiving the worship and homage from all the heavenly hosts; accept, we pray thee, these our invocations, offered with such reverence as befits thy dignity and greatness.
Three Ave Marias.

iii. Sovereign Queen of the universe; by that glory which thou hast by reason of thy high place in heaven, vouchsafe to take us into the number of thy servants, and obtain for us grace that, with quick and ready will, we may faithfully keep the precepts of our God and Lord.
Three Ave Maria's.

Let us take part in the joy of the angels praising Mary, and rejoice because we know that she is raised to the dignity of Queen of the universe; while with the seventh choir we sing:

Litanies. Then V. and R. and Oremus as before.

EIGHTH DAY. Aug. 13.

Veni Sancte Spiritus, &c., as above.

O gloriosa Virginum, &c. as above.

GLORY OF MARY AFTER DEATH.

For the crown which decks her brow.

Let us meditate how glorious Mary is in heaven by reason of the royal crown wherewith her Divine Son hath crowned her, and for the full knowledge which she now has of the deep mysteries of God, past, present, and to come; and, full of veneration for the incomparable honour bestowed upon our Queen, let us have recourse to her and say:

i. Queen unrivalled, who in heaven on high dost enjoy the high glory of being crowned by thy Divine Son with a royal diadem; help us to share thy matchless virtues, and ask for us that, purified in heart, we may be made worthy to be

crowned with thee in Paradise.
Three Ave Marias.

ii. Queen unrivalled in the full knowledge granted thee of all things upon earth; for thy own glory's sake obtain pardon for our past evil deeds, that we may never offend again by froward tongue or wanton thought.
Three Ave Marias.

iii. Queen unrivalled, whose desire it is to see men pure and clean of heart, that so they may be made worthy of thy God; obtain for us forgiveness of our sins, and help us, that all our looks, words, and deeds may please his heavenly Majesty.
Three Ave Maria's.

Let us then purify our hearts, in order that we may be worthy to give praise to Mary; and to the glory she possesses in that bright crown which decks her royal brow, let us add humble tokens of our love, while with the eighth choir we joyfully sing:

Litanies. Then V. and R. and Oremus as before.

NINTH DAY. Aug. 14.

Veni Sancte Spiritus, &c., as above.

O gloriosa Virginum, &c. as above.

GLORY OF MARY AFTER DEATH.

In her patronage of man.

Let us meditate how glorious Mary is in heaven, by reason of her patronage of man, and for the power she has to aid him, with great watchfulness in all his necessities; wherefore with lively confidence, in having for our patroness the very Mother of our God, let ns implore her:

i. Mary, our most powerful Patroness, whose glory it is in heaven to be the advocate of man; O take us from the hands of the enemy and place us in the arms of our God and Creator.
Three Ave Marias.

ii. Mary, our most powerful Patroness, who, being in heaven the advocate of man, wouldest that all men should be saved; make it thy care that none of us despair at the sight of our past relapses into sin.
Three Ave Marias.

iii. Mary, our most powerful Patroness, who, to fulfil thine office, dost love to be invoked by men; obtain for us such true devotion, that we may ever call upon thee in life, and above all at the awful moment of our death.
Three Ave Maria's.

Now with all our hearts let us celebrate the glories of Mary; and consoled at having Mary for our advocate in Heaven, let us join the ninth choir of the angels in praising her while we sing:

Litanies. Then V. and R. and Oremus as before.

109. VARIOUS OTHER NOVENAS.

The following Novenas were published in one volume by the Rev. Joseph Mary Falcone, of the Congregation of the Mission at Naples; and were printed in Naples in the year 1849:
His Holiness Pius IX., by a Rescript dated Gaeta, Jan. 5, 1849, granted to the faithful -
i. An indulgence of 300 DAYS for every day of each Novena, no matter at what time of the year it is made.
ii. A plenary indulgence for each Novena to be gained in the course of the Novena, or within the space of eight days after it, on that day when, after Confession and Communion, prayer be said for the Holy Church and Sovereign Pontiff.

These Novenas are -
1. Purification of our Blessed Lady.
2. St. Gabriel the Archangel.
3. St. Joseph, the Spouse of our Blessed Lady.
4. The Annunciation of our Blessed Lady.
5. The Seven Dolours of our Blessed Lady.
6. The Patronage of the Immaculate Heart of Mary.
7. The Holy Ghost.
S. The Sacred Heart of Jesus.
9. The Visitation of our Blessed Lady.
10. St. Vincent of Paul.
11. The Assumption of our Blessed Lady.
12. The Nativity of our Blessed Lady.
1:3. St. Michael the Archangel.
14. The holy Guardian Angels.
15. The Most Holy Rosary.
16. The holy Souls in Purgatory.
17. St. Raphael the Archangel.

18. The Presentation of our Blessed Lady.
19. The Immaculate Conception.
20. The Nativity of our Blessed Lord and Saviour Jesus Christ.

ST. MICHAEL THE ARCHANGEL

110. THE HYMN " TE SPLENDOR," ETC.

Pope Pius VII., by a Rescript of the S. Congr. of Indulgences, May 6, 1817, granted -
i. An indulgence of 200 days once a day to all the faithful who, with contrite hearts and devotion, say the following hymn, with the antiphon and prayer, in honour of St. Michael the Archangel; to obtain for themselves the mighty aid which his patronage affords to all in the assaults of the enemy of man, and iii all teuiuIitatIsi11s, whether in life or death.
ii. A plenary indulgence to all who shall have said this hymn every day for a month together, on any one day when, after Confession and Communion, they shall pray according to the intention of the Sovereign Pontiff.

Te splendor et virtus Patris,
Te vita, Jesu, cordium,
Ab ore qui pendent tuo,
Laudamus inter Angelos.

Tibi mille densa millium
Ducum corona militat:
Scul explicat victor crucem
Michael salutis signifer.

Draconis hic dirum caput
In ima pellit tartara,
Ducemque cum rebellibus
Coelesti ab arce fulminat.

Contra ducem superbiae
Sequamur hunc nos Principem,

196

Ut detur ex Agni throno
Nobis corona gloriae.

Patri, simulque Filio,
Tibique sancte Spiritus,
Sicut fuit, sit jugiter,
Saeclum per omne gloria. Amen.

Ant. Princeps gloriosissime, Michael Archangele, esto memor nostri: hic et ubique semper precare pro nobis Filium Dei.

V. In conspectu angelorum psallam tibi, Deus meus.
R. Adorabo ad templum sanctum tuum, et confitebor nomini tuo.

Oremus.
Deus, qui miro ordine angelorum ministeria hominumque dispensas: concede propitius, ut, a quibus tibi ministrantibus in coelo semper assistitur, ab his in terra vita nostra muniatur. Per Dominum nostrum, &c.

TRANSLATION.

O Jesu, lifespring of the soul,
The Father's power, and glory bright!
Thee with the angels we extol;
From Thee they draw their life and light.

Thy thousand thousand hosts are spread
Embattled o'er the azure sky;
But Michael bears Thy standard dread,
And lifts the mighty cries on high.

He in that sign the rebel powers
Did with their dragon prince expel;
And hurl'd them from the heaven's high towers
Down like a thunderbolt to hell.

Grant us with Michael still, O Lord,
Against the Prince of Pride to fight;
So may a crown be our reward,
Before the Lamb's pure throne of light.

To God the Father glory be,
And to his sole-begotten Son;
The same, O Holy Ghost, to Thee,
While everlasting ages run.

Ant. Most glorious Prince, Michael the Archangel, be thou mindful of us; here, and in all places, pray for us to the Son of God most high.

V. I wilt sing praises to Thee, my God, before the Angels.
R. I will adore Thee in Thy holy temple, and praise Thy Name.

Let us pray.
O God, who in the dispensation of Thy providence dost admirably dispose the ministry of angels and of men; mercifully grant that the Holy Angels, who ever minister before Thy throne in heaven, may be the protectors also of our life on earth. Through Jesus Christ our Lord.

111. ANGELICAL CROWN IN HONOUR OF ST. MICHAEL THE ARCHANGEL.

It is a pious tradition, that the Archangel Michael revealed to a holy person that he would he well pleased by his bringing into use the following prayers in his honour and in honour of all the angelic host; and that he would repay those who practised this devotion with signal favours, particularly in such times as the Catholic Church should experience some special trial. In this belief, a holy Carmelite nun, of the convent of Vetralla, in the diocese of Viterbo, who died with the reputation of sanctity in the year 1751, made it her delight to practise this method of prayer, commonly called the "Angelic Chaplet;" and it was at the instigation of the nuns of her convent that his Holiness Pins IX., by a decree of the S. Congr. of Rites, dated August 8, 1851, granted the following Indulgences -
i. An indulgence of seven years and seven quarantines every time the Chaplet is said.
ii. An indulgence of 100 days daily to any one who carries this Chaplet about him, or kisses the medal with the representation of the holy angels appended to the said Chaplet.
iii. A plenary indulgence once a month to every one who says daily this Chaplet, on any one day when, after Confession and Communion, he shall pray for the exaltation of our holy Mother the Church and the safety of the Sovereign Pontiff.
iv. A plenary indulgence, with the conditions above named, on -
1. The Feast of the Apparition of St. Michael. May 18.
2. The Dedication of St. Michael. September 29.
3. St. Gabriel the Archangel. March 18.
4. St. Raphael the Archangel. October 24.
5. Holy Angel Guardians. October 2.
To gain these Indulgences, a Chaplet must be used consisting of nine *Pater noster's,* and three *Ave Maria's* after each *Pater noster*, with four *Pater noster's* at the end; the following corresponding salutations being said at the same time in their proper order, with the antiphon and prayer at the end us

198

given below. These Chaplets must be blessed by the actual father confessor of the convent of Vetralla, or some other priest who has obtained faculties for this purpose.

METHOD OF PRACTISING THIS DEVOTION.

Let every one, according to his ability, begin with an act of sincere contrition, kneeling before a representation of the holy Archangel; then let him say with devotion the following salutations:

V. Deus in adjutorium meum intende.
R. Dontine ad adjuvandum me festina.

Gloria Patri, &c.

FIRST SALUTATION.

One Pater noster *and three* Ave Maria's, *to the First Angelic Choir.*

At the intercession of St. Michael and the heavenly choir of the Seraphim, may it please God to make us worthy to receive into our hearts the fire of His perfect charity. Amen.

SECOND SALUTATION.

One Pater noster *and three* Ave Maria's, *to the Second Angelic Choir.*

At the intercession of St. Michael and the heavenly choir of the Cherubim, may God grant us grace to abandon the ways of sin, and run the race of Christian perfection. Amen.

THIRD SALUTATION.

One Pater noster *and three* Ave Maria's, *to the Third Angelic Choir.*

At the intercession of St. Michael and the sacred choir of the Thrones, may it please God to infuse into our hearts a true and earnest spirit of humility. Amen.

FOURTH SALUTATION.

One Pater noster *and three* Ave Maria's, *to the Fourth Angelic Choir.*

At the intercession of St. Michael and the heavenly choir of the Dominations, may it please God to grant us grace to have dominion over our senses, and to correct our depraved passions. Amen.

FIFTH SALUTATION.

One Pater noster *and three* Ave Maria's, *to the Fifth Angelic Choir.*

At the intercession of St. Michael and the heavenly choir of the Powers, may God vouchsafe to keep our souls from the wiles and temptations of the devil. Amen.

SIXTH SALUTATION.

One Pater noster *and three* Ave Maria's, *to the Sixth Angelic Choir.*

At the intercession of St. Michael and the choir of the admirable celestial Virtues, may our Lord keep us from falling into temptation, and deliver us from evil. Amen.

SEVENTH SALUTATION.

One Pater noster *and three* Ave Maria's, *to the Seventh Angelic Choir.*

At the intercession of St. Michael and the heavenly choir of the Principalities, may it please God to fill our souls with the spirit of true and hearty obedience. Amen.

EIGHTH SALUTATION.

One Pater noster *and three* Ave Maria's, *to the Eighth Angelic Choir.*

At the intercession of St. Michael and the heavenly choir of Archangels, may it please God to grant its the gift of perseverance in the faith and in all good works, that we may thereby be enabled to attain unto the glory of Paradise. Amen.

NINTH SALUTATION.

One Pater noster *and three* Ave Maria's, *to the Ninth Angelic Choir.*

At the intercession of St. Michael and the Heavenly choir of Angels, may God vouchsafe to grant us the safe-conduct of the holy Angels through life, and after death a happy entrance into the everlasting glory of heaven. Amen.

Then say four Pater noster's *in conclusion; the first to St. Michael, the second to St. Gabriel, the third to St. Raphael, the fourth to your Angel Guardian.*

This exercise then ends with the following Antiphon.

ANTIPHON.

Michael, glorious Prince, chief and champion of the heavenly host, guardian of the souls of men, conqueror of the rebel angels, minister in the house of God, our worthy captain under Jesus Christ, endowed with superhuman excellence and virtue; vouchsafe to free us all from every evil, who with full confidence have recourse to thee; and by thy powerful protection enable us to make progress every day in the faithful service of our God.

V. Pray for us, most blessed Michael, prince of the Church of Jesus Christ.
R. That we may be made worthy of His promises.

PRAYER.

Almighty and eternal God, who in thine own marvellous goodness and pity
didst, for the common salvation of man, choose the glorious Archangel
Michael to be the prince of Thy Church; make us worthy, we pray Thee, to be
delivered by his beneficent protection from all our enemies, that at the hour of
our death no one of them may approach to harm us, and that by the same
Archangel Michael we may be introduced into the presence of Thy high and
heavenly Majesty. Through the merits of the same Jesus Christ our Lord.
Amen.

THE ANGEL GUARDIAN

112. "ANGEL OF GOD," ETC.

While we give thanks to God for having granted to each of us a holy angel for
our guardian, we ought ever to bear in mind the respect, devotion, and loving
confidence we owe to this blessed spirit; and with these feelings we should
often think of him, and implore his constant aid with the following well-known
invocation:

Angele Dei, qui custos es mei, me tibi commissum pietate superna, illumina,
custodi, rege, et guberna. Amen.

O angel of God, whom God hath appointed to be my guardian, enlighten and
protect, direct and govern me.

Or else.

Angel of God, my guardian dear,
To whom His love commits me here,

Ever this day be at my side,
To light and guard, to rule and guide. Amen.

Pope Pius VI., in order to kindle the fervour of the faithful to have frequent recourse to their holy Angel Guardian, granted, *motu proprio,* by a Brief of October 2, 1795 -

i. An indulgence of 100 days every time the above-named short prayer is said devoutly and with a contrite heart.

ii. A plenary indulgence to those who have been accustomed to say it morning and evening throughout the year, on the Feast of the Holy Guardian Angels, October 2; provided that on that day, after Confession and Communion, they visit a church or public oratory and pray for the Sovereign Pontiff.

iii. A plenary indulgence, *in articulo mortis,* was added by the same Pope, in another Brief of September 2, 1796, to all who had been accustomed during life frequently to say the said prayer. In this Brief also, *motu proprio,* he confirmed the Indulgences already granted.

His successor, Pius VII., afterwards, by a decree of the S. Congr. of Indulgences, of May 15, 1821, besides confirming afresh the above-named Indulgences, granted -

iv. A plenary indulgence to all the faithful who say at least once a day, for a month together, the said prayer, *Angele Dei,* &c., on any one day when, after Confession and Communion, they visit a church and pray as above.

ST. JOSEPH

113. THE FIVE PSALMS IN HONOUR OF HIS SACRED NAME.

The devotion of the faithful to Jesus and Mary having induced them to honour even their sacred names by reciting certain psalms and hymns, those who have had a devotion to St. Joseph have in like manner desired to honour that glorious patriarch, the adopted father of Jesus, and pure spouse of the ever-Virgin Mary, by saying five psalms, whose initial letters compose the name of Joseph. (F in the Italian standing for PH).

To encourage Christian People to practise this devotion to St. Joseph, thereby to obtain his efficacious protection in life, and still more in death, Pope Pius VII., by a Rescript and subsequent decree of June 26, 1809, issued by his Eminence the Cardinal-Vicar and preserved in his *Segretaria*, granted -

i. An indulgence of seven years and seven quarantines, every time these psalms are said devoutly and with a contrite heart, together with the hymn and prayer proper to the saint.

ii. A plenary indulgence once a month, to all who shall say them daily for a month together, on any one day when, after Confession and Communion, they shall, being truly penitent, pray according to the intention of the Sovereign Pontiff.

iii. A plenary indulgence on the Feast of the Patronage of St. Joseph (the third Sunday after Easter) was added by Pope Pius VII, by a Rescript of the S. Congr. of Indulgences of June 13, 1815, in which he also confirmed the above-named Indulgences. This may be gained by the faithful after Confession and Communion on that day, provided that they have said these five psalms frequently in the course of the year.

THE FIVE PSALMS.

Ant. Joseph virum Maria, de qua natus est Jesus, qui vocatur Christus.

J. *Ps.* 99

Jubilate Deo omnis terra: * servite Domino in laetitia.
Introite in conspectu ejus, * in exultatione.
Scitote, quoniam Dominus ipse est Deus: * ipse fecit nos, et non ipsi nos.
Populus ejus, et oves pascuae ejus: * introite portas ejus in confessione, atria ejus in hymnis; confitemni illi.
Laudate nomen ejus, quoniam suavis est Dominus, in aeternum misericordia ejus: * et usque in generationem et generationem veritas ejus.
Gloria Patri, et Filio, * et Spiritui Sancto.
Sicut erat in principio, et nunc, et semper, * et in saecula saeculorum. Amen.

Ant. Joseph virum Mariae, de qua natus est Jesus, qui vocatur Christus.

Ant. Joseph de domo David, et nomen Virginis Maria.

O. *Ps.* 46.

Omnes gentes plaudite manibus: * jubilate Deo in voce exultationis.
Quoniam Dominus excelsus, terribilis, * rex magnus super omnem terram.
Subjecit populos nobis, * et gentes sub pedibus nostris.
Elegit nobis hereditatem suam, * speciem Jacob, quam dilexit.
Ascendit Deus in jubilo, * et Dominus in voce tubae.
Psallite Deo nostro, psallite; * psallite regi nostro, psallite.
Quoniam rex omnis terrae Deus; * psallite sapienter.

Regnabit Deus super gentes; * Deus sedet super sedem sanctam suam.

Principes populorum congregati sunt cum Deo Abraham: * quoniam dii fortes terrae vehementer elevati sunt.

Gloria Patri, et Filio, * et Spiritui Sancto.

Sicut erat in principio, et nunc, et semper, * et in saecula saeculorum. Amen.

Ant. Joseph de domo David, et nomen Virginis Maria.

Ant. Joseph vir ejus, cum esset justus, et nollet eam traducere.

S. *Ps.* 128.

Saepe expugnaverunt me a juventute mea: * dicat nunc Israel.

Saepe expugnaverunt me a juventute mea: * etenim non potuerunt mihi.

Supra dorsum meum fabricaverunt peccatores: * prolongaverunt iniquitatem suam.

Dominus justus concidit cervices peccatorum: * confundantur, et convertantur retrorsum omnes, qui oderunt Sion.

Fiant sicut foenum tectorum, * quod priusquam evellatur, exaruit.

De quo non implevit manum suam, qui metit, * et sinum suum, qui manipulos colligit.

Et non dixerunt, qui praeteribant: Benedictio Domini super vos: * benediximus vobis in nomine Domini.

Gloria Patri, et Filio, * et Spiritui Sancto.

Sicut erat in principio, et nunc, et semper, * et in saecula saeculorum. Amen.

Ant. Joseph vir ejus, cum esset justus, et nollet eam traducere.

Ant. Joseph fili David, noli timere accipere Mariam conjugem tuam.

E. *Ps.* 80.

Exultate Deo adjutori nostro: * jubilate Deo Jacob.

Sumite psalmum, et date tympanum, * psalterium jucundum cum cithara.

Buccinate in Neomenia tuba, * in insigni die solemnitatis vestrae.

Quia praecptum in Israel est, * et judicium Deo Jacob.

Testimonium in Joscph posuit illud, cum exiret de terra Aegypti: * linguam, quam non noverat, audivit.

Divertit ab oneribus dorsum ejus: * manus ejus in cophino servierunt.

In tribulatione invocasti me, et liberavi te: * exaudivi te in abscondito tempestatis; probavi te apud aquam contradictionis.

Audi populus meus, et contestabor te: * Israel si audieris me, non erit in te deus recens, neque adorabis deum alienum.

Ego enim sum Dominus Deus tuus, qui eduxi te de terra Aegypti: * ditata os tuum, et implebo illud.

Et non audivit populus meus vocem meam: * et Israel non intendit mihi.

Et dimisi eos secundum desideria cordis eorum: * ibunt in adinventionibus suis.

Si populus meus audisset me, * Israel si in viis meis ambulasset

Pro nihilo forsitan inimicos eorum humiliassem: * et super tribulantos eos misissem manum meam.

Inimici Domini mentiti sunt ei: * et erit tempus eorum in saecula.

Et cibavit eos ex adipe frumenti; * et de petra melle saturavit eos.

Gloria Patri, et Filio, * et Spiritui Sancto.

Sicut erat in principio, et nunc, et semper, * et in saecula saeculorum. Amen.

Ant. Joseph fili David, noli timere accipere Mariam conjugem tuam.

Ant. Joseph exurgens a somno fecit, sicut praecepit ei angelus.

PH. *Ps.* 86.

Fundamenta ejus in montibus sanctis: * diligit Dominus portas Sion super omnia tabernacula Jacob.

Gloriosa dicta sunt de te: * civitas Dei.

Memor ero Rahab, et Babylonis: * scientium me.

Ecce alienigenae, et Tyrus, et populus Aethiopum: * hi fuerunt illic.

Numquid Sion dicet: Homo, et homo natus est in ea: * et ipse fundavit eam Altissimus?

Dominus narrabit in scripturis populorum, et principum: * horum, qui fuerunt in ea.

Sicut laetantium omnium: * habitatio est in te.

Gloria Patri, et Filio, * et Spiritui Sancto.

Sicut erat in principio, et nunc, et semper, * et in saecula saeculorum. Amen.

Ant. Joseph exurgens a somno fecit, sicut praecepit ei angelus.

V. Constituit eum dominum domus sui.
R. Et principem omnis possessionis sui.

Oremus.
Deus, qui ineffabili providentia beatum Joseph sacratissimae Genitricis tuae sponsum eligere dignatus es; praesta quaesumus, ut quem protectorem veneramur in terris, intercessorem habere mereamur in coelis. Qui vivis et regnas, &c.

V. He made him lord over His house.
R. And prince of all that was His.

Let us pray.
O God, who in Thine ineffable providence didst vouchsafe to choose blessed Joseph to be the husband of Thy most holy Mother; grant, we beseech Thee, that we may have him for our intercessor in heaven, whom on earth we

venerate as our holy protector. Who livest and reignest world without end. Amen.

HYMNUS

Dei qui gratiam impotes,
Coelestium dona expetunt,
Josephi nomen invocent,
Opemque poscant supplices.

Joseph vocato nomine
Deus adest petentibus,
Auget piis justitiam,
Culpamque delet impiis.

Josephi piis quaerentibus
Dantur beata munera,
Datur palma victoriae
Agonis in certamine.

Amplexus inter Virginis,
Castaeque prolis placido
Vitam sopore deserens,
Morientium fit regula.

Illo nihil potentius,
Cujus parentem nutibus,
Et subditum inuperiis
Deum viderunt Angeli.

Illo nihil perfectius,
Qui sponsus almae Virginis
Electus est, Altissimi
Custos parensque creditus.

O ter beata et amplius
Honor sit tibi, Trinitas,
Pater, Verbumque, et Spiritus,
Sanctoque Joseph nomini. Amen.

Ant. Adjutor est in tribulationibus, et protector omnibus beatus Joseph nomen suum pie invocantibus.

V. Sit nomen beati Josephi benedictum.
R. Ex hoc nunc et usque in saeculum.

Oremus.
Deus, qui mirabilis in sanctis tuis, mirabilior in beato Josepho, eum coelestium

dononum disponsatorem super familiam tuam constituisti; praesta quaesumus, ut cujus nomen devoti veneramur, ejus precibus et meritis adjuti ab portum salutis feliciter perveniamus. Per Dominum, &c.

HYMN.

Seek ye the grace of God,
And mercies from on high?
Invoke St. Joseph's holy name,
And on his aid rely.

So shall the Lord well-pleas'd
Your earnest prayer fulfil;
The guilty cleanse from guilt, and make
The holy holier still.

So shall his tender care
To you through life be nigh;
So shall his love with triumph crown
Your dying agony.

Lock'd in the Virgin's arms
Of Mary and her Son;-
Embracing each in speechless joy
And sweetest union.

O Joseph, in what peace
Was breath'd thy latest sigh!
Dear pattern of all those to come
Who should in Jesus die.

Hail, mightiest of saints!
To whom submissive bent
He whose Creator-hand outstretch'd
The starry firmament.

Hail, Mary's spouse elect!
Hail, guardian of the Word!
Nurse of the Highest, and esteem'd
The father of the Lord!

Blest Trinity to Thee,
From all in earth, in heaven,
And to St. Joseph's holy name,
Be praise and honour given.

Ant. Blessed Joseph is the helper in troubles and protector of all who piously call upon his name.

V. Blessed be the name of Joseph.
R. Henceforth and evermore.

Let us pray.
O God, wonderful in Thy saints, and more wonderful in blessed Joseph, who hast made him dispenser of heavenly gifts over Thy family; grant, we beseech Thee, that we who devoutly venerate his name on earth may, through the assistance of his prayers and merits, happily attain unto the haven of salvation. Through our Lord Jesus Christ. Amen.

114. RESPONSORIUM: "QUICUMQUE," ETC.

Pope Pius VII., by a Rescript of Sept. 6, 1804, given through his Eminence the Cardinal-Vicar, and kept in his *Segretaria*, granted -
An indulgence of one year to all the faithful in the whole Catholic world, every time that with contrite heart and devoutly they say the following Responsorium in honour of the glorious Patriarch St. Joseph, to implore his efficacious protection in life and in death:

THE RESPONSORIUM

Quicumque sanus vivere,
Cursumque vitae claudere
In fine laetus expetit,
Opem Josephi postulet.

Hic sponsus almae Virginis,
Paterque Jesu creditus,
Justus, fidelis, integer,
Quod poscit, orans impetrat.
Quicumque &c.

Foeno jacentem parvulum
Adorat, et post exulem
Solatur; inde perditum
Quaerit dolens, et invenit.
Quicumque &c.

Mundi supremus artifex
Ejus labore pascitur,
Summi Parentis Filius

Obedit illi subditus.
Quicumque, &c.

Adesse morti proximus
Cum Matre Jesu conspicit,
Et inter ipsos jubilans
Dulci sopore solvitur.
Quicumque, &c.

Gloria Patri, et Filio, ct Spiritui Sancto, &c.
Quicumque, &c.

Ant. Ecce fidelis servus, et prudeius, quem constituit Dominus super familiam suam.

V. Ora pro nobis, sancte Joseph.
R. Ut digni efficiamur promissionibus Christi.

Oremus.
Deus, qui ineffabili providentia beatum Joseph sacratissimae Genitricis tuae sponsum eligere dignatus es; praesta quaesumus, ut quem protectorem veneramur in terris, intercessorem habere mereamur in coelis. Qui vivis et regnas, &c.

TRANSLATION

To all who would holily live,
To all who would happily die,
St. Joseph is ready to give
Sure guidance, and help from on high.

Of Mary the spouse undefil'd,
Just, holy, and pure of all stain,
He asks of his own foster Child;
And needs but ask to obtain.

Here the first stanza is repeated:
To all who would holily live,
To all who would happily die,
St. Joseph is ready to give
Sure guidance, and help from on high

In the manger that Child he ador'd,
And nurs'd Him in exile and flight;
Him, lost in His boyhood, deplor'd,

And found with amaze and delight.
To all, &c.

The Maker of heaven and earth
By the labour of Joseph was fed;
The Son of an infinite birth
Submissive to Joseph was made.
To all, &c.

And when his last hour drew nigh,
O, full of all joy was his breast;
Seeing Jesus and Mary close by,
As he tranquilly slumber'd to rest.
To all, &c.

All praise to the Father above;
All praise to the glorious Son;
All praise to the Spirit of love,
While the days of eternity run.
To all, &c.

Ant. Behold the faithful and prudent servant whom the Lord set over His house.

V. Pray for us, Holy Joseph.
R. That we may be made worthy of the promises of Christ.

Let us pray.
O God, who in Thine ineffable providence didst vouchsafe to choose blessed Joseph to be the husband of Thy most holy Mother; grant, we beseech Thee, that we may have him for our intercessor in heaven, whom on earth we venerate as our holy protector. Who livest and reignest world without end. Amen.

115. SEVEN DOLOURS AND SEVEN JOYS.

The same Pope Pius VIII., by a Rescript of Dec. 9, 1819, issued through his Eminence the Cardinal-Vicar, and kept in the *Segretaria* of his court, granted -
i. An indulgence of 100 days, once a day, to all the faithful who with contrite heart practise the following devotion in honour of the Seven Sorrows and Seven Joys of the glorious Patriarch St. Joseph.
ii. An indulgence of 300 days, every Wednesday in the year, and every day of the two Novenas preceding the two feasts of St. Joseph, i.e. his principal feast, March 19, and the feast of his Patronage, third Sunday after Easter.

iii. A plenary indulgence, on each of these two feasts, to such as, after Confession and Communion, shall say the prayers.

iv. A plenary indulgence once a month to all who say these prayers daily for a month, on any one day in the month when, after confession and Communion, they shall pray according to the intention of the Sovereign Pontiff.

Pope Gregory XVI, of holy memory, granted farther Indulgences to all the faithful who say the prayers on any seven consecutive Sundays in the year, sic. -

v. A 300 days indulgence on each of these Sundays, and -

vi. A Plenary indulgence on the seventh, after confession, communion. and prayers for the Sovereign Pontiff. Vide Rescript of the S. Congr. of Indulgences, Jan 22, 1836.

In addition to this grant, his Holiness Pope Pius IX., by two decrees of the S. Cong. of Indulgences, Feb. 1 and March 22, 1847, after confirming the above, granted -

vii. A Plenary indulgence, on each of the seven Sundays kept as above in honour of the holy Patriarch St Joseph, at any time in the year whatever, provided only they be kept consecutively, and provided also the usual conditions are observed of Confession, Communion, visit to a church, and prayer according to the mind of his Holiness. The same Indulgence is also granted by him to the poor and illiterate, wherever this devotion is not publicly practised, provided only they say seven *Pater noster's*, seven *Ave Maria's,* and seven *Gloria Patri's,* instead of the prayers above enjoined, and provided also they fulfil the other prescribed conditions.

THE SEVEN DOLOURS AND SEVEN JOYS.

i. St. Joseph, pure spouse of most holy Mary, the trouble and anguish of thy heart were great, when, being in sore perplexity, thou wast minded to put away thy stainless spouse: but this joy was inexpressible when the archangel revealed to thee the high mystery of the Incarnation.

By this thy sorrow and thy joy, we pray thee comfort our souls now and in their last pains with the consolation of a well-spent life, and a holy death like unto thine own, with Jesus and Mary at our side.

Pater, Ave, *and* Gloria.

ii. St. Joseph, Blessed Patriarch, chosen to the office of Father of the Word made Man, the pain was keen that thou didst feel when thou didst see the Infant Jesus born in abject poverty; but thy pain was changed into heavenly joy when thou didst hear the harmony of angel-choirs, and behold the glory of that night when Jesus was born.

By this thy sorrow and thy joy, we pray thee obtain for us, that, when the journey of our life is ended, we too may pass to that blessed land where we

shall hear the angel-chants, and rejoice in the bright light of heavenly glory.
Pater, Ave, *and* Gloria.

iii. St. Joseph, who wast ever most obedient in executing the law of God, thy heart was pierced with pain when the Precious Blood of the Infant Saviour was shed at His Circumcision; but with the Name of Jesus new life and heavenly joy returned to thee.
By this thy sorrow and thy joy, obtain for us, that, being freed in our life from every vice, we too may cheerfully die, with the sweet Name of Jesus in our hearts and on our lips.
Pater, Ave, *and* Gloria.

iv. St. Joseph, faithful Saint, who wast admitted to take part in the redemption of man; the prophecy of Simeon foretelling the sufferings of Jesus and Mary caused thee a pang like that of death; but at the same time his prediction of the salvation and glorious resurrection of innumerable souls filled thee with a blessed joy.
By this thy sorrow and thy joy, help us with thy prayers to be of the number of those who, by the merits of Jesus and his Virgin Mother, shall be partakers of the resurrection to glory.
Pater, Ave, *and* Gloria.

v. St. Joseph, watchful Guardian, friend of the Incarnate Son of God, truly thou didst greatly toil to nurture and to serve the Son of the Most High, especially in the flight thou madest with Him unto Egypt; yet didst thou rejoice to have God Himself always with thee, and to see the overthrow of the idols of Egypt.
By this thy sorrow and thy joy, obtain for us grace to keep far out of the reach of the enemy of our souls, by quitting all dangerous occasions, that so no idol of earthly affection may any longer occupy a place in our hearts, but that, being entirely devoted to the service of Jesus and Mary, we may live and die for them alone.
Pater, Ave, *and* Gloria.

vi. St. Joseph, angel on earth, who didst so wonder to see the King of heaven obedient to thy bidding, the consolation thou hadst at His return was disturbed by the fear of Archelaus, but nevertheless, being reassured by the angel, thou didst go back and dwell happily at Nazareth, in the company of Jesus and of Mary.
By this thy sorrow and thy joy, obtain for us, that, having our hearts freed from idle fears, we may enjoy the peace of a tranquil conscience, dwelling safely with Jesus and Mary, and dying at last between them.
Pater, Ave, *and* Gloria.

vii. St. Joseph, example of all holy living, when, though without blame, thou didst lose Jesus, the Holy Child, thou didst search for Him for three long days in great sorrow, until with joy unspeakable thou didst find him, who was as thy life to thee, amidst the doctors in this Temple.

By this thy sorrow and thy joy, we pray thee with our whole heart so to interpose always in our behalf, that we may never lose Jesus by mortal sin; and if (which God avert) we are at any time so wretched as to do so, that we pray thee to aid us to seek Him with such ceaseless sorrow until we find Him, particularly in the hour of our death, that we may pass from this life to enjoy Him for ever in heaven, there to sing with thee His divine mercies without end. Pater, Ave, *and* Gloria.

Ant. Ipse Jesus erat incipiens quasi annorum triginta, ut putabatur filius Joseph.

V. Ora pro nobis, sancte Joseph.
R. Ut digni efficiamur promissionibus Christi.

Oremus.
Deus, qui ineffabili providentia beatum Joseph sanctissimae Genitricis tuae sponsum eligere dignatus es; praesta quaesumus, ut quem protectorem veneramur in terris, intercessorem habere mereamur in coelis. Qui vivis et regnas in saecula saeculorum. R. Amen.

Ant. Jesus Himself was about thirty years old, being, as was supposed, the son of Joseph.

V. Pray for us, holy Joseph.
R. That we may be made worthy of the promises of Christ.

Let us pray.
O God, who in Thine ineffable providence didst vouchsafe to choose blessed Joseph to be the husband of Thy most holy Mother; grant, we beseech Thee, that we may have him for our intercessor in heaven, whom on earth we venerate as our holy protector. Who livest and reignest world without end. Amen.

116. THE PRAYER "VIRGINUM CUSTOS," TO BE SAID BY PRIESTS.

Pope Pius VII., by a Rescript of Sept. 23, 1802, issued through his Eminence the Cardinal-Vicar, and kept in his *Segretaria,* granted to all priests, secular and regular -
An indulgence of one year each time they say with devotion tine following prayer to St. Joseph.

The other prayer, "O felicem virum," with the indulgence, to be said by priests before saying Mass, is to be found above.

EFFICAX ORATIO.

Virginum custos, et pater Sancte Joseph, cujus fideli custodiae ipsa innocentia Christus Jesus, et Virgo virginum Maria commissa fuit; te per hoc utrumque carissimum pignus Jesum et Mariam, obsecro, et obtestor, ut me ab omni immunditia preservatum, mente incontaminata, puro corde et casto corpore Jesu et Marae semper facias castissime famulari. R Amen.

THE PRAYER.

Guardian of virgins, and holy father Joseph, to whose faithful custody Christ Jesus, Innocence itself, and Mary, Virgin of virgins, were committed; I pray much beseech thee by these dear pledges, Jesus and Mary, that being preserved from all uncleanness, I may with spotless mind, pure heart, and chaste body, ever most chastely serve Jesus and Mary all the days of my life. Amen.

For the Ejaculatory Prayers, Jesus, Mary, Joseph, *&c. and the Indulgences attached to them, see <u>above</u>.*

APPENDIX

179. THE MONTH OF MARCH, DEDICATED TO ST. JOSEPH.

By a Rescript of June 12, 1855, his Holiness Pope Pius IX. granted -
The plenary indulgence to all the faithful who shall have dedicated the whole month of March to the glorious patriarch St. Joseph, on condition of their making use of the pious devotions and meditations which are found collected in a little book on sale at the publisher's, No. 153 Piazza di S. Ignazio, printed in 1855 (in which book is transcribed the Rescript of the grant), provided that, being truly penitent, they shall, after Confession and Communion, pray according to the mind of the Sovereign Pontiff. He granted also a partial indulgence of 300 days every time that they practise this pious exercise. He granted, moreover, the same indulgences to those of the faithful who, being lawfully hindered during the month of March, shall dedicate some other month to the honour of the same glorious patriarch, making use of the above-named little book.

His Holiness Pope Pius IX,, by a decree, *Urbis et Orbis*, of the Holy Congregation of Indulgences of April 27, 1865, extended this Indulgence to any devotional exercise which shall be made every day in the month of March in honour of St. Joseph, just as in the case of the pious exercise in the month of May in honour of most Holy Mary.

180. PIOUS EXERCISE OF THE PERPETUAL CULTUS IN HONOUR OF ST. JOSEPH.

His Holiness Pope Pius IX., by a Rescript of Jan. 20, 1856, which is kept in the Secretary's office of the Sacred Congregation of Propaganda, vouchsafed to approve the following practice, and to enrich it with various indulgences; as,
i. Plenary indulgence on the day of enrolment, on any day selected to be kept holy once in the year, and *in articulo mortis*.
ii. Plenary indulgence on March 19, on the Feast of the Patronage of St. Joseph; on Jan. 23, the Feast of the Espousals of most Holy Mary; and on all the Feasts of Obligation of our Lady. (The Feasts meant are the Feast of the Purification, Annunciation, Assumption. Nativity, and Immaculate Conception of our Lady. In England, the Assumption only is of obligation.)
iii. The indulgence of seven years and seven quarantines every day on which any of the things prescribed below are performed.
By another Brief of July 5, 1861, the same Sovereign Pontiff approved afresh of the pious exercise, or *cultus perpetuus*, in honour of St. Joseph, in favour of all the faithful in the Catholic world; and whilst he confirmed the above-named indulgences, he added the Plenary Indulgence for any one day in each month, to be chosen at the pleasure of the members enrolled.

THE PIOUS EXERCISE.

This devout exercise consists in each one of the associated selecting one day of the year, or else day of each month, at pleasure, in order to consecrate it, by different acts of piety, to the special honour of St. Joseph; and it is called perpetual, because if as many persons as there are days in the year, or as there are days in the month, agree together each to select his own one particular different day in order to dedicate it to St. Joseph, there will be an uninterrupted series of special venerators of the holy patriarch. And still greater amid more continuous will be the *cultus* in proportion as the number of persons who adopt this exercise becomes greater.

The Exercise is as follows:

N. N., a devout client of St. Joseph, is invited to honour him with a special *cultus* on one day at pleasure in the year, and on one day in each month, thereby to console him in those afflictions of his, of which our sins were the cause. For this object he will take care to perform the following practices with the greater diligence and fervour:
i. To approach the holy Sacraments, - i.e. of Confession and Communion, - and, if unable to do so, to supply for their omission with an act of contrition, and with a spiritual communion.
ii. To assist at Holy Mass with special devotion, in memory of the Presentation of Jesus in the Temple.

iii. To make one quarter of an hour's meditation on the afflictions of St. Joseph.
iv. To keep himself recollected in soul, and to pass the day in union with St. Joseph,
v. To do some act of mortification, or some work of spiritual or corporal mercy.
vi. To say seven *Paters, Aves,* and *Glorias* in honour of his afflictions and his joys.
vii. To finish the day with a visit to the Blessed Sacrament, and with an offering of the heart to St. Joseph.
Whosoever consoles St. Joseph in life shall be aided by him in death.

181. EJACULATION IN HONOUR OF ST. JOSEPH

By a Brief of Jan. 27, 1863, the Sovereign Pontiff Pius IX. granted to all the faithful, collectively and individually, who are enrolled in the Pious Exercise of the Cultus Perpetuus in honour of St. Joseph -
50 days indulgence every time that with contrite hearts and devotion they shall say, in any language, the following ejaculation.

THE EJACULATION.

Alme Joseph, dux noster, nos et sanctam Ecclesiam protege.
Foster-father Joseph, our guide, protect us and the holy Church.

182. PRAYER TO ST. JOSEPH, "O GLORIOUS ST. JOSEPH, FATHER AND PROTECTOR," ETC.

By a Brief of Feb. 3, 1863, the Sovereign Pontiff Pius IX. granted to all the faithful who, with contrite hearts and devotion, shall say the following prayer in honour of St. Joseph, in any language, provided the translation be a faithful one -
100 days indulgence, to be gained once a day.

THE PRAYER.

O glorious St. Joseph, father and protector of virgins, faithful guide, to whom God intrusted Jesus, very innocence, and Mary, Virgin of virgins; by this twofold deposit to thee so dear, make it thy care that I, preserved from every defilement, pure in heart and chaste, may serve with constancy Jesus and Mary in perfect chastity. Amen.

183. ANOTHER PRAYER TO ST. JOSEPH, "REMEMBER, MOST PURE HUSBAND OF MARY."

By a Brief of June 26, 1863, the Sovereign Pontiff Pius IX. granted - 300 days indulgence, to be gained once a day, to all the faithful who, with contrite hearts and devotion, shall say the following prayer.

THE PRAYER.

Remember, most pure husband of Mary ever-Virgin, my loving protector Joseph, that never hath it been heard that any one invoked thy protection or asked aid of thee who has not been consoled. In this confidence I come before thee, I fervently recommend myself to thee. Despise not my prayer, reputed father of the Saviour of men, but do thou in thy pity receive it. Amen.

THE HOLY APOSTLES PETER AND PAUL.

117. VISIT TO THEIR CHURCHES ON THEIR FEAST AND ITS OCTAVE.

If the solemn festival of the holy Apostles Peter and Paul ought to be celebrated with feelings of gratitude and veneration throughout the whole Catholic world, as the first preachers of the faith of Jesus Christ and of the holy Gospel, much more ought it to be so celebrated in this our city of Rome; for it was Rome, which, being first enlightened by the heavenly teaching of these Apostles, became, from a disciple of error, Mistress of the Truth; and it was this city of Rome that these Apostles consecrated with their blood. The more, then, to augment the gratitude and devotion of the people of Rome towards these holy Apostles, and the more always to implore their efficacious protection with God, Pope Benedict XIV., in his Constitution *Admirabiles* of April 1, 1743, granted -
i. An indulgence of 100 days, to all the faithful who, being truly penitent and having confessed, shall visit the under mentioned churches on their festival and during its octave.
ii. An indulgence of seven years and seven quarantines, to those who shall

make this visit *processionally*, with their respective Archconfraternity or Confraternity.

CHURCHES TO BE VISITED.

June 29, St. Peter *in Vaticano*; where lies the body of the Apostle St. Peter. These is also a Plenary indulgence to be obtained by those who make this visit after Confession and Communion. See Note.
June 30, St. Paul outside the walls; where rests his holy body.
July 1, St. Pudenziana; once the house of St. Pudens, Roman senator, where St. Peter lodged the first time he came to Rome.
July 2, St. Mary *in Via Lata*; in the crypt of which church St. Paul was imprisoned.
July 3, St. Peter *in Vinculi*s; where are venerated the chains of St. Peter.
July 4, St. Peter *in Carcere*; where St. Peter and St. Paul were kept in prison.
July 5, St. Peter *in Montorio*; in which place this Apostle was crucified with his head downwards.
July 6, St. John *in Laterano*; where are venerated the sacred heads of the two great Apostles.

NOTE.- Pope Urban VIII., in his Constitution *Inter primarias*, Nov. 15, 1630 (Bullar. *Basil. Vatic*., tom. iii. p. 242, edit. Rom. 1752), granted to all faithful Christians who, devoutly visiting the sacred Confession of St. Peter the Apostle in the Vatican Basilica, shall say the prayer, "Ante oculos tuos, Domine," &c., or who, not being able to do so from not knowing how to read, shall say twelve *Pater noster's* and twelve *Ave Maria's* to implore the divine mercy - i. A plenary indulgence, after Confession and Communion, on all the following festivals, viz.
The Most Holy Trinity.
All the Feasts of our Lord Jesus Christ and of the Blessed Virgin Mary.
The Feast of St. John Baptist
The Feast of the holy Apostles SS. Peter and Paul, and the Feasts of all the other holy Apostles.
The Feast of All Saints.
All the Fridays in March.
ii. An indulgence of seven years and seven quarantines, on all other days, to those who have a firm purpose of confessing.
To this Prayer, composed by St. Augustine in a time of grievous public calamity, the same Pope Urban VIII. added the versicles, &c., recommending then to be inserted at the end of all Roman breviaries. The prayer hangs on a board by the side of the altar of the said Confession.

THE PRAYER, EXTRACTED FROM THE ROMAN BREVIARY.

(As this prayer is little known, it is here given at length in Latin and English, though only referred to in the Roman Raccolta.)

Ante oculos tuos, Domine, culpas nostras ferimus; et plagas quas accepimus, conferimus.
Si pensamus malum quod fecimus, minus est quod patimur, majus est quod meremur.
Gravius est quod commisimus, levius est quod toleramus.
Peccati poenam sentimus, et peccandi pertinaciam non vitamus.
In flagellis tuis infirmitas nostra teritur, et iniquitas non mutatur.
Mens aegra torquetur, et cervix non flectitur.
Vita in dolore suspirat, et in opere non se emendat.
Si expectas, non corrigimur; si vindicas, non duramus.
Confitemur in correctione quod egimus; obliviscimur post visitationem quod flevimus.
Si extenderis manum, facienda promittimus; si suspenderis gladium, promissa non solvimus.
Si ferias, clamamus ut parras; si peperceris, iterum provocamus ut ferias.
Habes, Domine, confitentes reos; novimus quod nisi dimittas, recte nos perimus.
Praesta, Pater omnipotens, sine merito quod rogamus, qui fecisti ex nihilo qui te rogarent. Per Christum Dominum nostrum. Amen.

V. Gregem tuam, Pastor aeterne, non deseras.
R. Sed inter beatos Apostolos tuos perpetua defensione custodias.
V. Protege, Domine, populum tuum ad te clainantem, et Apostolorum tuorum patrocinio confidentem.
R. Perpetua defensione custodias.
V. Orate pro nobis, sancti Apostoli Dei.
R. Ut digni efficiamur promissionibus Christi.

ORATIO.

Praesta, quaesumus, omnipotens Deus, ut nullis nos permittas perturbationis concuti, quos in Apostolicae confessionis petra solidasti. Per Dominum. R. Amen.

Imploret, clementissime Domine, nostris opportunam necessitatibus opem devote a nobis prolata meditatio, qua sanctus olim Joannes Chrysostomus, in hac basilica conditus, te cum beatissimis Apostolis Petro et Paulo repraesentavit sic colloquentem: "Circumdate hanc novam Sion et cirumvallate eam: hoc est, custodite, munite, precibus firmante; ut quando irascor in tempore, et orbem terrae concutio, aspiciens sepulcrum vestrum numquam desiturum, et quae libenter propter me geritis stigmata, iram misericordia vincam, et ob hanc te percipiam vestram intercessionem. Etenim quando Sacerdotium et Regnum video lacryimari, statim quasi compatiens ad commiserationem flector, et illius meae vocis remniscor: 'Protegam urbem hanc propter David servum tuum et Aaron sanctum tuum.'" Domine, fiat, fiat. Amen, Amen.

TRANSLATION

Lord, before Thine eyes we bring our sins, and with them we compare the stripes which we have received.
When we think of the evil we have done, little is that which we suffer, great that which we deserve.
Heaviest are our offences, lightest our burden.
We are afflicted by the punishment of our sin, yet we avoid not the obstinate desire of sinning.
The weakness of our flesh faints under Thy scourges, yet is not our iniquity changed.
The sick soul is sore tormented, yet is not the neck bent.
In pain our life sighs heavily; yet are its deeds in no wise amended.
If Thou waitest for us, we are not corrected; if Thou takest vengeance, we bear it not.
When we are corrected, we confess our shortcomings; after Thou hast visited us, we forget that which we bewailed.
If Thou stretchest forth Thy hand, we promise what we will do; if Thou delayest to draw Thy sword, we perform not our promises.
If Thou strikest us, we cry unto Thee to spare; if Thou sparest, we provoke Thee again to strike.
Lord, hear the confession of Thy guilty people; for we know well that unless Thou shouldest pardon, Thou dost righteously consume us.
Almighty Father, grant us that which though we pray we do not deserve to obtain; Thou who didst create men of nothing, that they might pray to Thee. Through Jesus Christ our Lord. Amen.

V. Eternal Shepherd, desert not Thy flock.
R. But by thy blessed Apostles guard and defend it evermore.
V. Protect, O Lord, Thy people, who cry unto Thee, trusting in the patronage of Thy Apostles.
R. Yea, guard them with an everlasting defence.
V. Pray for us, O holy Apostles of God.
R. That we may be made worthy of the promises of Christ.

Let us pray.
O Almighty God, we beseech Thee, suffer us not, whom Thou hast firmly founded upon the rock of the apostolical confession, ever to be shaken by any storms of the enemy. Through our Lord Jesus Christ. Amen.

O most merciful God, let us obtain timely help in our necessity, whilst we devoutly proffer to Thee the meditation which blessed John Chrysostom, who lies buried in this basilica, has represented Thee thus addressing Thy most holy Apostles Peter and Paul: "Surround this new city of Zion, and compass it about; guard it, fortify it, establish it with your prayers; that when, in time to come, My wrath is kindled within Me, and I begin to shake terribly the earth, I may look on the place where your bodies are lying, and beholding the wounds which ye willingly bear in them for My sake, I may overcome anger with mercy, and so accept your intercession. For indeed, when I behold the tears of the Kingdom and of the Priesthood, straightway My heart is moved to compassion, and I call to mind the words of my mouth: 'I will protect this city for the sake of David My servant, and Aaron My holy one.'" Amen, O Lord, and Amen.

118. PRAYER, "O BLESSED APOSTLES," WITH A PATER NOSTER, AVE MARIA, AND GLORIA PATRI.

Pope Pius VI., by a Rescript of July 28, 1778, issued through the *Segretaria* of the memorials, granted -
i. An indulgence of 100 days to all the faithful who, being contrite, shall say at least once a day the following prayer, with one *Pater, Ave*, and *Gloria*, in honour of the blessed Apostles Peter and Paul.
ii. A plenary indulgence, on all Feasts of SS. Peter and Paul, provided that, after Confession and Communion, they shall on such feast-day itself, or one of the nine days preceding it, or eight days following it, visit a church or altar dedicated to those Saints, saying there the following prayer, and remembering the Holy Church and its Sovereign Pontiff.

THE PRAYER

O blessed Apostles Peter and Paul, I, NN., elect you this day for my special protectors and advocates with God. In all humility I rejoice with thee, blessed Peter, Prince of the Apostles, because thou art the rock whereon God hath built his Church; and I rejoice with thee too, blessed Paul, because thou wast chosen of God for a Vessel of election, and a preacher of the truth throughout the world. Obtain for me, I beseech you both, a lively faith, firm hope, and perfect charity, entire detachment from myself, contempt of the world, patience in adversity, humility in prosperity, attention in prayer, purity of heart, right intention in my works, diligence in the fulfilment of all the duties of my state of life, constancy in my good resolutions, resignation to the holy will of God, perseverance in Divine grace unto death; that, having overcome by your joint intercession and your glorious merits, the temptations of the world, the flesh, and the devil, I may be made worthy to appear before the face of the chief and eternal Bishop of Souls, Jesus Christ our Lord, to enjoy Him and to love Him for all eternity, who with the Father and the Holy Ghost liveth and reigneth ever world without end. Amen.

Pater, Ave, *and* Gloria

---

119. RESPONSORIUM: "SI VIS PATRONUM."

Pius VI., in order to increase the devotion of the faithful to Peter, Prince of the Apostles, granted my a Rescript of the S. Congr. of Indulgences, Jan. 19. 1782
-
i. An indulgence of 100 days to all who shall devoutly say daily the following Responsorium.
in. A plenary indulgence, on the Feast of St. Peter's Chair in Rome, Jan. 18, and also on the Feast of St. Peter's Chains, August 1; provided that on those days, being truly penitent, after Confession and Communion, they visit a church or altar dedicated to St. Peter, and pray according to the intention of the Sovereign Pontiff.

THE RESPONSORIUM.

Si vis patronum quaerere,
Si vis potentem vindicem,
Quid jam moraris? invoca
Apostolorum Principem.

O sancte coeli Claviger,
Tu nos precando subleva;
Tu redde novis pervia
Aulae supernae limina.

Ut ipse multis poenitens
Culpam rigasti lacrymis,
Sic nostra tolli poscimus
Fletu perenni crimina.

O sancte coeli.&c.

Sicut fuisti ab angelo
Tuis solutus vinculis,
Tu nos iniquis exue
Tot implicatos nexibus.

O sancte coeli. &c.

O firma Petra Ecclesiae,
Columna flecti nescia,
Da robur et constantiam,
Error fidem ne subruat.

O sancte coeli. &c.

Romam tuo qui sanguine
Olim sacrasti, protege;
In teque confidentibus
Praesta salutem gentibus.

O sancte coeli. &c.

Tu rem tuere publicam,
Qui te colunt, fidelium,
Ne laesa sit contagiis,
Ne scissa sit discordiis.

O sancte coeli. &c.

Quos hostis antiquus dolos
Instruxit in nos, destrue;
Truces et iras comprime,
Ne clade nostra saeviat.

O sancte coeli. &c.

Contra furentis impetus
In morte vires suffice,
Ut et supremo vincere
Possimus in certamine.

O sancte coeli. &c.

Gloria Patri, &c.

O sancte coeli. &c.

Ant. Tu es Pastor ovium, Princeps Apostolorum tibi traditae sunt claves regni coelorum.

V. Tu es Petrus.
R. Et super hanc petram aedificabo ecclesiam meam.

Oremus.
Apostolicis nos, Domine quaesumus, beati Petri Apostoli tui attolle praesidiis: ut quanto fragiliores sumus, tanto ejus intercessione validioribus auxiliis

foveamur; et jugiter apostolica defensione muniti, nec succumbamus vitiis, nec opprimamur adversis. Per Christum, &c.

THE RESPONSORY OF ST. PETER.

Seek ye a patron to defend -
Your cause? - then, one and all,
Without delay upon the Prince
Of the Apostles call.

Blest holder of the heavenly keys,
Thy prayers we all implore
Unlock to us the sacred bars
Of heaven's eternal door.

By penitential tears thou didst
The path of life regain;
Teach us with thee to weep our sins,
And wash away their stain.

Blest holder, &c.

The angel touch'd thee, and forthwith
Thy chains from off thee fell;
O, loose us from the subtle coils
That bind us fast to hell.

Blest holder, &c.

Firm rock whereon the Church is based,
Pillar that cannot bend,
With strength endue us; and the faith
From heresy defend.

Blest holder, &c.

Save Rome, which from the days of old
Thy blood hath sanctified;
And help the nations of the earth
That in thy help confide.

Blest holder, &c.

O, worshipped by all Christendom,
Her realms in peace maintain;
Let no contagion sap her strength,
No discord rend in twain.

Blest holder, &c.

The weapons which our ancient foe
Against us doth prepare,
Crush thou; nor suffer us to fall
Into his deadly snare.

Blest holder, &c.

Grant us through life; and in that hour
When our last fight draws nigh,
O'er death, o'er hell, o'er Satan's power,
Gain us the victory.

Blest holder, &c.

All glory to the Father be;
Praise to the Son sin who rose;
Praise to the Spirit Paraclete;
While age on ages flows.

Blest holder, &c.

Glory be to the Father, &c.

Blest holder, &c.

Ant. Thou art the shepherd of the sheep, Prince of the Apostles; to thee were given the keys of the kingdom of heaven.

V. Thou art Peter.
R. And upon this rock will I build My Church.

Let us pray.
O Lord, we beseech Thee, raise us up by the Apostolic might of Blessed Peter Thine Apostle; that the weaker we are in ourselves, the more powerful may be the assistance whereby we are strengthened through his intercession; that thus, ever fortified by the protection of Thine Apostle, we may neither yield to sin, nor be overwhelmed by adversity. Through Christ our Lord. Amen.

120. THE RESPONSORIUM: "PRESSI MALORUM," ETC.

Pope Pius VII., through his Eminence the Cardinal Vicar, by a Rescript of Jan. 23, 1806, kept in the Archivium of the Pious Union of St. Paul aforementioned, granted, in order to increase in all the faithful devotion towards the blessed Apostle Paul, Vessel of Election and Doctor of the Gentiles -
i. An indulgence of 100 days to all those who shall devoutly say daily the following Responsorium.

ii. A plenary indulgence on the 25th of January, the Feast of the Conversion of the Apostle, and on June the 30th, the Feast of his Commemoration, to all who on those days, being truly penitent, shall, after Confession and Communion, visit some church or altar dedicated to the Apostle, and pray according to the intention of the Sovereign Pontiff.

DICTUM RESPONSORIUM.

Pressi malorum pondere
Adite Paulum supplices,
Qui certa largus desuper
Dabit salutis pignora.

O grata coelo Victima,
Doctorque, amorque gentium,
O Paule, nos te vindicem,
Nos te patronum poscimus.

Nam tu beato concitus
Divini amoris impetu,
Quos insecutor oderas,
Defensor inde amplcteris.

O grata. &c.

Non te procellae, et verbera,
Non vincla, et ardor hostium,
Non dira mors deterruit,
Ne sancto adesses coetui.

O grata. &c.

Amoris eja pristini
Ne sis, precamur, immemor,
Et nos supernae languidos
In spem reducas gratiae.

O grata.

Te destruantur auspice
Saevae inferorum machinae,
Et nostra templa publicis
Petita votis insonent.

O grata. &c.

Te deprecante floreat
Ignara damni charitas,

Quam nulla turbent jurgia,
Nec ullus error sauciet.

O grata. &c.

Qua terra cumque diditur,
Jungatur uno foedere,
Tuisque semper afflat
Salubre nectar litteris.

O grata. &c.

Det velle nos quod imperat,
Det posse Summus Arbiter,
Ne fluctuantes horridae
Caligo noctis obruat.

O grata. &c.

Gloria Patri, &c.

O grata. &c.

Ant. Vas electionis est mihi iste, ut portet nomen meum coram gentibus, et regibus, et filiis Israel.

V. Ora pro nobis S. Paule Apostole.
R. Ut digni efficiamur promissionibus Christi.

Oremus.
Omnipotens sempiterne Deus, qui beato Apostolo tuo Paulo, quid faceret ut impleretur Spiritu Sancto, divina miseratione praecepisti: ejus dirigentibus monitis, et suffragantibus meritis concede, ut servientes tibi in timore, et tremore coelestium donorum consolatione repleamur. Per Christum Dominum nostrum. R. Amen.

THE RESPONSORY OF ST. PAUL.

All ye who groan beneath
A load of ills oppress'd,
Entreat St. Paul, and he will pray
The Lord to give you rest.

O victim, dear to Heaven
O Paul, thou teacher true
Thou love and joy of Christendom,
To thee for help we sue.

Pierced by the flame of love,
Descending from on high
Twas thine to preach the faith which once
Thou soughtest to destroy.

O victim, &c.

Nor toil, nor threaten'd death,
Nor tempest, scourge, or chain,
Could from th' assembly of the saints
Thy loving heart detain.

O victim, &c.

O, by that quenchless love
Which burnt in thee of yore,
Take pity on our miseries,
Our fainting hope restore.

O victim, &c.

True champion of the Lord,
Crush thou the schemes of hell;
And with adoring multitudes
The sacred temples fill.

O victim, &c.

Through thy prevailing prayer,
May charity abound
Sweet charity, which knows no ill,
Which nothing can confound.

O victim, &c.

To earth's remotest shores
May one same faith extend;
And thy epistles through all climes
Their blessed perfume send.

O victim, &c.

Grant us the will and power
To serve Thee, God of might;
Lest, wav'ring still and unprepar'd,
We sink in depths of night.

O victim, &c.

Praise to the Father be;
Praise to the Son who rose
Praise to the Spirit Paraclete;
While age on ages flows.

O victim, &c.

Glory be to the Father, &c.

O victim, &c.

Ant. This is My vessel of election, to carry My Name among the Gentiles and kings and the children of Israel.

V. Pray for us, O blessed Apostle Paul.
R. That we may be made worthy of the promises of Christ.

Let us pray.
Almighty and Eternal God, who in Thy divine compassion didst direct Thy blessed Apostle Paul what to do that He might be filled with Thy Holy Spirit; grant that we may be so counselled by his teaching, and aided by the suffrage of his merits, that, serving Thee in fear and trembling, we may be filled with the consolation of Thy heavenly gifts. Through Christ our Lord. Amen.

APPENDIX

184. THREE " PATERS" ETC. BEFORE HIS TOMB.

By a Brief of May 15, 1857, the Sovereign Pontiff Pius IX. granted -
 The indulgence of seven years and seven quarantines to all the faithful who, with contrite heart and devotion, shall say three *Paters*, three *Aves,* and three *Glorias* before the tomb of St. Peter, the Prince of the Apostles, in the Vatican Basilica, to render thanks to God for the favours granted to this holy Apostle.
Moreover, to any one who shall, with contrite heart and devotion, kiss the foot of the bronze statue of this Apostle in the aforesaid Basilica he granted -
50 days indulgence, provided he prays at the same time for peace among Christian princes, for the extirpation of heresy, and for the exaltation of our Holy Mother the Church.

121. THE HYMN "BELLI TUMULTUS," ETC.

Pope Pius VII., by his Rescript of August 14,1801, granted -
i. A plenary indulgence to all the faithful who, on the Feast of St. Pius V., May 5, being truly penitent, shall, after Confession and Communion, say on this day with devotion the following hymn before an altar or greater relic of this Saint, or else in some church dedicated to his honour, praying according to the intention of the Sovereign Pontiff.
ii. An indulgence of forty days, once a day, on saying this hymn with devotion. These Indulgences Pope Pius VIII. of blessed memory granted afresh for ever by a decree of the S. Congr. of Indulgences of Oct. 2, 1830.

HYMNUS

Belli tumultus ingruit,
Cultus Dei contemnitur;
Ultrixque culpam persequens
Jam poena terris imminet.

Quem nos in hoc discrimine
Coelestium de sedibus
Praesentiorem vindicem,
Quam te, Pie, invocabimus?

Nemo, beate Pontifex,
Intensiore robore
Quam tu, superni numinis
Promovit in terris decus.

Quem nos. &c.

Ausisve fortioribus
Avertit a cervicibus,
Quod Christianis gentibus
Jugum parabant barbari.

Quem nos. &c

Tu comparatis classibus,
Votis magis sed fervidis
Ad insulas Echinadas
Fundis tyannum Thraciae.

Quem nos. &c.

Absensque eodem tempore,
Hostis fuit quo perditus,
Vides, et adstantes doces
Pugnae secundos exitus.

Quem nos. &c.

Majora qui coelo potes,
Tu supplices nunc aspice,
Tu civium discordias
Compesce, et iras hostium.

Quem nos. &c.

Precante te, pax aurea
Terris revisat; ut Deo
Tuti queamus reddere
Mox laetiora cantica.

Quem nos. &c.

Tibi, Beata Trinitas
Uni Deo sit gloria,
Laus, et potestas omnia
Per saeculorum saecula. Amen.

V. Ora pro nobis, Beate Pie.
R. Ut digni efficiamur promissionibus Christi.

Oremus.
Deus, qui ad conterendos ecclesiae tuae hostes, et ad divinum cultum reparandum beatum Pium pontificem maximum eligere dignatus es: fac nos ipsius defendi praesidiis, et ita tuis inhaerere obsequiis, ut omnium hostium superatis insidiis perpetua pace laetemur. Per Dominum nostrum Jesum Christum Filium tuum, &c. R. Amen.

THE HYMN.

Wars and tumults fill the earth;
Men the fear of God despise;
Retribution, vengeance, wrath,
Brood upon the angry skies.

Holy Pius! Pope sublime!
Whom, in this most evil time,
Whom, of saints in bliss, can we
Better call to aid than thee?

None more mightily than thou
Hath, by holy deed or word,
Through the spacious earth below
Spread the glory of the Lord.

Holy Pius, &c.

Thine it was, O pontiff brave!
Pontiff of eternal Rome!
From barbaric yoke to save
Terror-stricken Christendom.

Holy Pius, &c.

When Lepanto's gulf beheld,
Strewn upon its waters fair,
Turkey's countless navy yield
To the power of thy prayer.

Holy Pius, &c.

Who meanwhile with prophet's eye
Didst the distant battle see;
And announce to standers-by
That same moment's victory.

Holy Pius, &c.

Mightier now and glorified,
Hear the suppliant cry we pour;
Crush Rebellion's haughty pride;
Quell the din of rising war.

Holy Pius, &c.

At thy prayer may golden peace
Down to earth descend again:
License, discord, trouble cease;
Justice, truth, and order reign.

Holy Pius, &c.

To the Lord of endless days,
One Almighty Trinity,
Sempiternal glory, praise,
Honour, might, and blessing be.

Holy Pius, &c.

V. Pray for us, blessed Pius.
R. That we may be made worthy of the promises of Christ.

Let us pray.
God, who to the destruction of the enemies of Thy Church, and to the restoration of Thy holy worship, didst vouchsafe to elect blessed Pius to be Thy high-Priest; grant us so to be defended by his protection, and so to remain steadfast in Thy service, that overcoming the snares of all our enemies, we may enjoy perpetual peace. Through our Lord Jesus Christ Thy Son. Amen.

ST. NICHOLAS OF BARI.

122. PRAYER IN HONOUR OF ST. NICHOLAS OF BARI

Pope Gregory XVI., of blessed memory, by a Rescript of the S. Congr. of Indulgences of Dec. 22, 1832, granted -
An indulgence of fifty days once a day, to all the faithful who, with a contrite heart and devoutly, shall say the following prayer in honour of St. Nicholas of Bari, with one *Pater* and *Ave*.

St. Nicholas, my special Protector, from that bright throne where thou dost enjoy the vision of thy God, in pity turn thine eyes upon me; obtain for me from God that grace and assistance of which, in my present necessities, spiritual and temporal, I am most in want, and specially the grace of N. ... , if such be expedient for my eternal welfare. Remember, moreover, O saintly Bishop, our Sovereign Pontiff; the Holy Church, and this city of Rome. Bring back to the right way of salvation those who live steeped in sin, or buried in the darkness of ignorance, error, and heresy. Comfort the sorrowing, provide for the needy, strengthen the weak-hearted, defend the oppressed, help the sick; let all experience the effects of thy powerful intercession with Him who is Supreme Giver of all good. Amen.

One *Pater* and one *Ave*.

V. Ora pro nobis beate Nicolae.
R. Ut digni efficiamur promissionibus Christi.

Oremus.
Deus, qui beatum Nicolaum gloriosum Confessorem tuum atque Pontificem innumeris decorasti, et quotidie non cessas illustrare miraculis: tribue quaesumus, et ejus meritis et precibus a gehennae incendiis, et a periculis omnibus liberemur. Per Christum Dominum nostrum. Amen.

TRANSLATION.

V. Pray for us, blessed Nicholas.
R. That we may be made worthy of the promises of Christ.

Let us pray.
O God, who hast honoured, and ceasest not daily to honour, Thy High-Priest and glorious Confessor blessed Nicholas with innumerable miracles; grant, we beseech Thee, that by his merits and prayers we may be delivered from the fire of hell and from all other dangers. Through Christ our Lord. Amen.

ST. FRANCIS OF PAOLA

123. DEVOTION OF THE THIRTEEN FRIDAYS.

Pope Clement XII., in the Brief *Coelestium munerum dispensatio* of Dec. 2, 1738, granted -
i. A plenary indulgence to all the faithful who, upon thirteen Fridays continuously preceding the Feast of St. Francis of Paola (April 2), or at any other time of the year, shall, in honour of this Saint, being truly penitent, visit, after Confession and Communion, a church of the Minims, commonly called the Paolotti, either already erected or hereafter to be erected, and pray there for our Holy Mother Church; this Indulgence may be gained on any one of the said Fridays; and
ii. An indulgence of seven years and seven quarantines on all other Fridays.

Moreover, wherever there are not churches of the above named order, or where they are distant at least a mile from a person's own dwelling, the same Clement XII. granted in these two cases, by a Brief *Nuper editae* of March 20, 1739, the same indulgences to the faithful as are mentioned above, conditional of course upon their previous Confession and Communion. In this Brief permission is given to visit any other church whatsoever dedicated to God in honour of St. Francis of Paola, or any altar existing in any church where there is a picture of this glorious Saint; and if none of these conditions can be complied with, the visit may be made to their own parish church. This devotion originated with St. Francis himself, who practised it in honour of our Lord .Jesus Christ and His twelve Apostles with this intent, on each of the thirteen Fridays he used to recite thirteen Pater noster's and as many Ave Maria's, and this devotion he promulgated by word of mouth and by letter to his own devout followers, as an efficacious means of obtaining from God the graces they desired, provided they were for the greater good of their souls. Since the death of the Saint, which took place April 2, 1507, the day on which Good Friday fell in that year, this devotion has always been practised by the faithful throughout the whole Catholic world in honour of the holy Founder; and so it came at last to be approved by the said Clement XII., who granted the Indulgences above named, in order to animate good Christians to adopt it.

ST. ALOYSIUS GONZAGA

124. THE SIX SUNDAYS AND HIS FEAST.

Pope Clement XII., in order to inspire the faithful, and especially the young, with greater devotion towards the angelic youth St. Aloysius Gonzaga, granted by two decrees of time S. Congr. of Indulgences, Dec. 11, 1739, and Jan. 17, 1740 -
i. A Plenary Indulgence on each of the six Sundays which are wont to be kept in honour of this Saint, either immediately before his Feast, on June 21, or else at some other time of the year. In order to gain *this Plenary Indulgence,* it is

requisite that the six Sundays should be kept consecutively; and that on each of them the faithful, being truly penitent, should, after Confession and Communion, employ themselves in pious meditations or vocal prayers, or other works of Christian piety, in honour of the Saint. There are several books of devotion on the subject, pointing out what pious exercises are to be done on these six Sundays.

ii. A Plenary Indulgence may also be gained on his Feast by all the faithful who, after Confession and Communion, shall make a visit to the Saint and pray for the Holy Church, &c. This Indulgence may be gained on that day in the year when, and in that place or at that altar where, his Feast is celebrated *de licentia Ordinarii,* whenever and wheresoever that day and place may be. See Brief of Benedict XIII., Nov. 22, 1729; of Clement XII., Nov. 21, 1737; and Benedict XIV., April 22, 1712.

125. PRAYER, "O BLESSED ALOYSIUS," ETC., WITH ONE "PATER" AND ONE "AVE."

Pope Pius VII., at the prayer of many bishops, the more to increase devotion towards St. Aloysius Gonzaga, who from the the of his canonisation was given by Benedict XIII. as the special protector of the young, granted, by a decree of the S. Congr. of Indulgences, March 6, 1802 -

An indulgence of 100 days, once a day, to all the faithful who, being contrite, shall devoutly say the following prayer, with one *Pater noster* and one *Ave Maria*.

THE PRAYER.

O blessed Aloysius, adorned with angelic virtues, I thy most unworthy suppliant recommend specially to thee the chastity of my soul and body, praying thee by thy angelic purity to plead for me with Jesus Christ the Immaculate Lamb, and His most Holy Mother, Virgin of virgins, that they would vouchsafe to keep me from all grievous sin. Never suffer me to be defiled with any stain of impurity; but when thou dost see me in temptation, or in danger of falling, then remove far from my mind all evil thoughts and unclean desires, and awaken in me the memory of eternity to come, and of Jesus crucified; impress deeply in my heart a sense of the holy fear of God; and kindling in me the fire of Divine love, enable me
so to follow thy footsteps here on earth, that in heaven I may be made worthy to enjoy with thee the vision of our God for ever. Amen.

One Pater noster *and one* Ave Maria.

126. ST. STANISLAS KOSTKA

At the repeated prayer of the Father Procurator-General of the Venerable Congregation called *Pii Operarii* (Pious Labourers) here in Rome, to propagate amongst the faithful the devotion towards St. Stanislas Kostka, as especially calculated to augment the love of our blessed Lady, Pope Pius VII., by two decrees, April 3 and May 1, 1821, and Leo XII., by two other decrees, Jan. 21 and Feb. 25, 1826 (all of which were published by the S. Congr. of Indulgences, May 13,1826), granted -

i. A plenary indulgence on the Feast of the Saint, Nov. 13, or on that Sunday on which, for the convenience of the people, this feast shall be celebrated *de licentia Ordinarii,* to all the faithful who, after Confession and Communion, shall visit the church or public oratory where it is celebrated, and pray according to the intention of the Sovereign Pontiff.

ii. An indulgence of seven years and seven quarantines on every one of the ten Sundays before his feast, kept in honour of the ten months of novitiate made by the Saint; to be gained by visiting the church or oratory where these Sundays are kept, and praying as above.

iii. An indulgence of 100 days every day of the Novena preceding his feast, for assisting devoutly at the said Novena with contrite heart, and praying as above.

iv. An indulgence of 100 days, once a day, to all who shall say a *Pater* and *Ave* before a picture of the Saint exposed in any church or public oratory, and pray as above, &c.

v. A plenary indulgence may be gained by the faithful by practising this exercise for a month continuously, on any one day in the month when, after Confession and Communion, they shall pray as above. Whoever, by reason of a lawful impediment, shall be unable to say in church the *Pater* and *Ave* prescribed, may say it wherever he likes on such days in the month as he is so hindered, and by so doing he shall gain this *Plenary Indulgence.*

vi. An indulgence of 100 days, in addition to the seven years and seven quarantines granted for the above-named ten Sundays, to all who, being contrite in heart, shall assist at the day's Retreat called "the Retreat of St. Stanislas," wherever it is made, once in the week, and who shall pray according to the mind of the Sovereign Pontiff.

All these Indulgences, at first granted for the kingdom of the Two Sicilies, were afterwards extended to the Pontifical States for any church or public oratory where the devotion to St. Stanislas is or shall be introduced, as appears from the decree above named, Feb. 25, 1826; and the same Pope Leo XII., by another decree of the S. Congr. of Indulgences, March 3, 1827, made them available for the whole Catholic world, even for private monastic churches and oratories of seminaries, colleges, refuges, monasteries and houses of retreat for both sexes.

Furthermore the Sovereign Pontiff Pope Pius IX., by an autograph Rescript kept in the *Segretaria* of the S. Congr. of Indulgences, dated March 22, 1847, granted -

vii. An indulgence of 300 days, to be gained once a day by all the faithful who in honour of this Saint shall say the three following prayers for Purity, Charity, and a Good Death, adding to each one *Pater*, one *Ave*, and one *Gloria*.

And the same Pope, by a decree of the same S. Congr. of July 10, 1854, has vouchsafed to add -

viii. A plenary indulgence to all the faithful who shall say these prayers, with the *Pater, Ave*, and *Gloria*, once a day for a month together; to be gained by them on that day in each month when, after Confession and Communion, they shall visit a church or public oratory, and pray there for a time according to the mind of his Holiness.

THE PRAYERS.

For Purity.

St. Stanislas, my most pure patron, Angel of purity, I rejoice with thee at the extraordinary gift of virginal purity which graced thy spotless heart; I humbly pray thee, obtain for me strength to overcome all impure temptations, and inspire me with constant watchfulness to guard my purity, - that virtue so glorious in itself, and so acceptable to God.
Pater. Ave. Gloria.

For Charity.

St. Stanislas. my most loving patron, Seraph of charity, I rejoice with thee at the ardent fire of charity which kept thy pure and innocent heart always at peace and united to God; I humbly pray thee, obtain for me such ardour of divine love, that it may consume away every other earthly affection, and kindle in me the fire of His love alone.
Pater. Ave. Gloria.

For a Good Death.

St. Stanislas, my most tender and most mighty patron, Angel of purity and Seraph of charity, I rejoice with thee at thy most happy death, which arose from thy desire to contemplate our Lady assumed into heaven, and was caused by the excess of thy love for her. I give thanks to Mary, because she thus accomplished thy desires; and I pray thee, by the lustre of thy happy death, to be my advocate and my patron in my death. Intercede with Mary for me, to obtain for me a death, if not all happiness like thine, yet calm and peaceful,

under the protection of Mary my advocate, and thee, my special patron.
Pater. Ave. Gloria.

ST. PHILIP NERI

127. PRAYERS FOR EVERY DAY IN THE WEEK

The Holy Father Pius IX, by a rescript of the Sacred Congregation of
Indulgences, dated May 17, 1852, granted -
An indulgence of fifty days; to be gained once a day for saying with a contrite
heart the following prayers, each on its appointed day, in order to obtain
thereby the intercession of this Saint for the acquisition of certain special
virtues.

THE PRAYERS.

FOR SUNDAY.

Prayer to obtain the virtue of Humility.

St, Philip, my glorious Patron, who on earth didst so love humility as to count
the praise and even the good esteem of men as dross; obtain for me also this
virtue by thy prayers. Thou knowest how haughty I am in my thoughts, how
contemptuous in my words, how ambitious in my doings. Ask for me humility
of heart; that my mind may be freed from all pride, and impressed with the
same low esteem of self which thou hadst of thyself, counting thyself the worst
of all men, and for that reason rejoicing when thou didst suffer contempt, and
seeking out for thyself occasions of enduring it. Great Saint, obtain for me a
true humble heart and the knowledge of my own nothingness; that I may
rejoice when I am despised, and resent not when others are preferred before
me; that I may never be vain when I am praised, but may ever seek only to be
great in the eyes of God, desiring to receive from Him alone all my exaltation.

Pater, Ave, Gloria.

FOR MONDAY

Prayer to obtain the virtue of Patience.

St. Philip, my Patron Saint, whose heart was ever so constant in time of trouble, and whose spirit was so loving under suffering, that, when persecuted by the jealous, or calumniated by the wicked who thought to discredit thy sanctity, or when tried by God with many long, painful infirmities, thou didst always bear thy trials with wonderful tranquillity of heart and mind; pray for me that I may have a spirit of true courage in every adversity. Alas, how much I stand in need of patience! I shrink from every little trouble; I sicken under every light affliction; I fire up at and resent every trifling contradiction; never willing to learn that the road to paradise lies amidst the thorns of tribulation. Yet this was the path our Diving Master deigned to tread, and this too, my Saintly Patron, was thy path also. Obtain for me, then, this courage, that with good hearty will I may embrace the crosses which every day I receive from God, and bear them all with the same endurance and ready will as thou didst when thou wast on earth; that so I may be made worthy to enjoy the blessed fruit of sufferings with thee in heaven above.

Pater, Ave, Gloria.

FOR TUESDAY

Prayer to obtain the virtue of Purity.

St. Philip, who didst always preserve the white lily of thy purity unsullied, with such great honour to thyself that the brightness of this fair virtue dwelt in thine eyes, shone forth from thy hands, and cast its fragrance over thy whole body, causing it to emit so sweet a perfume that it gave consolation, fervour, and devotion to all who conversed with thee; obtain me from the Holy Spirit of God so true a love for that virtue, that neither the words nor bad examples of sinners may ever make any impression upon my soul. Never permit me in any way to lose that lovely virtue; and since avoidance of occasions, prayer, labour, humility, frequent use of the Sacraments, were the arms with which thou didst conquer the flesh, which is our worst enemy, so do thou obtain for me grace to use the same arms to vanquish the same foe. Take not away thy help from me; but be as zealous for me as thou wast during thy life for thy penitents, keeping them far removed from all sensual infection. Do this for me, my holy Patron; and be ever my protector in respect of this fair virtue.

Pater, Ave, Gloria.

FOR WEDNESDAY.

Prayer to obtain the Love of God.

St. Philip, I am filled with wonder at the great miracle which was wrought in thee by the Holy Spirit when He poured into thy heart such a flood of heavenly charity, that in order to contain it two of thy ribs were broken by the power of Divine love; and I am confounded when I compare thy heart with mine own. I see thy heart all burning with love; and mine, all frozen and taken up with creatures. I see thine inflamed with a fire from heaven, which so filled thy body that it radiated like flames from thy countenance; while mine is full of earthly love. I love the world, which allures me and can never make me happy; I love the flesh, which ever wears me with its cares, and can never render me immortal; I love riches, which I can enjoy but for a moment. O when shall I learn of thee to love nothing but God, my incomprehensible and only Good! Help me, then, blessed Patron, that by thy intercession I may begin at once: obtain for me an efficacious love, manifesting itself by works; a pure love, making me love God most perfectly; a strong love, enabling me to surmount all obstacles hindering my union with God in life, that so I may be wholly united to Him for ever after my death.

Pater, Ave, Gloria.

FOR THURSDAY

Prayer to obtain the Love of our Neighbour.

Glorious Saint, who didst employ thyself wholly in the good of thy neighbour, thinking well of all, sympathising with all, helping all, who throughout thy whole life didst ever try to secure the salvation of all, never shrinking from labour or trouble, keeping for thyself no time or comfort, that thou mightest win all hearts to God; pray for me, that together with the pardon of my sins I may have charity for my neighbour, and be henceforth more compassionate to him in his necessities, and obtain for me grace that I may love every man with pure, unselfish love, as mine own brother, succouring each one, if I am unable to do it with temporal goods, at least with prayers and good advice. And teach me too on every occasion to defend the honour of my neighbour, and never to say to him a hurtful or displeasing word; but ever to maintain, even with my enemies, sweetness of spirit like thine own, whereby thou didst triumph over thy persecutors. Blessed Saint, ask of God for me also this lovely virtue, which already thou hast gained for so many of thy clients; that so we may all one day come to praise our God with thee in an eternity of bliss.

Pater, Ave, Gloria.

FOR FRIDAY

Prayer to obtain detachment from temporal goods.

Great Saint, who didst prefer a poor and austere life to the comforts of thy home, despising the honour and glory of thy station; obtain for me grace ever to keep my heart detached from transitory goods of this life. St. Philip, whose desire it ever was to become so poor as one day to have to beg thy bread, and find no charitable hand to offer thee a crumb wherewith to support life; ask of God for me such love of poverty that I may turn all my thoughts to goods which never fail. St. Philip, who didst prefer to live unknown, to promotion to the highest honours of the Church; intercede for me, that I may never seek after dignities, but always content myself with that state where God has set me. My heart is too
anxious for the empty fleeting things of earth; but thou - ah, what a maxim didst thou leave us by thy two words: "And then-" ! O wonder-working words! may they ever be deeply impressed upon my soul; that, despising the nothingness of earth, God alone may reign sole object of my affections and my thoughts.

Pater, Ave, Gloria.

FOR SATURDAY

Prayer to obtain perseverance in good works.

St. Philip, my holy Patron, who, ever constant in good works and full of merit, didst receive from Most High God the crown of glory in reward of all thy labours; obtain for me grace never to weary in His service. St. Philip, who didst recompense those who loved thee by acquiring for them the gift of perseverance in good, ask of God this gift for me; stand by me, dear father, at the last moment of my life, and pray for me that I may depart this life
strengthened with the grace of the Holy Sacraments. Meanwhile intercede for me, that I may do penance for my sins, and deplore them bitterly all my days. St. Philip, who from on high beholdest all my miseries, and the chains which yet bind me to my sins and to this earth; pray for me that I may be liberated from them, and be constantly devoted to my God. Obtain for me an ardent desire to co-operate in my own salvation, and unshaken firmness in the good which I have begun; that so by thy intercession I may deserve to be for ever in thy company in an eternity of bliss.

Pater, Ave, Gloria.

128. ST. CAMILLUS OF LELLIS.

The Sovereign Pontiff Pius IX., by a decree of the S. Congr. of Indulgences, August 8, 1853, granted, at the prayer of the Clerks Regulars, ministers of the sick, thereby to augment devotion towards this Saint -

i. An indulgence of seven years and seven quarantines, whenever any one shall, at any time of the year, in public or in private, practise the pious exercise of keeping seven Sundays in honour of St. Camillus, saying some devout prayer in honour of this Saint. This Indulgence may be gained on each of these Sundays, provided the prayer be said with contrite heart.

ii. A plenary indulgence, instead of the seven years &c., on the seventh Sunday, to all the faithful who, after Confession and Communion, and having said the prayer as above, shall visit a church or public oratory and pray there according to the intention of his Holiness.

FOR THE FAITHFUL IN THEIR AGONY.

129. THREE " PATER NOSTER'S," IN MEMORY OF THE AGONY OF OUR LORD JESUS CHRIST, AND THREE "AVE MARIA'S," IN MEMORY OF THE DOLOURS OF THE BLESSED VIRGIN MARY.

Pope Pius VII., by a Rescript and subsequent decree dated April 18, 1809, of his Eminence the Pro-Vicar (kept in the *Segretaria* of his Vicariate), granted-

i. An indulgence of 300 days to all Christians every time that, praying for the faithful in their agony, they shall say, with contrite heart and with devotion, three *Pater noster's* in remembrance of the Passion and Agony of Jesus Christ, and three *Ave Maria's* in memory of the bitter sorrows undergone by most holy Mary whilst assisting at the agony of her beloved Son Jesus.

ii. A plenary indulgence and remission of all sins to those who shall practise this pious exercise once a day at least for an entire month to be gained on any one day at the month when, after Confession and Communion, they shall pray according to the mind of the Sovereign Pontiff. These Indulgences may be also applied to the souls in purgatory.

PIOUS EXERCISE IN MEMORY OF THE AGONY OF OUR LORD JESUS CHRIST.

For this devout exercise, and the notices respecting the Indulgences attached to it, see above.

PRAYER "DEUS QUI PRO REDEMPTIONE," ETC., WITH FIVE "PATER'S," "AVE'S" AND "GLORIA'S."

For the prayer and Indulgences, see above.

---

130. PRAYER "O CLEMENTISSIME JESU," ETC.

In order to animate the faithful to pray many times a day for those who are in their agony, thereby to obtain for them the aid of divine grace, the Sovereign Pontiff Pius IX,, by a Rescript dated from Portici near Naples, Feb. 2, 1850, granted -

i. An indulgence of 100 days every time the following prayer is said with contrite heart and devotion.

ii. A plenary indulgence to those who shall say it at least three times a day, for a mouth together, at three distinct intervals, to be gained on that day when, after Confession and Communion, they shall visit a church or public oratory, and pray there for a time according to the mind of His Holiness.

THE PRAYER.

O clementissime Jesu, amator animarum; obsecro Te per agoniam cordis tui sanctissimi, et per dolores Matris tuae immaculatae, lava in sanguine tuo peccatores totius mundi, nunc positos in agonia et hodie morituros. Amen.

Cor Jesu in agonia factum, miserere morientium.

TRANSLATION.

O most merciful Jesus, Lover of souls; I pray Thee by the agony of Thy most sacred Heart, and by the sorrows of Thy Immaculate Mother, cleanse in Thine own Blood the sinners of the whole world who are now in their agony amid are to die this day. Amen.

Heart of Jesus, once in agony, pity the dying.

FOR A GOOD DEATH.

131. PRAYER "LORD JESUS," ETC.

In order to implore the divine assistance in the last moments of our life, Pius VII., by a Rescript of May 12, 1802, granted -
i. An indulgence of 100 days, once a day, to all the faithful who with contrite heart shall say these following prayers.
ii. A plenary indulgence to those who say them every day for a month, on any one day in the said month when, after Confession and Communion, they shall visit a church or public oratory, and offer up prayer to God according to the intention of the Sovereign Pontiff.
The grant of these Indulgences was renewed by Pope Leo XII., by a decree of the S. Congr. of Indulgences, August 11, 1824. The original decree is preserved in the Archivium of the Pious Union of St. Paul, of which mention has already been frequently made above, the priests of the said Pious Union being the petitioners for this grant.

THE PRAYERS.

O Lord God of goodness, and Father of mercies, I draw nigh to Thee with a contrite and humble heart; to Thee I recommend the last hour of my life, and that judgment which awaits me afterwards.
Merciful Jesus, have mercy on me.
When my feet, benumbed with death, shall admonish me that my course in this life is drawing to an end,
Merciful Jesus, have mercy on me.
When my hands, cold and trembling, shall no longer be able to clasp the crucifix, and shall let it fall against my will on my bed of suffering,
Merciful Jesus, have mercy on me.
When my eyes, dim with trouble at the approach of death, shall fix themselves on Thee my last and only support,
Merciful Jesus, have mercy on me.
When my ups, cold and trembling, pronounce for the last time Thy adorable Name,
Merciful Jesus, have mercy on me.
When my face, pale and livid, shall inspire the beholders with pity and dismay; when my hair, bathed in the sweat of death, and stiffening on my head, shall forebode my approaching end,
Merciful Jesus, have mercy on me.
When my ears, shall to be for ever shut to the discourse of men, shall be open to that irrevocable decree, which is to fix my doom for all eternity,

Merciful Jesus, have mercy on me.

When my imagination, agitated by dreadful spectres, shall be sunk in an abyss of anguish; when my soul, affrighted by the sight of my iniquities and the terrors of Thy judgments, shall have to fight against the angel of darkness, who will endeavour to conceal from my eyes Thy mercies, and to plunge me into despair,

Merciful Jesus, have mercy on me.

When my poor heart, oppressed with suffering and exhausted by its continual struggles with the enemies of its salvation, shall feel the pangs of death,

Merciful Jesus, have mercy on me.

When the last tear, the forerunner of my dissolution, shall drop from my eyes, receive it as a sacrifice of expiation for my sins; grant that I may expire the victim of penance; and then in that dreadful moment,

Merciful Jesus, have mercy on me.

When my friends and relations, encircling my bed, shall be moved with compassion for me, and invoke Thy clemency in my behalf,

Merciful Jesus, have mercy on me.

When I shall have lost the use of my senses, when the world shall have vanished from my sight, when my agonising soul shall feel the sorrows of death,

Merciful Jesus, have mercy on me.

When my last sighs shall force my soul to issue from my body, accept them as the children of a loving impatience to come to Thee.

Merciful Jesus, have mercy on me.

When my soul, trembling on my lips, shall bid adieu to the world, and leave my body lifeless, pale, and cold, receive this separation as a homage which I willingly pay to Thy Divine Majesty, and in that last moment of my mortal life,

Merciful Jesus, have mercy on me.

When at length my soul, admitted to Thy presence, shall first behold the splendour of Thy Majesty, reject me not, but receive me into Thy bosom, where I may for ever sing Thy praises, and in that moment when eternity shall begin to me,

Merciful Jesus, have mercy on me.

Let us pray.

O God, who hast doomed all men to die, and hast concealed from all the hour of their death, grant that I may pass my days in the practice of holiness and justice, and that I may be made worthy to quit this world in the peace of a good conscience, and in the embrace of Thy love, through Christ our Lord. Amen.

THREE OFFERINGS TO THE MOST HOLY TRINITY TO OBTAIN A GOOD DEATH.

See above for the prayers themselves, and the Indulgences attached to them.

132. PRAYERS, ETC. FOR DELIVERANCE FROM UNPREPARED DEATH

Pope Pius VII, by a decree of the S. Congr. of Indulgences, March 2, 1816, granted -

i. An indulgence of 100 days to all the faithful every time that, praying to God for this intention, that shall with contrite heart and devotion say the following prayers and antiphons, first collected by the blessed Cardinal Joseph Mary Tommassi, by order of Pope Clement XI., and published in the two languages, Latin and Italian.

ii. A plenary indulgence to all who say them every day for a year to be gained on the two Feasts of the holy Cross, viz. May 3 and Sept. 14, on Holy Thursday, and on Good Friday, provided that on those days, being penitent, and after Confession and Communion, they pray according to the intention of the Sovereign Pontiff in any church where there is the Blessed Sacrament: for the Indulgence on Good Friday, the Confession and Communion required may be made on the preceding day.

DD. ORATIONES.

1. Exaudi nos, Deus salutaris nostri, et ne dies nostros ante finiri jubeas, quam peccata dimittas: et quia in inferno superflua poenitentia est, et nullum spatium corrigendi; hinc te supplices rogamus et petimus, ut ubi das spatium supplicandi, jubeas et peccata dimitti. Per Dominum, &c.

2. Averte Domine, quaesumus, a fidelibus tuis cunctos miseratus errores; et saeventium morborum repentinam depelle perniciem, ut quos merito flagellas devios, foveas tua miseratione correctos. Per Dominum, &c.

ANTIPHONA.

3. Anima mea cessa jam peccare; cogita de subitanea transpositione ad aeterna tormenta. Ibi enim non suscipitur poenitentia, lice lucrifaciunt lacrymae. Dum tempus adest convertere, clama dicens: Deus meus, miserere mei.

ANTIPHONA.

4. Media vita in morte sumus: quem quaesumus adjutorem nisi te, Domine, qui pro peccatis nostris irasceris? Sanctus Deus, sanctus fortis, sanctus misericors, Salvator, amarae morti ne tradas nos.

5. V. Ne subito praeoccupati die mortis quaeramus spatium poenitentiae, et invenire non possimus.
R. Attende, Domine, et miserere, quia peccavimus tibi.

6. Populum tuum, quaesumus, omnipotens Deus, ab ira tua ad te confugientem paterna recipe pietate: ut qui tuae majestatis flagella in repentina morte formidant, de tua mereantur venia gratulari. Per Dominum, &c.

7. Ecclesiae tuae, quaesumus, omnipotens Deus, placatus intende conventum, et misericordia tua nos potius quam ira praeveniat; quia si iniquitates nostras observare volueris, nulla poterit creatura subsistere: sed admirabili pietate, qua nos fecisti, ignosce peccantibus, ut opera manuum tuarum repentia morte non facias interire. Per Dominum, &c.

8. Exaudi, Domine, preces nostras, et ne velis cum servis tuis adire judicium: quia sicut in nobis nulla justitia reperitur, de qua praesumere valeamus; ita te fontem pietatis agnoscimus, a quo et a peccatis nostris ablui, et ab infirmitatibus, ac repentina morte liberari confidimus. Per Dominum, &c.

9. Deus, sub cujus oculis omne cor trepidat, et omnes conscientiae pavescunt, misericordiam tuam effunde supplicibus; ut qui de meritorum qualitate diffidimus, non judicium tuum in repentina morte nostra, sed indulgentiam tuam sentiamus. Per Dominum, &c.

THE PRAYERS.

1. Hear us, O God of our salvation, and issue not the decree for the completion of our days before Thou forgivest us our sins; and because penance avails not in hell, and there is no room for amendment in the pit, therefore we humbly pray and beseech Thee here on earth, that giving us time to pray for pardon, Thou wouldst give us all forgiveness of our sins. Through our Lord Jesus Christ. Amen.

2. Take away, merciful Lord, all errors from Thy faithful people, avert from them the sudden destruction of the wasting pestilence; and those whose wanderings Thou dost justly chastise, do Thou mercifully pity when corrected. Through Jesus Christ our Lord.

ANTIPHON.

3. Sin no longer, O my soul; think upon the sudden change from sin to endless torments. There, in hell, penance is not accepted, and tears profit not. Turn, then, whilst thou hast time; cry out and say, Have mercy upon me, O my God.

ANTIPHON.

4. In the midst of life we are in death; but to whom can we look to be our helper save Thee, O Lord, who art justly angry with us because of our sins? O holy God, holy and strong, holy and merciful Saviour, deliver us not over to a bitter death,

5. V. Lest, overtaken by the day of death, we seek time for penance, and be unable to find it.

R. Hearken, O Lord, and have mercy on us; for we have sinned against Thee.

6. We beseech Thee, Almighty God, receive in Thy fatherly pity Thy people who flee unto Thee from Thine anger; that those who fear to be chastised by the rod of Thy majesty through unprepared death, may be made worthy to rejoice in Thy pardon. Through our Lord Jesus Christ, &c.

7. We beseech Thee, Almighty God, graciously incline Thine ear to the assembly of Thy Church, and let Thy mercy to us anticipate Thine anger; for if Thou shouldst mark iniquities, there shall no creature be able to stand before Thee: but in that same admirable charity whereby Thou didst create us, pardon us sinners, and destroy not the work of Thine own hands in an unprepared death. Through our Lord Jesus Christ, &c.

8. Hear our prayers, O Lord, and enter not into judgment with Thy servants; for, knowing that there is no justice in us on which we can dare to presume, We acknowledge no other fount of mercy whereby we can he washed from our sins, delivered from our infirmities, and espcially from unprepared death, but only Thou, O Lord. Through Jesus Christ our Lord.

9. O God, before whom every heart trembles and ever conscience is awed; show forth Thy mercy upon us Thy suppliants, that we who trust not in the excellence of our own merit, may never experience unprepared death, but may receive Thy pardon. Through our Lord Jesus Christ, &c.

PRAYER.

Most merciful Lord ,Jesus, by Thy agony and bloody sweat, and by Thy death, deliver me, I beseech Thee, from sudden and unprepared death. O most gentle Lord Jesus, by Thy cruel and ignominious scourging and crowning with thorns, by Thy cross and bitter passion, and by Thine own great goodness, I humbly pray Thee, let me not die unprepared, and pass from this life without the Holy Sacraments. Jesus, my best beloved, my Lord! by all Thy travails and all Thy sorrows, by Thy Precious Blood, and by Thy most holy wounds, and by those last words spoken by Thee upon the cross, - "My God, My God, why hast Thou forsaken Me?" and again, Father, into Thy hands I commend My spirit," - most ardently I pray Thee, free me from unprepared death. Thy hands, O my Redeemer, have wholly made and formed me; O suffer not death to take me unawares; grant me, I beseech Thee, time for penance; vouchsafe me a happy passage in Thy grace, that in the world to come I may love Thee with My whole heart, and praise and bless Thee for ever and for ever. Amen.

Then say five Pater noster's *and five* Ave Maria's *in memory of the Passion of Our Lord Jesus Christ, and three* Ave Maria's *to the Blessed Virgin Mother of Sorrows.*

133. EJACULATION OF RESIGNATION TO THE WILL OF GOD.

At the prayer of the priests devoted to the instruction of the poor in the church of St. Galla here in Rome, Pope Pius VII., by a decree of the S. Congr. of Indulgences, May 19, 1815, granted -
i. An indulgence of 100 days once a day to all the faithful who say with contrite hearts and devotion the following ejaculation of resignation to the will of God.
ii. A plenary indulgence, once a year, to all who say it daily; to be gained on any one day when, after Confession and Communion, they shall pray according to the intention of the Sovereign Pontiff.
iii. Lastly, a plenary indulgence *in articulo mortis* to those who during life shall have frequently recited this ejaculation, provided they accept death with resignation from the hands of God.

Fiat, laudetur, atque in aeternum superexaltetur justissima, altissima, et amabilissima voluntas Dei in omnibus.

May the most just, most high, most adorable will of God be in all things done, and praised, and magnified for ever.

134. PLENARY INDULGENCE AT THE HOUR OF OUR DEATH. *(In articulo mortis.)*

The origin of this Plenary Indulgence is most ancient, as appears from the thirteenth letter of St. Cyprian, martyr, written in the latter half of the third century of the Church; mention is also made of it by Baronius in the year 878 of his history, when speaking of John VIII., who granted it to those Christians who died in the war against the Saracens. It was granted also by Clement VI., created Pope in time year 1342, on occasion of a pestilence; and by Gregory XI., who was created in the year 1370. In after ages, bordering upon our own times, Paul V., Alexander VII., and all other succeeding Popes, have with pious liberality granted this Indulgence, in order that the faithful, by the acquisition of it at the end of their lives, may be able to satisfy the justice of God for the temporal punishment due to their sin, and so pass at once to eternal bliss. [P. Theodore de Indulg. pars ii. cap. ii. art. v. $$ 1 et seq.]
This Plenary Indulgence, which may also be gained by any one who

receives *in articulo mortis* the benediction given by the Sovereign Pontiff, by bishops, parish priests, or others who have the necessary faculties) having been frequently mentioned in these pages, it will be well to observe here, that in order to gain it, the faithful, besides being in the grace of God, ought - *first,* to have fulfilled, or to be fulfilling, the good works enjoined in the grant of this Indulgence, as, for example, they ought either "to have frequently said such and such a prayer as above," or "to invoke at the moment of death with their mouth and with their heart the most Holy names of Jesus and Mary," or, "do so at least internally with contrite hearts," &c.; and secondly, it is requisite that the dying person should accept deaths from the hands of God with resignation and in conformity to the divine pleasure. See the thirty-fourth Constitutions of Benedict XIV., *Pia Mater,* April 5, 1747; and note that this Plenary Indulgence *in articulo mortis* is not suspended in the year of the Jubilee, according to the special declarations of Benedict XIV., of Clement XIV. and of Leo XII., in their respective Bulls above named on the suspension of Indulgences during the year of the Jubilee.

APPENDIX

187. PRAYER, "O MARY, CONCEIVED WITHOUT STAIN," ETC.

His Holiness Pope Pius IX., by a Rescript of March 11, 185;, granted - 100 days indulgence, to be gained once a day by all the faithful who, with contrite heart and devotion, say the following prayer to obtain a good death.

THE PRAYER.

O Maria, sine labe concepta, ora pro nobis, qui confugimus ad te. O Refugium peccatorum, Mater agonizantium, noli nos derelinquere in horâ exitus nostri, sed impetra nobis dolorem perfectum, sinceram contritionem, remissionem peccatorum nostrorum, Sanctissimi Viatici dignam receptionem, Extremae Unctionis Sacramenti corroborationem, quatenus securi praesentari valeamus ante thronum justi sed et misericordis Judicis, Dei et Redemptoris nostri. Amen.

TRANSLATION.

Mary, conceived without stain, pray for us, who fly to thee. Refuge of sinners, Mother of those who are in their agony, leave us not in the hour of our death, but obtain for us perfect sorrow, sincere contrition, remission of our sins, a worthy reception of the most holy Viaticum, the strength of the Sacrament of Extreme Unction, in order that we may be able to stand with safety before the throne of the just but merciful Judge, our God and our Redeemer. Amen.

FOR THE FAITHFUL DEPARTED.

135. THE OFFICE.

St. Pius V., in his Bull *Quod a nobis,* July 9, 1568, granted -
i. An indulgence of 100 days to all the faithful, as often as they shall devoutly say of obligation the Office of the Dead on the days prescribed by the rubrics of the Roman Breviary.
ii. Forty days indulgence, to all the faithful, every time they say it out of their own devotion. See another Bull, *Superni omnipotentis Dei,* April 8, 1571.

136. THE "DE PROFUNDIS" AT THE FIRST HOUR AFTER THE "AVE MARIA."

Pope Clement XII. was the first who, in order to move the piety of Christians to pray for the souls in Purgatory, granted, by a Brief of Aug. 4, 1736, *Coelestes Ecclesiae thesauros* -
i. The indulgence of 100 days to all the faithful, every time that at the sound of the bell, at the first hour after the evening *Ave Maria,* they say devoutly on their knees the psalm *De profundis,* with a *Requiem aeternam* at the end of it. (The evening Ave Maria in Rome varies with the season; it is commonly taken as 6 o'clock.)
ii. A plenary indulgence to those who perform this pious exercise for a year at the hour appointed, once in the year, on any one day, after Confession and Communion. Those who do not know by heart the *De Profundis,* may gain these Indulgences by saying in the way already mentioned for the *De profundis*, one *Pater noster* and one *Ave Maria,* with the *Requiem aeternam.* Observe also, that the aforesaid Clement XII. declared, Dec. 12, 1736, that these Indulgences might be gained by saying the *De profundis,* &c., as above, although, according to the custom of a particular church or place, the "signal for the dead," as it is called, be given by the sound of the bell either before or after one hour after the evening *Ave Maria.*
Pope Pius VI., by a Rescript of March 18, 1781, granted the above-named Indulgences to all the faithful who should chance to dwell in any place where no bell for the dead is sounded, and who shall say the *De profundis* or *Pater noster,* as aforesaid, about the time specified above.

Ps. 129.

De profundis clamavi ad te, Domine: * Domine, exaudi vocem meam.
Fiant aures tuae intendentes: * in vocem deprecationis meae.

252

Si iniquitates observaveris, Domine: * Domine, quis sustinebit?
Quia apud te propitiatio est: * propter legem tuam sustinui te, Domine.
Sustinuit anima mea in verbum ejus: * speravit anima mea in Domino.
A custodia matutina usque ad noctem: * speret Israel in Domino.
Quia apud Dominum misericordia: * et copiosa apud eum redemptio.
Et ipse redimet Israel: * ex omnibus iniquitatibus ejus.
Requiem aeternam * dona eis, Domine.
Et lux perpetna luceat eis.
Requiescant in pace.
Amen.

End at pleasure with the following:

V. Domine, exaudi orationem meam,
R. Et clamor meus ad te veniat.

Oremus.
Fidelium Deus omnium conditor et redemptor, animabus famulorum
famularumque tuarum remissionem cunctorum tribue peccatorum: ut
iudulgentiam, quam semper optaverunt, piis supplicationibus consequantur.
Qui vivis et regnas in saecula saeculorum. R. Amen.

V. Requiem aeternam dona eis, Domine.
R. Et lux perpetua luceat eis.
V. Requiescant in pace.
R. Amen.

TRANSLATION.

Ps., 129.

Out of the depths I have cried unto Thee, O Lord, Lord, hear my voice.
Let Thine ears be attentive: to the voice of my supplication.
If Thou, O Lord, shalt mark our iniquities: O lord, who can abide it?
For with Thee there is mercy: and by reason of Thy law I have waited on Thee,
O Lord.
My soul hath waited on His word : my soul hath hoped in the Lord.
From the morning watch even unto night: let Israel hope in the Lord.
For with the Lord there is mercy: and with Him is plenteous redemption.
And He shall redeem Israel: from all his iniquities.
Eternal rest give to them, O Lord.
And let perpetual light shine upon them.
May they rest in peace.
Amen.

V. Lord, hear my prayer.
R. And let my cry come unto Thee.

Let us pray.
O God, the Creator and Redeemer of all the faithful; grant to the souls of Thy servants departed the remission of all their sins, that by our devout supplications they may obtain that pardon which they have always desired. Who livest and reignest world without end. Amen.

V. Eternal rest give unto them, O Lord.
R. And let perpetual light shine upon them.
V. May they rest in peace.
R. Amen.

137. FIVE PATER'S AND AVE'S, WITH THE V. TE ERGO, ETC.

Pope Pius VII., by a Brief dated Feb,. 7, 1817, the original of which is kept in the Archivium of the Chapter of the Cathedral Church of Arezzo, whose bishop first prayed for this Indulgence, granted -
i. An indulgence of 300 days, to all the faithful who, being contrite in heart, and devoutly meditating on the Passion of our Lord Jesus Christ, shall say in suffrage for the faithful departed five *Pater noster's* and five *Ave Maria's*, with the versicle *Te ergo quaesumus, tuis famulis subveni, quos pretioso sanguine redemisti*, or, who shall say the ejaculation, "Eternal Father, we pray Thee help the souls of Thy servants, whom Thou hast redeemed with the blood of Jesus Christ;" and the *Requiem aeternam*.
ii. A plenary indulgence and remission of all sins to all who shall have practised this pious exercise every day for a month, on any one day in each month when, being repentant, they shall, after Confession and Communion, pray for our holy Mother the Church, &c., and for the eternal repose of the departed.

138. PRAYERS FOR THE WHOLE WEEK.

"Purgatory opened to the Piety of the Living, or a Brief daily Exercise in aid of the Souls in Purgatory," as the title of a little book of which many editions have been printed in Rome and elsewhere, and which is in the hands of many a devout person.
Pope Leo XII., in order to hold out a greater inducement to the faithful to pray for the faithful departed, granted by a Rescript of the S. Congr. of Indulgences, Nov, 18, 1826 -

An indulgence of 100 days, to all who say with contrite heart and devotion once a day the prayers assigned in the above mentioned exercise to each day in the week, with one *Pater, Ave,* and the *De profundis;* and his holiness expressed at the same time his desire that the little books containing these devotions should be distributed *gratis*, as indeed has hitherto been the constant practice. Those, however, who use these prayer-books, are therein exhorted to say every day two Ave Maria's additional; one for all those who are associated in the exercise, and the other for all those who of their charity assist in promulgating it.

THE PRAYERS.

For Sunday.

O Lord God Almighty, I pray Thee, by the Precious Blood which Thy Divine Son Jesus shed in the garden, deliver the souls in purgatory, and especially that soul amongst them all who is most destitute of spiritual aid; and vouchsafe to bring it to Thy glory, there to praise and bless Thee for ever. Amen.
Pater, Ave *and* De Profundis.

For Monday.

O Lord God Almighty, I pray Thee, by the Precious Blood which Thy Divine Son Jesus shed in His cruel scourging, deliver the souls in purgatory, and that soul especially amongst them all which is nearest to its entrance into Thy glory; that so it may forthwith begin to praise and bless Thee for ever. Amen.
Pater, Ave *and* De Profundis.

For Tuesday.

O Lord God Almighty, I pray Thee, by the Precious Blood which Thy Divine Son Jesus shed in His bitter crowning with thorns, deliver the souls in purgatory, and in particular that one amongst them all which would be the last to depart out of these pains, that it may not tarry so long a time before it come to praise Thee in Thy glory and bless Thee for ever. Amen.
Pater, Ave *and* De Profundis.

For Wednesday.

O Lord God Almighty, I pray Thee, by the Precious Blood which Thy Divine Son Jesus shed in the streets of Jerusalem when He carried the cross upon His sacred shoulders, deliver the souls in purgatory, and especially that soul which is richest in merits before Thee; that so, in that throne of glory which awaits it, it may magnify Thee and bless Thee for ever. Amen.
Pater, Ave *and* De Profundis.

For Thursday.

O Lord God Almighty, I pray Thee by the Precious Body and Blood of Thy Divine Son Jesus, which He gave with His own Hand upon the eve of His Passion to His beloved apostles to be their meat and drink, and which He left to His whole Church to be a perpetual sacrifice and the life-giving food of His own faithful people, deliver the souls in purgatory, and especially that one which was most devoted to this Mystery of infinite love, that it may with the same Thy Divine Son, and with The Holy Spirit, ever praise Thee for Thy love therein in eternal glory. Amen.

Pater, Ave *and* De Profundis.

For Friday.

O Lord God Almighty, I pray Thee, by the Precious Blood which Thy Divine Son shed upon the wood of the cross, especially from his most sacred Hands and Feet, deliver the souls in purgatory, and in particular that soul for which I am most bound to pray; that no neglect of mine may hinder it from praising Thee in Thy glory and blessing Thee for ever. Amen.

Pater, Ave *and* De Profundis.

For Saturday.

O Lord God Almighty, I beseech Thee, by the Precious Blood which gushed forth from the Side of Thy Divine Son Jesus, in the sight of, and to the extreme pain of his most holy Mother, deliver the souls in purgatory, and especially that one amongst them all which was the most devout to her; that it may soon attain unto Thy glory, there to praise Thee in her and her in Thee world without end. Amen.

Pater, Ave *and* De Profundis.

139. THE HOUR OF PRAYER ON THE THREE LAST DAYS OF HOLY WEEK.

By a decree of the Sacred Congregation of Indulgences for Italy and the adjacent islands, April 6, 1745, Benedict XIV. granted -

An indulgence of seven years and seven quarantines to all the faithful, on each and all of the three days, Thursday, Friday, and Saturday in Holy Week, provided that on those days they devoutly make an hour's mental or oral prayer for the benefit of the souls in purgatory.

140. HEROIC ACT OF CHARITY, OR, OFFERING OF ALL WORKS OF SATISFACTION AND SUFFRAGE IN BEHALF OF THE SOULS IN PURGATORY.

This heroic act of charity in behalf of the souls in purgatory consists in a voluntary offering made in their favour by any one of the faithful of all works of satisfaction done by him in this life, as well as of all suffrages which shall be offered for him after his death; by this act he deposits them all into the hands of the Blessed Virgin, that she may distribute them in behalf of those holy souls whom it is her good pleasure to deliver from the pains of purgatory, at the same time that he declares that by this offering he only foregoes in their behalf the special and personal fruit of each satisfactory work; so that, being a priest, he is not hindered from applying the Holy Sacrifice of the Mass according to the intentions of those who give him alms.

This heroic act of charity, called also a vow or oblation, was instituted by F. Gaspar Oliden, a Theatine; for although it was not unknown in former ages, it was he who propagated it, and it was at his prayer that it was enriched with many indulgences first by Pope Benedict XIII. in his decree of August 23, 1728; and then by Pope Pius VI., in a decree of Dec. 12, 1788; these indulgences were finally specified by our Sovereign Pontiff Pius IX, in a decree of the S. Congr. of Indulgences of Sept. 30, 1852. They are as follows:

i. An indult of a privileged altar, personally, every day in the year, in all priests who have made this offering.

ii. A plenary indulgence, applicable only to the departed, to all the faithful who have made this offering, whenever they go to Holy Communion, provided they visit a church or public oratory, and pray there for a time according to the mind of His Holiness.

iii. A Plenary indulgence, every Monday, to all who hear Mass in suffrage for the souls in purgatory, provided they visit the church, and pray as above.

iv. All Indulgences granted or to be granted, even though not applicable to the dead, which are gained by the faithful who have made this offering, may be applied to the holy souls in purgatory.

v. Lastly, the same Sovereign Pontiff, Pope Pius IX., having regard to the young who are not yet communicants, as well as to the poor sick, to those who are afflicted with chronic disorders, to the aged, to farm-labourers, prisoners, and others who are debarred from communicating and unable to hear Mass on Mondays, vouchsafed by another decree of the S. Congr. of Indulgences, of November 20, 1854, to declare that for all the faithful who cannot hear mass on Mondays, the mass heard on Sundays should be available for gaining the Indulgence no. iii; and that in favour of those who are not yet communicants, or who are hindered from communicating, he leaves it at the disposal of their respective ordinaries to authorise confessors to commute the works enjoined. And note lastly, that although this act of charity is denominated a vow in some printed tracts, in which also is given a formula for making the offering, no inference is to be drawn therefrom that this offering binds under sin; neither is it necessary to make use of the said formula, since, in order to share in the said indulgences, no more is required than a hearty act of our will.

141. ALL INDULGENCES DURING THE HOLY YEAR OF THE JUBILEE, APPLICABLE IN SUFFRAGE FOR THE SOULS IN PURGATORY.

Pope Benedict XIII,, in the Bull, *Salvatoris,* April 28, 1725, granted to all the faithful power to apply in suffrage for the souls in purgatory all the indulgences which are suspended throughout the whole Catholic world during the year of the Universal Jubilee, and this even although in the grant of any of these Indulgences there should never have been given the power to apply them for this purpose. Benedict XIV, Clement XIV., and Leo XII., renewed this grant in their respective Bulls, quoted above, on the suspension of Indulgences during the Holy Year.

THE DIVINE OFFICE AND THE OFFICE OF THE BLESSED VIRGIN.

142. THE PRAYER "SACROSANCTAE," WITH "PATER,"AND "AVE," AFTER THE OFFICE.

Pope Leo X. granted to all persons under obligation to recite the Divine Office, or the Office of the Blessed Virgin. provided that, kneeling, and with devotion, they say after it the following prayer, *Sacrosanctae*, composed by Saint Bonaventura, Doctor of the Church, together with one *Pater noster* and one *Ave Maria,* the remission of all defects and faults committed through human frailty in reciting it. And as this grant is not properly an Indulgence, but rather a compensation for, or a supplying of the defects committed in the recitation of the Office, it follows that it is not suspended during the Holy Year like the other Indulgences.

258

DICTA ORATIO.

Sacrosanctae et indviduae Trinitati, Crucifixi Domini nostri Jesu Christi humanitati, beatissimae et gloriosissimae semperque Virginis Mariae fecundae integritati, et omnium sanctorum universitati sit sempiterna laus, honor, virtus, te gloria ab omnia creatura; nobisque remissio omnium peccatorum, per infinita saecula saeculorurn. Amen.

V. Beata viscera Mariae Virginis, quae portaverunt aeterni Patris Filium.
R. Et beata ubera quae lactaverunt Christum Dominum.

Pater noster. Ave Maria.

THE PRAYER.

To the most holy and undivided Trinity, to the Humanity of our Crucified Lord Jesus Christ, to the fruitful virginity of the most blessed and glorious Mary ever Virgin, and to the whole company of saints, be for ever praise, honour, power, and glory from every creature; and to us be remission of all our sins, world without end. Amen.

V. Blessed is the womb of Mary the Virgin, which bore the Son of the Eternal Father.
R. And blessed are the breasts which gave suck to Christ the Lord.

Pater noster. Ave Maria.

THE GRADUAL AND PENITENTIAL PSALMS

143. THE GRADUAL AND PENITENTIAL PSALMS.

St. Pius V., in his Bull *Quod a nobis*, July 9, 1568, granted -
i. An indulgence of fifty days, to all the faithful, every time that under obligation they say devoutly the Gradual or Penitential Psalms on the days prescribed by the rubrics of the Renian Breviary.
ii. Forty days indulgence to those who say them at any other time for their own devotion. See his Bull *Superni omnipotentis Dei,* April 5, 1571.

144. MENTAL PRAYER

Pope Benedict. XIV., in his Bull *Quamadmodum* of Dec. 16, 1746, granted -
A plenary indulgence once a month, to all the faithful who make mental prayer devoutly for half an hour, or at least a quarter of an hour a day; to be gained on that day when, after Confession and Communion, they shall pray to God for the Holy Church, &c.

145. TEACHING AND LEARNING MENTAL PRAYER.

The same Pope Benedict XIV., in the above-named Bull, granted -
i. A plenary indulgence, once a month, as well to those who frequently teach, either in public or private, the way to meditate or make mental prayer, as to those who frequently learn it; to be gained on the day when, being penitent, they shall, after Confession and Communion, pray for time Holy Church, &c.
ii. An indulgence of seven years and seven quarantines, every time that, being truly penitent, and after Confession and Communion, they teach or are present at the instruction on meditation.

DEVOUT VISITS

146. VISIT TO THE CHURCHES OF THE STATIONS.

The practice of visiting the churches of the Stations, where are preserved the sacred memorials of the saints, and especially of the martyrs, dates its institution from the first ages of Christianity; and on certain days in the year the people, clergy, and even Popes, used to go there in procession to pray. This pious and time-honoured devotion, constantly maintained, moved Pope Gregory the Great to make a list of the Stations, assigning time churches to be visited, not only during Lent, but also on certain other days and times in the year and these days he ordered to be inserted in the Roman Missal, as is related by John the Deacon in his *Life of St. Gregory,* book ii. cc. 2 and 6.

In order to induce the faithful to make these visits to the churches of the Stations on the appointed days, and to pray there according to the intention of the Sovereign Pontiff, the same Pope St. Gregory, and others his successors, granted various Indulgences, which were all confirmed afresh for ever by Pope Pius VI. in a decree of the S. Congr. of Indulgences, July 9, 1777; a list of these Indulgences will presently be given, as well as of the days and churches of the Stations.

Afterwards, Leo XII., *motu proprio,* given through the same S. Congr. of Indulgences, Feb. 28, 1827, granted -

i. An indulgence of forty years and as many quarantines, to all the faithful, every time that during Lent, with contrite hearts and devotion, they visit the churches of the Stations in the manner he prescribed; and he ordered this method of visiting the churches to be published in a book for the purpose printed at the press of the Camera Apostolica. He granted also -

ii. A plenary indulgence to all persons who shall have made the visit as above three times, each visit on a different day; to be gained on any one day when, being penitent, they shall, after Confession and Communion, visit some church or public oratory, and pray there for our holy mother the Church, &c.

The method prescribed to be used is as follows: First, to visit some church, and say there the prayers appointed in the book, to the Blessed Sacrament, to the Blessed Virgin, and to the holy martyrs; then to go to the church of the Station, saying on the way the psalm *Miserere,* five *Pater noster's*, five *Ave Maria's,* and five *Gloria Patri's,* and then the *Steps of the Passion of Our Lord Jesus Christ;* and lastly, whilst at the church itself, to say the Litanies of the Saints with the versicles and prayers assigned, and at the end the psalm *De profundis,* &c. All unlearned persons, however, and others who do not possess this book of the Stations, may gain the same Indulgences by saying at the two churches which they visit such prayers as their own devotion suggests to them and as are suitable to their capacity; and while they go from one church to the other, they are to say a third part of their rosary with the Litanies; and on leaving the church of the Station, to end their visit with the psalm *De profundis,* or else with one *Pater noster,* one *Ave Maria,* and a *Requiem aeternam* for the holy souls in purgatory.

The same Pontiff declared his will that all nuns and others dwelling in monasteries and communities should participate in the benefit of these Indulgences, provided that they keep the method prescribed and visit their own churches; and he also extended these Indulgences to the sick and to prisoners, provided they supply what they are unable to perform by doing some good

261

work enjoined them by their own confessor.

Note, that although it is only necessary to visit one church in order to gain the Indulgences, there are on certain days, besides the churches set down in the Roman Missal for the Stations, several other churches enjoying the same Indulgences through grants of various Sovereign Pontiffs; thus we may instance the grant of Leo XII. above named, who, by a Brief of Jan. 8, 1828, confirmed a privilege already granted by Clement VIII., Feb. 4, 1603, viz, that the church of St. Gregory on the Celian Hill should be one of the stational churches for the Friday after Ash-Wednesday whilst at time same time he desired that on the second Sunday in Lent there should be another Station at this church, as appears from a notice of his Eminence the Cardinal-Vicar, Feb. 20, 1828.

DAYS AND CHURCHES OF THE STATIONS IN ROME.

Jan. 1. Circumcision of our Lord Jesus Christ. Station, St. Mary beyond the Tiber. Indulgence of thirty years and thirty quarantines.

Jan. 6. The Epiphany of our Lord. St. Peter, on the Vatican. The same indulgence.

Septuagesima Sunday. St. Laurence, outside the Walls. The same indulgence.

Sexagesima. St. Paul, outside the Walls. The same indulgence.

Quinquagesima. St. Peter, on the Vatican. The same indulgence.

Ash-Wednesday. St. Sabina in St. Alexius, and St. Mary in Cosmedin, called Bocca della Verità. Indulgence of fifteen years and fifteen quarantines.

Thursday after Ash Wednesday. St. George in Velabro, and the church of Jesus and Mary. Indulgence of ten years and ten quarantines.

Friday. SS. John and Paul, and St. Gregory, on the Celian Hill. The same indulgence.

Saturday. St. Tryphon, and St. Augustine. The same indulgence.

First Sunday in Lent. St. John Lateran. The same indulgence.

Monday. St. Peter's Chains and St. John della Pigna. The same indulgence.

Tuesday. St. Anastasia. The same indulgence.

Wednesday (Ember day). St. Mary Major. The same indulgence.

Thursday. St. Laurence in Pane e Perna. The same indulgence.

Friday (Ember day). The Twelve Holy Apostles. The same indulgence.

Saturday (Ember day). St. Peter, on the Vatican. The same indulgence.

Second Sunday in Lent. St. Mary in Domnica, called the Church of the Navicella, and St. Gregory, on the Celian. The same indulgence.

Monday. St. Mary Major and St. Clement. The same indulgence.

Tuesday. St. Balbina. The same indulgence.

Wednesday. St. Cecilia beyond the Tiber. The same indulgence..

Thursday. St. Mary beyond the Tiber. The same indulgence.

Friday. St. Vitalis. The same indulgence.

Saturday. SS. Marcellinus and Peter', near the Lateran Basilica. The same indulgence.

Third Sunday in Lent. St. Laurence, outside the Walls. Indulgence of ten years and ten quarantines.

Monday. St. Mark, The same indulgence.

Tuesday. St. Pudentiana. The same indulgence.

Wednesday. SS. Sixtus, Nereus, and Achilleus. The same indulgence.

Thursday. SS. Cosmas and Damian, in the Forum. The same indulgence.

Friday. St. Laurence in Lucina. The same indulgence.

Saturday. SS. Caius and Susanna, and St. Mary of time Angels, at the Baths. The same indulgence.

Fourth Sunday in Lent. The Holy Cross in Jerusalem. Indulgence of fifteen years and fifteen quarantines.

Monday. The Four Saints crowned with Martyrdom. Indulgence of ten years and ten quarantines.

Tuesday. St. Laurence ins St. Damasus, and St. Andrew della Valle. The same indulgence.

Wednesday. St. Paul, outside the Gates. The same indulgence.

Thursday. SS. Martin and Silvester, on the Hills, and St. Silvester in Capite. The same indulgence.

Friday. St. Eusebius and St. Bibiana. The same indulgence.

Saturday. St. Nicholas in Carcere. The same indulgence.

Passion Sunday. St. Peter, on the Vatican, and St. Lazarus. The same indulgence.

Monday. St. Crysogonus, beyond the Tiber. The same indulgence.

Tuesday. St. Cyriacus, and St. Mary on the Broad Way, and SS. Quiricus and Julitta, on the Hills. The same indulgence.

Wednesday. St. Marcellus. The same indulgence.

Thursday. St. Apollinaris. The same indulgence.

Friday. St. Stephen, on the Celian, called the Round Church of Stephen. The same indulgence.

Saturday. St. Johns before the Latin Gate, and St. Caesareus. The same indulgence.

Palm Sunday. St. John Lateran. Indulgence of twenty-five years and twenty-five quarantines.

Monday in Holy Week. St. Praxede. Indulgence of ten years and ten quarantines.

Tuesday in Holy Week. St. Prisca, and St. Mary at the Gate of the People. The same indulgence.

Wednesday in Holy Week. St. Mary Major. The same indulgence.

Thursday in Holy Week. St. .John Lateran. Plenary indulgence, after Confession and Communion.

Good Friday. Holy Cross at Jerusalem. Indulgence of thirty years and thirty quarantines.

Holy Saturday. St. John Lateran. The same indulgence.

Easter Day. St. Mary Major. Plenary indulgence; after Confession and Communion.

Easter Monday. St. Peter, on the Vatican, and St. Onuphrius. Indulgence of thirty years and thirty quarantines.

Easter Tuesday. St. Paul, outside the Walls, The same indulgence.

Wednesday in Easter Week. St. Laurence, outside the the Walls. The same indulgence.

Thursday in Easter Week. The Twelve Holy Apostles. The same indulgence.

Friday in Easter Week. St. Mary of the Martyrs, called La Rotunda (The Round Church). The same indulgence.

Saturday in Easter Week. St. John Lateran. The same indulgence.

Low Sunday. St. Pancratius and St. Mary della Scala. The same indulgence.

April 25. *Feast of St. Mark the Evangelist.* St. Peter, on the Vatican. The same indulgence.

Rogation Monday. St. Mary Major. The same indulgence.

Rogation Tuesday. St. John Lateran. The same indulgence.

Rogation Wednesday. St. Peter, on the Vatican. The same indulgence.

Ascension Day. St. Peter, on the Vatican. Plenary indulgence; after Confession and Communion.

Saturday, Vigil of Pentecost. St. John Lateran. Indulgence of ten years and ten quarantines.

Whit-Sunday. St. Peter, on the Vatican. Indulgence of thirty years and thirty quarantines.

Whit-Monday. St. Peter's Chains. The same indulgence.

Whit-Tuesday. St. Anastasia, The same indulgence.

Wednesday in Whitsun-Week (Ember Day). St. Mary Major. The same indulgence.

Thursday in Whitsun-Week. St. Laurence, outside the Walls. The same indulgence.

Friday in Whitsun-Week (Ember Day). The Twelve Holy Apostles. The same indulgence.

Saturday in Whitsun-Week (Ember Day). Eve of the Feast of the Most Holy Trinity. St. Peter, on the Vatican. The same indulgence.

Wednesday in September (Ember day). St. Mary Major. Indulgence of ten years and ten quarantines.

Friday in September (Ember day). The Twelve Holy Apostle's, The same indulgence.

Saturday in September (Ember day). St. Peter, on the Vatican. The same indulgence..

First Sunday in Advent. St. Mary Major. The same indulgence.

Second Sunday in Advent. Holy Cross in Jerusalem. The same indulgence.

Third Sunday in Advent. St. Peter, on the Vatican. Indulgence of fifteen years and fifteen quarantines.

Wednesday in December (Ember day). St. Mary Major. Indulgence of ten years and ten quarantines.

Friday in December (Ember day). The Twelve Holy Apostles. The same indulgence.

Saturday in December (Ember day). St. Peter, on the Vatican The same indulgence.

*Fourth Sunday in Advent. T*he Twelve Holy Apostles. The same indulgence.

Dec. 24. *Christmas Eve.* St. Mary Major. Indulgence of fifteen years and fifteen quarantines.

Dec. 25. *Christmas Day. First Mass.* Altar of the Holy Crib, in St. Mary Major. The same indulgence.

Second Mass. St. Anastasia. The same indulgence.

Third Mass and the rest of the day . St. Peter, on the Vatican, and St. Mary Major. Plenary indulgence, after Confession and Communion.

Dec. 26. *St. Stephen the First Martyr.* St. Stephen on the Celian Hill, commonly called the Round Church of St. Stephen. Indulgence of thirty years and thirty quarantines.

Dec. 27. *St. John the Apostle and Evangelist.* St. Mary Major. The same indulgence..

Dec. 28. *The Holy Innocents.* St. Paul, outside the Walls. The same indulgence.

---

147. VISIT TO THE SEVEN CHURCHES AND SEVEN PRIVILEGED ALTARS.

The custom of visiting the Seven principal churches in Rome is of most ancient institution:- They are as follows: St. Peter, on the Vatican; St. Paul, and St. Sebastian, outside the Walls; St. John Lateran; the Holy Cross in Jerusalem; St. Laurence, outside the Walls; and St. Mary Major. This devotion was introduced by the piety of our ancestors; and it has the authoritative approval of the Sovereign Pontiffs, as Sixtus V. observes in his Bull *Egregia Populi Romani Pietas*, Feb. 13, 1586, in which he speaks of the visit to the seven churches. It was almost the daily devotion of St. Joseph Calasactius, it was frequently practised by St. Philip Neri as well as by other Saints, and it is now in continual use with persons of every rank, not only those who dwell in Rome, but with strangers also, who come to Rome in order to venerate in these churches the relics deposited there, especially those of the holy apostles and martyrs. Whoever, having Confessed and Communicated, shall visit these seven churches after this pious custom, and pray there according to the intention of the Sovereign Pontiff, may gain the many indulgences, with which these churches have been enriched for every day in the year. See Several Bulls and Pontifical Briefs, the originals of which are to be found in the archives of these churches.

Most ancient also is the custom of visiting the seven privileged altars in these churches, but especially in St. Peter, on the Vatican; a record of this custom being found in the archives of this church as far back as the times of Pope Innocent II., who flourished in 1130. These seven altars in St. Peter's are -

1. The Altar of Our Lady, commonly called the "Gregoriana;"
2. Of SS. Processus and Martinianus;
3. Of St. Michael the Archangel;
4. Of St. Petronilla, Virgin;
5. Of Our Lady, commonly called "of the Pillar;"
6, Of the Holy Apostles St. Simon and St. Jude; and
7. Of St. Gregory the Great.

Any of the faithful who shall visit devoutly these seven altars with due dispositions, and (if intending to gain the plenary indulgence) having Confessed and Communicated, may obtain many indulgences granted by various Sovereign Pontiffs, and confirmed by St. Pius V., by Sixtus V., Paul V., Clement VIII,, and Urban VIII. This last Pope issued many Bulls in favour of the churches outside the walls, in which he grants to the seven altars of these churches the same Indulgences as are granted to the seven altars in St. Peter, on the Vatican.

148. FOR THE INDULGENCE COMMONLY CALLED "IL PERDONO," "THE PARDON."

The little church of Our Lady of the Angels, near Assisi, commonly called *Della Porziuncula,* from a villa near it, was given to St. Francis by the Benedictine monks. It was in this holy chapel, or rather little church, as it them was, that the seraphic father so urgently besought our Lord Jesus Christ that all the faithful who should visit it after Confession and Communion might obtain a Plenary Indulgence.

His prayers, made in union with the prayers of our Blessed Lady, were answered; and the Indulgence he had asked was granted by our Divine Lord, who ordered it to be confirmed by His Vicar Honorius III., at that time Sovereign Pontiff, who, having ascertained that such was the Divine pleasure, did, in the year 1223, confirm for ever this Plenary indulgence for the 2d of August, beginning with the First Vespers, the anniversary of the dedication of this church, which was afterwards magnificently enlarged and decorated with the title of Basilica. (1)

This Indulgence, commonly called the Indulgence of the Sacred Pardon, or of the *Sacro Perdono,* was afterwards extended by many Popes to all the churches of the three orders instituted by St. Francis, more particularly by Gregory XV, in a Bull, *Splendor Paternae Gloriae,* July 4, 1622, who prescribed Communion as well as Confession as a good work to be done for gaining this Indulgence.

The Venerable Innocent XI., by a brief of Jan. 22, 1689, confirming this Bull of Gregory XV., declared that this Indulgence might also be applied in suffrage for the holy souls in purgatory. (2)

The peculiarity of this Indulgence is, that it may be gained *toties quoties,* that is, as many times as it is visited, though on the same day; and this pious custom of visiting again and again many times the same chapel or church of the *Porziuncula*, or any other of the churches of the order of St. Francis, in order to gain this Indulgence in suffrage for the departed on each of these visits, has never been prohibited; (3) this has been twice decided by the S. Congr. of the Council - on July 17, 1700, and on Dec, 4, 1723;. (4) Nay more, when in the S. Congr. of Indulgences, held Feb. 22, 1847, the question was proposed, "Whether in visiting on the 2d of August churches of the order of St. Francis, the Plenary indulgence could be gained every time the visit was repeated;" the S. Congr. decided in the affirmative, and at the same time declared that the Holy Communion, requisite for the indulgence, need not be made in the Franciscan church. These declarations were all confirmed by the Sovereign Pontiff Pius IX., in a decree of the said S. Congr., July 12, 1847.

NOTES.

(1) Lections of the 2d Noct. for Aug. 2, in the Breviary and Martyrology of the Franciscan Order.

(2) See Lambertini (afterwards Benedict XIV.) as promoter of the faith, in the petitions concerning this Indulgence addressed to a special Congregation deputed for this purpose my Pope Clement XI., in the year 1700, § ii. no. 26.

(3) See the same author, in his Report to the S. Congr. of the Council, of which he was at that the secretary, in the year 1723, on the ancient custom *toties quoties* of the said Indulgence.

(4) Thesaurus of the Resolutions of the S. Congr. of the Council, vol. ii. Dec. 4, 1723, p. 398.

149. CHRISTIAN DOCTRINE. FOR TEACHING AND LEARNING IT.

On Sundays and other Festivals it is the duty of all parish priests, in their respective parishes, to teach children Christian doctrine (see *Council of Trent,* sess. xxiv. cap. iv. *De Reform.*): and all masters of schools are under the same obligations towards their scholars, and all fathers of families towards their children and domestics, &c. St. Pius V., in his Constitution *Ex debito pastoralis officii,* Oct. 6, 1571, calls this "a most holy work." "His work is the salvation of souls and the preservation of Christian commonwealths," says Paul V., in his Constitution *Ex credito nobis,* Oct. 6, 1607. For the same reason this Pope, besides erecting into an arch-confraternity, in the patriarchal basilica of St. Peter, a Congregation of Christian Doctrine, which was held there under the directions of the *Padri Dottrinarij,* or Fathers of Christian Doctrine, and endowing it with various privileges and indulgences communicable to similar confraternities aggregated to it in any diocese out of Rome, granted in the aforesaid Constitution, "in order to animate the faithful the more diligently to teach and to learn Christian Doctrine," the following Indulgence -

i. An indulgence of seven years and seven quarantines, to all masters of schools who, on feast-days, shall take their scholars to be instructed in Christian doctrine, or shall themselves instruct them in it; and to those masters who, on working days, explain Christian doctrine in their schools, 100 days indulgence.

ii. The indulgence of 100 days to fathers and mothers every time they instruct their children and domestics in Christian doctrine.

iii. An indulgence of 100 days to all the faithful every that they employ themselves for half an hour in teaching or learning Christian doctrine.

iv. An indulgence of three years, on all the feasts of the Blessed Virgin, to the faithful of every age who are accustomed to assemble in school or church to learn Christian doctrine, provided they confess on the said feasts; and an indulgence of seven years to those who, being of age to communicate, shall on those days receive the Blessed Sacrament.

v. An indulgence of seven years and seven quarantines was added to these Indulgences by Clement XII., by a Brief, June 27, 1732, to all the faithful every time that after Confession and Communion, they assist at catechism, or doctrinal teaching, or catechise, or teach doctrine.

vi. He granted also a plenary indulgence, after Confession and Communion, to those who have the pious custom of assisting at or teaching Christian doctrine, on the Feast of the Nativity of our Lord Jesus Christ, on Easter Day, and on the Feast of the Holy Apostles SS. Peter and Paul.

EXPLANATION OF THE GOSPEL.

150. EXPLANATION OF THE GOSPEL. FOR ASSISTING AT THE SAME.

Pope Benedict XIV., by a decree, July 31, 1736, of the S. Congr. of Indulgences. granted -

i. An indulgence of seven years and seven quarantines, to all the faithful every time they devoutly assist at the Explanation of the Gospel, which is made by the Parish Priests, in their respective parishes, on Sundays and the greater festivals of the year, according to the decrees of the holy Council of Trent. (Sess. v. *De Reform.* cap. ii., and sess. xxii. cap. viii.)

ii. A plenary indulgence on the Feast of the Nativity of our Lord Jesus Christ, on Easter Day, and on the Feast of time Holy Apostles SS. Peter and Paul, provided that on those days, after Confession and Communion, they also assist at the said Explanation.

At the prayer of the venerable College of the Parish Priests of Rome, Pius VI., by a Rescript of the S. Congr. of Indulgences, Dec. 12, 1784, (which is preserved in the *Segretaria* of the Vicariate), confirmed these indulgences, and granted also an additional plenary indulgence; on the Epiphany of our Lord, Jan. 6, and on Whit-Sunday, on the same conditions as above.

These Indulgences may likewise be gained by the Parish Priests themselves, or by others who from time to time supply their place in the Explanation of the Holy Gospel; as appears from the said decree.

WORKS OF MERCY.

151. VISITS TO THE SICK IN THE HOSPITALS.

By an Edict of his Eminence the Cardinal-Vicar, Feb. 28, 1778, regarding the spiritual and temporal assistance of the sick in the hospitals in Rome, Pope Pius VI. exhorts in an especial manner all ecclesiastics and congregations of seculars, and in general all the faithful, to frequent the hospitals, each one those of his or her own sex, instructing, consoling, and serving the sick, or ministering to them some restorative, medicine, &c.

and the more to animate the faithful to these charitable duties, he granted -

An indulgence of 100 days every time they do this good work.

152. FOR THE PIOUS HOUSE OF THE REFUGE.

Pius VII., by a Rescript of the *Segretaria* of the Memorials, Sept. 16, 1806, granted the following Indulgences to all the faithful who shall co-operate in the spiritual or temporal welfare of the pious house called the *Refuge*, erected in Rome in the same year 1806, near St. Mary, beyond the Tiber, solely for those women who, after the expiration of their sentences in the public gaol of St. Michael, desire of their own accord to enter this pious house, and to live there removed from dangerous occasions of sin, doing penance for their past transgressions.

i. A plenary indulgence on the day on which, after Confession and Communion, they are enrolled as Deputies or Benefactors.

ii. A plenary indulgence on the Feast of St. John, Evan., Dec. 27; provided that, after Confession and Communion, they visit the church of St. John *in Ayno*, now *in S. Nicola degli Incoronati*, where the divine offices are celebrated by the directors of the said pious house of "the Refuge."

iii. A plenary indulgence *in articulo mortis*, if, being penitent, they invoke with contrite hearts the most holy Names of Jesus and Mary.

iv. An indulgence of 200 days, to those who themselves shall give, or in any other way make it their care that spiritual or corporal assistance is given to these poor penitent women.

v. An indulgence of sixty days, to those who shall give bread to these poor women, or alms to this pious house, as well as every time they shall prevail on others to give, or in any other way contribute to the support of the house.

vi. An indulgence of sixty days every time they give alms to settle them in honourable marriage, or in a cloistered monastery.

vii. An indulgence of 100 days every time they shall assist at, or, if priests, say Mass on the anniversaries, or recite the office for the deputies or benefactors deceased.

viii. Finally, those who are deputies or benefactors shall during life share in all the prayers, works of piety, &c., which shall be done by these women; and at the death of each deputy or benefactor three Masses shall be celebrated for his soul, provided that this charity of his shall have been persevered in up to the moment of his death.

153. ALMSGIVING IN HONOUR OF JESUS, MARY AND JOSEPH.

Pope Pius VII., by a Rescript of June 13, 1815, of the S. Congr. of Indulgences, confirmed the following Indulgences previously granted to any one who shall feed three poor persons in memory of, and to the special honour of Jesus, Mary, and Joseph -

i. An indulgence of seven years and seven quarantines every time he does this with a heart penitent for its sins.

ii. A plenary indulgence, if on the same day, after Confession and Communion, he shall pray according to the intention of the Sovereign Pontiff.

iii. An indulgence of 100 days to all the members of the family, or domestics of him, by whom this charitable work is done, as well as to all who shall contribute to this work of mercy, whether by lending their own services, or by their mere presence.

Thus Rescript is kept in the *Segretaria* of the Tribunal of his Eminence the Cardinal-Vicar, and an authentic copy ins the Archivium of the Pious Union of St. Paul, elsewhere named.

TIMES OF CALAMITY.

154. TIMES OF CALAMITY.

The following prayers and ejaculations are suggested to the faithful, that they may thereby have recourse to God to vouchsafe to free them, through the Passion of Jesus Christ, and through the intercessions of most holy Mary, from any scourge which they have too justly deserved for their sins; and to all who say them with a contrite heart and with devotion, Pope Gregory XIV., of holy memory, by a Rescript of the S. Congr. of Indulgences, Aug. 21, 1837, granted -

An indulgence of forty days, once a day.

PRAYERS AND EJACULATIONS.

Mercy of our God, encompass us, and deliver us from every plague.

Gloria Patri, &c.

Eternal Father, sign us with the Blood of the Immaculate Lamb, its Thou didst sign the dwellings of Thy people.

Gloria Patri, &c.

Most precious Blood of Jesus our Love, cry for mercy for us from Thy Divine Father, and deliver us.

Gloria Patri, &c.

Wounds of my Jesus, mouths of love and mercy, speak for us, in pity, to the Eternal Father; hide us within yourselves, and deliver us.

Gloria Patri, &c.

Eternal Father, Jesus is ours; ours His Blood, ours His infinite Merits; to Thee we offer ourselves wholly: then if Thou lovest Him, and holdest precious this gift we make Thee, Thou oughtest to deliver us; and for this we hope with fullest confidence.

Gloria Patri, &c.

Eternal Father, Thou desirest not the death of a sinner, but rather that he should be converted and live: in Thy mercy grant that we may live before Thee and be ever Thine.

Gloria Patri, &c.

Salva nos, Christe Salvator, per virtutem sanctae crucis; qui salvasti Petrum in mari, miserere nobis.

Save us, Christ our Saviour, by the virtue of Thy holy cross; Thou who didst save Peter in the sea, have mercy upon us.

Mary, Mother of mercy, pray for us, and we shall be delivered; Mary, our advocate, speak for us, and we shall be saved.

The Lord justly scourgeth us for our sins; but do thou, Mary, plead for us, for thou art our most tender Mother.

Mary, in thy Jesus, and in thee, have we put our hope; O, let us never be confounded.

Salve Regina, &c.

155. FOR TROUBLED TIMES.

His Holiness Pope Pius IX., by an Autograph Rescript, kept in the *Segretaria* of the S. Congr. of Indulgences, of April 6, 1848, grants -

i. The indulgence of seven years and seven quarantines, to all the faithful every time they say the following prayers with devotion, or make the accompanying pious intention and offering, especially in times of trouble and of the merited chastisement of Christ.

ii. The plenary indulgence, once a month, to those who shall have said them

272

once a day for a month together; to be gained on that day when, after having Confessed and Communicated, they shall pray according to the mind of his Holiness.

PRAYERS.

Respice, Domine, sancte Pater, de sanctuario tuo et de excelso coelorum habitaculum, et vide hanc sacrosanctam Hostiam, quam tibi offert Magnus Pontifex noster sanctus, innocens, dilectus Filius tuus Dominus noster Jesus Christus pro peccatis fratrum suorum, et esto placabilis super multitudinem malitiae mundi. Ecce vox sanguinis fratris nostri Primogeniti Jesu clamat ad te de cruce. Exaudi Domine, placare Domine, attende, et fac; ne moreris propter temetipsum, Deus noster, quia nomen tuum invocatum est super domum et civitatem istam, et super universum populum tuum, et fac nobiscum secundum infinitam misericordiam tuam. Per eundem Christum Dominum nostrum. Amen.

V. Ut ad veram poenitentiam nos perducere digneris.
R. Te rogamus audi nos.
V. Ut domum, civitatem istam, et universum populum tuum, Domine, defendere, pacificare, custodire, conservare, et piissima misericordia tua respicere digeris,
R. Te rogamus audi nos.
V. Per sacrosancta humanae redemptionis Mysteria,
R. Cito anticipent nos, Domine, misericordiae tuae, et parce populo tuo.
V. Per merita, et intercessionem Beatissimae Genitricis tuae, et omnium Angelorum atque Sanctorum,
R. Cito anticipent nos, Domine, misericordiae tuae, et parce populo tuo.
V. Sancta Maria sine labe originali concepta, et omnes Angeli et Sancti, intercedite pro nobis ad Dominum,
R. Ut cito anticipent nos misericordiae Dornini, et parcat populo suo; ut omnes cum ipso gaudere possimus in saecula saeculorum. Amen.

Oremus.
Omnipotens et misericors Deus, fiat semper et in omnibus sanctissima voluntas tua secundum infinitam et aeternam misericordiam tuam. Per Christum Dominum nostrum. Amen.

TRANSLATION. *

Look down, O Lord, from Thy sanctuary, and from Heaven Thy dwelling-place on high, and behold this sacred Victim which our great High-Priest, Thy holy Child, our Lord Jesus, offers up to Thee for the sins of This brethren; and be appeased for the multitude of our transgressions. Behold the voice of the Blood of Jesus, our Brother, cries to Thee from the Cross. Give ear, O Lord! be appeased, O Lord! hearken, and do not tarry for Thine own sake, O my God, for Thy Name is invoked upon this city and upon Thy people; and deal with us according to Thy mercy. Amen.

V. That Thou wouldst vouchsafe to bring us to true penance,
R. We beseech Thee, hear us.
V. That Thou wouldst vouchsafe to defend this house and city, and all Thy people, to keep them in peace, to guard, preserve, and look down on them with Thy most tender pity,
R. We beseech Thee, hear us.
V. Through the holy Mysteries of the redemption of man.
R. Let Thy mercies come quickly to aid us, O Lord, and spare Thy people.
V. Through the merit and intercession of Thy most blessed Mother, and all the angels and saints.
R. Let Thy mercies come quickly to aid us, O Lord, and spare Thy people.
V. Holy Mary, conceived without original sin, and all ye Angels and Saints, intercede for us to our Lord.
R. That the mercies of our Lord may come quickly to aid us, and that He may spare His people; that so we all may rejoice with Him for ever and ever. Amen.

Let us pray.
Almighty and merciful God, may Thy most holy will be done, at all times and in all things, according to Thine infinite and eternal mercy. Through Christ our Lord. Amen.

* See also above, the same prayer with Notice of the Indulgence annexed to it.

DEVOUT INTENTION AND OFFERING.

Eternal Father, in union with all the heavenly host, and with the Hearts of Jesus and of Mary, I desire that from all eternity, and for eternity, the most Precious Blood of Jesus Christ, his infinite merits, and the merits of His Church be offered to Thee, in discharge of our debt of sin, of the sin of the whole world, for the deliverance of the holy souls in purgatory, and in thanksgiving, first, that Thou hast granted to us, and to all who are at present in this world, and wilt grant to all who shall hereafter be born, such gifts, graces, and mercies as redound to Thine own greater glory and the greater sanctification of all souls in these present tribulations, justly deserved as Thy chastisements; and, secondly, that Thou hast formed of the whole world one Fold and one Shepherd, that all who on earth live in the faith, hope, and charity of our Lord Jesus Christ may meet together in heaven, to sing Thy divine mercies for ever and ever. Amen.

156. ANOTHER PRAYER IN ANY PLAGUE OR TROUBLE.

In order that the faithful may with the greater fervour address their humble supplications to God, and by the invocation of His holy Name may mercifully be delivered from the scourge of His divine wrath, as well as from every other trouble, our holy Father Pope Pius IX., by a decree of Nov. 8, 1849, dated from Portici in the kingdom of Naples, granted -
The indulgence of 100 days every time the following prayer is said with contrite heart and devotion.

THE PRAYER.

Adjuva nos, Deus salutaris nostri, et propter gloriam nominis tui libera nos; et propitius esto peccatis nostris propter nomen tuum.

Ps. 53.

Deus, in nomine tuo salvum me fac: * et in virtute tua judica me
Deus, exaudi orationem meam: * auribus percipe verba oris mei.
Quoniam alieni insurrexerunt adversum me, et fortes quaesierunt animam meam: * et non proposuerunt Deum ante conspectum suum.
Ecce enim Deus adjuvat me: * et Dominus susceptor est animae meae.
Averte mala inimicis meis: * et in veritate tua disperde illos.
Voluntarie sacrificabo tibi: et confitebor nomini tuo, Domine, quoniam bonum est.
Quoniam ex omni tribulatione eripuisti me: * et super inimicos meos despexit oculus meus.
Gloria Patri, et Filio: * et Spiritui Sancto.
Sicut erat in principio, et nunc, et semper: * et in saecula saeculorum. Amen.

V. Propter gloriam nominis tui libera nos.
P. Et propitius esto peceatis nostris propter nomen tuum.

Oremus.
Preces populi tui, quaesumus, Domine, clementer exaudi: ut qui juste pro peecatis nostris affligimur, pro gloria nominis tui misericorditer liberemur. Per Christum Dominum nostrum. R. Amen.

To ergo quaesumus tuis famulis subveni, quos Pretioso Sanguine redemisti.

TRANSLATION.

Help us, O God of our salvation, and for the glory of Thy Name deliver us: be merciful to our sins for Thy Name's sake.

Ps. 53.

Save me, O Lord, in Thy Name; and judge me in Thy strength.

O God, hear my prayer; give ear to the words of my mouth

For strangers have risen up against me, and the mighty have sought after my soul, and they have not set God before their eyes.

For behold, God is my helper, and the Lord is the protector of my soul.

Turn away evil from me upon my enemies, and scatter them in Thy truth.

I will freely sacrifice to Thee; and will give praise, O God, to Thy Name, because it is good.

For Thou hast delivered me out of all my trouble, and mine eye hath looked down upon mine enemies.

Glory be to the Father, &c.

V. For the glory of Thy Name, deliver us.

R. And deal mercifully with our sins for Thy Name's sake.

Let us pray.

Lord, we beseech Thee, in Thy pity hear the prayers of Thy people; that we who suffer justly for our sins, may for the glory of Thy Name mercifully be delivered. Through Christ our Lord. R. Amen.

We beseech Thee, therefore, help Thy servants, whom Thou hast redeemed with Thy Precious Blood.

---

157. PRAYER TO OBTAIN A GRACE AND THE MERCY OF GOD IN EVERY NECESSITY, PLAGUE, AND TROUBLE.

The Sovereign Pontiff Pius IX., by a Rescript of his Reverence the Cardinal-Vicar of August 5, 1854, kept in the Archivium of the Venerable Congregation of Missionaries of the Most Precious Blood in Rome, granted to the faithful - The indulgence of 100 days every time that, with contrite hearts and devotion, they say the following prayer so efficaciously worded by the Venerable Benedict Joseph Labrè.

THE PRAYER.

Jesus Christus, Rex gloriae, venit in pace.
Deus homo factus est.
Verbum caro factum est.
Christus de Maria Virgine natus est.
Christus per medium illorum ibat in pace.
Christus crucifixus est.
Christus mortuus est.
Christus sepultus est.
Christus resurrexit.

Christus ascendit in coelum.
Christus vincit.
Christus regnat.
Christus imperat.
Christus ab omni malo nos defendat.
Jesus nobiscum est.

Pater, Ave, *and* Gloria.

TRANSLATION.

Jesus Christ, the King of Glory, hath come in peace.
God was made man.
The Word was made flesh.
Christ was born of Mary the Virgin.
Christ went through the midst of them in peace.
Christ was crucified.
Christ died.
Christ was buried.
Christ rose from the dead.
Christ ascended into heaven.
Christ is victorious.
Christ reigns.
Christ is Lord of all.
May Christ defend us from all evil.
Jesus is with us.

Pater, Ave, *and* Gloria.

Eternal Father, by the Blood of Jesus have mercy; sign us with the Blood of the Immaculate Lamb Jesus Christ, as Thou didst sign the people of Israel, in order to deliver them from death: and do thou, Mary, Mother of mercy, pray to God and appease him for us, and obtain for us the grace we ask.
Gloria Patri, &c.

Eternal Father, by the Blood of Jesus have mercy; save us from the shipwreck of the world, as Thou didst save Noe from the universal deluge: and do thou, Mary, Ark of salvation, pray to God and appease Him for us, and obtain for us the grace we ask.
Gloria Patri, &c.

Eternal Father, by the Blood of Jesus have mercy; deliver us from the plagues which we have deserved for our sins, as Thou didst deliver Lot from the flames of Sodom: and do thou, Mary, our Advocate, pray to God and appease Him for us, and obtain for us the grace we ask.
Gloria Patri, &c.

Eternal Father, by the Blood of Jesus have mercy; comfort us under our present necessities and troubles, as Thou didst comfort Job, Anna, and Tobias in their afflictions: and do thou, Mary, Comforter of the afflicted, pray to God and appease Him for us, and obtain for us the grace we ask.
Gloria Patri, &c.

Eternal Father, by the Blood of Jesus have mercy; Thou who wouldest not the death of a sinner, but rather that he should be converted and live, grant us through Thy mercy time for penance; that, filled with contrition and penance for our sins, which are the cause of all our evils, we may live in the holy faith, hope, charity, and peace of our Lord Jesus Christ: and do thou, Mary, Refuge of sinners, pray to God and appease Him for us, and obtain for us the grace we ask.
Gloria Patri, &c.

Precious Blood of Jesus, our Love, cry unto the Diviue Father for mercy, pardon, grace, and peace for , sfor N., and for all the world.
Gloria Patri, &c.

Mary, our Mother and our Hope, pray to God for us, for N., and for all, and obtain for us the grace we ask.
Gloria Patri, &c.

Eternal Father, I offer Thee the Blood of Jesus Christ in discharge of all my debt of sin, for the wants of Holy Church, and for the conversion of sinners.
Gloria Patri, &c.

Mary Immaculate, Mother of God, pray to Jesus for us, for N., and for all.
Jesu, Mary, mercy!
St. Michael Archangel, St. Joseph, SS. Peter and Paul, protectors of all the faithful in the Church of God, and all ye Angels and Saints of Paradise, men and women, pray to God, and by your intercession obtain grace and mercy for us, for N., and for all. Amen.

158. TO IMPLORE PEACE.

The same Sovereign Pontiff Pius IX., by a decree of the S. Congr. of Indulgences of May 18 and Sept. 18,1848, grants -
i. The indulgence of 100 days, to all the faithful, every time that with contrite hearts they say the following Antiphon and Prayer to implore peace from God.
ii. The plenary indulgence to those who shall have said it once a day for a whole month; to be gained on the day when, having Confessed and Communicated, they shall visit a public church, and pray there for a time according to the mind of his Holiness.

Ant. Da pacem, Domine, in diebus nostris: quia non est alius qui pugnet pro nobis, nisi tu Deus noster.

V. Fiat pax in virtute tua,
R. Et abundantia in turribus tuis.

Oremus.
Deus, a quo sancta desideria, recta consilia, et justa sunt opera: da servis tuis illam, quam mundus dare non potest, pacem: ut et corda nostra mandatis tuis dedita, et hostium sublata formidine, tempora sint tua protectione tranquilla. Per Christum Dominum nostrum. Amen.

TRANSLATION.

Ant. Give peace, O Lord, in our days; for there is none other to fight for us, but only Thou, our God.

V. Let peace be in Thy strength, O Lord,
R. And plenty in Thy strong places.

Let us pray.
O God, from whom proceed all holy desires, all right counsels and just works; grant unto us Thy servants that peace which the world cannot give, that our hearts may be devoted to Thy commands, and that, being delivered from the fear of our enemies, we may pass our time in peace under Thy protection. Through Christ our Lord. Amen.

TIMES OF CALAMITY.

154. TIMES OF CALAMITY.

The following prayers and ejaculations are suggested to the faithful, that they may thereby have recourse to God to vouchsafe to free them, through the Passion of Jesus Christ, and through the intercessions of most holy Mary, from any scourge which they have too justly deserved for their sins; and to all who say them with a contrite heart and with devotion, Pope Gregory XIV., of holy memory, by a Rescript of the S. Congr. of Indulgences, Aug. 21, 1837, granted -

An indulgence of forty days, once a day.

PRAYERS AND EJACULATIONS.

Mercy of our God, encompass us, and deliver us from every plague.
Gloria Patri, &c.
Eternal Father, sign us with the Blood of the Immaculate Lamb, its Thou didst sign the dwellings of Thy people.
Gloria Patri, &c.
Most precious Blood of Jesus our Love, cry for mercy for us from Thy Divine Father, and deliver us.
Gloria Patri, &c.
Wounds of my Jesus, mouths of love and mercy, speak for us, in pity, to the Eternal Father; hide us within yourselves, and deliver us.
Gloria Patri, &c.
Eternal Father, Jesus is ours; ours His Blood, ours His infinite Merits; to Thee we offer ourselves wholly: then if Thou lovest Him, and holdest precious this gift we make Thee, Thou oughtest to deliver us; and for this we hope with fullest confidence.
Gloria Patri, &c.
Eternal Father, Thou desirest not the death of a sinner, but rather that he should be converted and live: in Thy mercy grant that we may live before Thee and be ever Thine.
Gloria Patri, &c.
Salva nos, Christe Salvator, per virtutem sanctae crucis; qui salvasti Petrum in mari, miserere nobis.
Save us, Christ our Saviour, by the virtue of Thy holy cross; Thou who didst save Peter in the sea, have mercy upon us.
Mary, Mother of mercy, pray for us, and we shall be delivered; Mary, our advocate, speak for us, and we shall be saved.
The Lord justly scourgeth us for our sins; but do thou, Mary, plead for us, for thou art our most tender Mother.
Mary, in thy Jesus, and in thee, have we put our hope; O, let us never be confounded.
Salve Regina, &c.

155. FOR TROUBLED TIMES.

His Holiness Pope Pius IX., by an Autograph Rescript, kept in the *Segretaria* of the S. Congr. of Indulgences, of April 6, 1848, grants -

i. The indulgence of seven years and seven quarantines, to all the faithful every time they say the following prayers with devotion, or make the accompanying pious intention and offering, especially in times of trouble and of the merited chastisement of Christ.

ii. The plenary indulgence, once a month, to those who shall have said them once a day for a month together; to be gained on that day when, after having Confessed and Communicated, they shall pray according to the mind of his Holiness.

PRAYERS.

Respice, Domine, sancte Pater, de sanctuario tuo et de excelso coelorum habitaculum, et vide hanc sacrosanctam Hostiam, quam tibi offert Magnus Pontifex noster sanctus, innocens, dilectus Filius tuus Dominus noster Jesus Christus pro peccatis fratrum suorum, et esto placabilis super multitudinem malitiae mundi. Ecce vox sanguinis fratris nostri Primogeniti Jesu clamat ad te de cruce. Exaudi Domine, placare Domine, attende, et fac; ne moreris propter temetipsum, Deus noster, quia nomen tuum invocatum est super domum et civitatem istam, et super universum populum tuum, et fac nobiscum secundum infinitam misericordiam tuam. Per eundem Christum Dominum nostrum. Amen.

V. Ut ad veram poenitentiam nos perducere digneris.
R. Te rogamus audi nos.
V. Ut domum, civitatem istam, et universum populum tuum, Domine, defendere, pacificare, custodire, conservare, et piissima misericordia tua respicere digeris,
R. Te rogamus audi nos.
V. Per sacrosancta humanae redemptionis Mysteria,
R. Cito anticipent nos, Domine, misericordiae tuae, et parce populo tuo.
V. Per merita, et intercessionem Beatissimae Genitricis tuae, et omnium Angelorum atque Sanctorum,
R. Cito anticipent nos, Domine, misericordiae tuae, et parce populo tuo.
V. Sancta Maria sine labe originali concepta, et omnes Angeli et Sancti, intercedite pro nobis ad Dominum,
R. Ut cito anticipent nos misericordiae Dornini, et parcat populo suo; ut omnes cum ipso gaudere possimus in saecula saeculorum. Amen.

Oremus.
Omnipotens et misericors Deus, fiat semper et in omnibus sanctissima voluntas tua secundum infinitam et aeternam misericordiam tuam. Per Christum Dominum nostrum. Amen.

TRANSLATION. *

Look down, O Lord, from Thy sanctuary, and from Heaven Thy dwelling-place on high, and behold this sacred Victim which our great High-Priest, Thy holy Child, our Lord Jesus, offers up to Thee for the sins of This brethren; and be appeased for the multitude of our transgressions. Behold the voice of the Blood of Jesus, our Brother, cries to Thee from the Cross. Give ear, O Lord! be appeased, O Lord! hearken, and do not tarry for Thine own sake, O my God, for Thy Name is invoked upon this city and upon Thy people; and deal with us according to Thy mercy. Amen.

V. That Thou wouldst vouchsafe to bring us to true penance,
R. We beseech Thee, hear us.
V. That Thou wouldst vouchsafe to defend this house and city, and all Thy people, to keep them in peace, to guard, preserve, and look down on them with Thy most tender pity,
R. We beseech Thee, hear us.
V. Through the holy Mysteries of the redemption of man.
R. Let Thy mercies come quickly to aid us, O Lord, and spare Thy people.
V. Through the merit and intercession of Thy most blessed Mother, and all the angels and saints.
R. Let Thy mercies come quickly to aid us, O Lord, and spare Thy people.
V. Holy Mary, conceived without original sin, and all ye Angels and Saints, intercede for us to our Lord.
R. That the mercies of our Lord may come quickly to aid us, and that He may spare His people; that so we all may rejoice with Him for ever and ever. Amen.

Let us pray.
Almighty and merciful God, may Thy most holy will be done, at all times and in all things, according to Thine infinite and eternal mercy. Through Christ our Lord. Amen.

* See also above, the same prayer with Notice of the Indulgence annexed to it.

DEVOUT INTENTION AND OFFERING.

Eternal Father, in union with all the heavenly host, and with the Hearts of Jesus and of Mary, I desire that from all eternity, and for eternity, the most Precious Blood of Jesus Christ, his infinite merits, and the merits of His Church be offered to Thee, in discharge of our debt of sin, of the sin of the whole world, for the deliverance of the holy souls in purgatory, and in thanksgiving, first, that Thou hast granted to us, and to all who are at present in this world, and wilt grant to all who shall hereafter be born, such gifts, graces, and mercies as redound to Thine own greater glory and the greater sanctification of all souls in these present tribulations, justly deserved as Thy chastisements; and, secondly, that Thou hast formed of the whole world one Fold and one Shepherd, that all who on earth live in the faith, hope, and charity of our Lord Jesus Christ may meet together in heaven, to sing Thy divine mercies for ever and ever. Amen.

156. ANOTHER PRAYER IN ANY PLAGUE OR TROUBLE.

In order that the faithful may with the greater fervour address their humble supplications to God, and by the invocation of His holy Name may mercifully be delivered from the scourge of His divine wrath, as well as from every other trouble, our holy Father Pope Pius IX., by a decree of Nov. 8, 1849, dated from Portici in the kingdom of Naples, granted -
The indulgence of 100 days every time the following prayer is said with contrite heart and devotion.

THE PRAYER.

Adjuva nos, Deus salutaris nostri, et propter gloriam nominis tui libera nos; et propitius esto peccatis nostris propter nomen tuum.

Ps. 53.

Deus, in nomine tuo salvum me fac: * et in virtute tua judica me
Deus, exaudi orationem meam: * auribus percipe verba oris mei.
Quoniam alieni insurrexerunt adversum me, et fortes quaesierunt animam meam: * et non proposuerunt Deum ante conspectum suum.
Ecce enim Deus adjuvat me: * et Dominus susceptor est animae meae.
Averte mala inimicis meis: * et in veritate tua disperde illos.
Voluntarie sacrificabo tibi: et confitebor nomini tuo, Domine, quoniam bonum est.
Quoniam ex omni tribulatione eripuisti me: * et super inimicos meos despexit oculus meus.
Gloria Patri, et Filio: * et Spiritui Sancto.
Sicut erat in principio, et nunc, et semper: * et in saecula saeculorum. Amen.

V. Propter gloriam nominis tui libera nos.
P. Et propitius esto peceatis nostris propter nomen tuum.

Oremus.
Preces populi tui, quaesumus, Domine, clementer exaudi: ut qui juste pro peecatis nostris affligimur, pro gloria nominis tui misericorditer liberemur. Per Christum Dominum nostrum. R. Amen.

To ergo quaesumus tuis famulis subveni, quos Pretioso Sanguine redemisti.

TRANSLATION.

Help us, O God of our salvation, and for the glory of Thy Name deliver us: be merciful to our sins for Thy Name's sake.

Ps. 53.

Save me, O Lord, in Thy Name; and judge me in Thy strength.
O God, hear my prayer; give ear to the words of my mouth
For strangers have risen up against me, and the mighty have sought after my soul, and they have not set God before their eyes.
For behold, God is my helper, and the Lord is the protector of my soul.
Turn away evil from me upon my enemies, and scatter them in Thy truth.
I will freely sacrifice to Thee; and will give praise, O God, to Thy Name, because it is good.
For Thou hast delivered me out of all my trouble, and mine eye hath looked down upon mine enemies.
Glory be to the Father, &c.

V. For the glory of Thy Name, deliver us.
R. And deal mercifully with our sins for Thy Name's sake.

Let us pray.
Lord, we beseech Thee, in Thy pity hear the prayers of Thy people; that we who suffer justly for our sins, may for the glory of Thy Name mercifully be delivered. Through Christ our Lord. R. Amen.

We beseech Thee, therefore, help Thy servants, whom Thou hast redeemed with Thy Precious Blood.

157. PRAYER TO OBTAIN A GRACE AND THE MERCY OF GOD IN EVERY NECESSITY, PLAGUE, AND TROUBLE.

The Sovereign Pontiff Pius IX., by a Rescript of his Reverence the Cardinal-Vicar of August 5, 1854, kept in the Archivium of the Venerable Congregation of Missionaries of the Most Precious Blood in Rome, granted to the faithful - The indulgence of 100 days every time that, with contrite hearts and devotion, they say the following prayer so efficaciously worded by the Venerable Benedict Joseph Labrè.

THE PRAYER.

Jesus Christus, Rex gloriae, venit in pace.
Deus homo factus est.
Verbum caro factum est.
Christus de Maria Virgine natus est.
Christus per medium illorum ibat in pace.

Christus crucifixus est.
Christus mortuus est.
Christus sepultus est.
Christus resurrexit.
Christus ascendit in coelum.
Christus vincit.
Christus regnat.
Christus imperat.
Christus ab omni malo nos defendat.
Jesus nobiscum est.

Pater, Ave, *and* Gloria.

TRANSLATION.

Jesus Christ, the King of Glory, hath come in peace.
God was made man.
The Word was made flesh.
Christ was born of Mary the Virgin.
Christ went through the midst of them in peace.
Christ was crucified.
Christ died.
Christ was buried.
Christ rose from the dead.
Christ ascended into heaven.
Christ is victorious.
Christ reigns.
Christ is Lord of all.
May Christ defend us from all evil.
Jesus is with us.

Pater, Ave, *and* Gloria.

Eternal Father, by the Blood of Jesus have mercy; sign us with the Blood of the Immaculate Lamb Jesus Christ, as Thou didst sign the people of Israel, in order to deliver them from death: and do thou, Mary, Mother of mercy, pray to God and appease him for us, and obtain for us the grace we ask.
Gloria Patri, &c.

Eternal Father, by the Blood of Jesus have mercy; save us from the shipwreck of the world, as Thou didst save Noe from the universal deluge: and do thou, Mary, Ark of salvation, pray to God and appease Him for us, and obtain for us the grace we ask.
Gloria Patri, &c.

Eternal Father, by the Blood of Jesus have mercy; deliver us from the plagues which we have deserved for our sins, as Thou didst deliver Lot from the flames of Sodom: and do thou, Mary, our Advocate, pray to God and appease Him for us, and obtain for us the grace we ask.
Gloria Patri, &c.

Eternal Father, by the Blood of Jesus have mercy; comfort us under our present necessities and troubles, as Thou didst comfort Job, Anna, and Tobias in their afflictions: and do thou, Mary, Comforter of the afflicted, pray to God and appease Him for us, and obtain for us the grace we ask.
Gloria Patri, &c.

Eternal Father, by the Blood of Jesus have mercy; Thou who wouldest not the death of a sinner, but rather that he should be converted and live, grant us through Thy mercy time for penance; that, filled with contrition and penance for our sins, which are the cause of all our evils, we may live in the holy faith, hope, charity, and peace of our Lord Jesus Christ: and do thou, Mary, Refuge of sinners, pray to God and appease Him for us, and obtain for us the grace we ask.
Gloria Patri, &c.

Precious Blood of Jesus, our Love, cry unto the Diviue Father for mercy, pardon, grace, and peace for , sfor N., and for all the world.
Gloria Patri, &c.

Mary, our Mother and our Hope, pray to God for us, for N., and for all, and obtain for us the grace we ask.
Gloria Patri, &c.

Eternal Father, I offer Thee the Blood of Jesus Christ in discharge of all my debt of sin, for the wants of Holy Church, and for the conversion of sinners.
Gloria Patri, &c.

Mary Immaculate, Mother of God, pray to Jesus for us, for N., and for all.
Jesu, Mary, mercy!
St. Michael Archangel, St. Joseph, SS. Peter and Paul, protectors of all the faithful in the Church of God, and all ye Angels and Saints of Paradise, men and women, pray to God, and by your intercession obtain grace and mercy for us, for N., and for all. Amen.

158. TO IMPLORE PEACE.

The same Sovereign Pontiff Pius IX., by a decree of the S. Congr. of Indulgences of May 18 and Sept. 18,1848, grants -

i. The indulgence of 100 days, to all the faithful, every time that with contrite hearts they say the following Antiphon and Prayer to implore peace from God. ii. The plenary indulgence to those who shall have said it once a day for a whole month; to be gained on the day when, having Confessed and Communicated, they shall visit a public church, and pray there for a time according to the mind of his Holiness.

Ant. Da pacem, Domine, in diebus nostris: quia non est alius qui pugnet pro nobis, nisi tu Deus noster.

V. Fiat pax in virtute tua,
R. Et abundantia in turribus tuis.

Oremus.
Deus, a quo sancta desideria, recta consilia, et justa sunt opera: da servis tuis illam, quam mundus dare non potest, pacem: ut et corda nostra mandatis tuis dedita, et hostium sublata formidine, tempora sint tua protectione tranquilla. Per Christum Dominum nostrum. Amen.

TRANSLATION.

Ant. Give peace, O Lord, in our days; for there is none other to fight for us, but only Thou, our God.

V. Let peace be in Thy strength, O Lord,
R. And plenty in Thy strong places.

Let us pray.
O God, from whom proceed all holy desires, all right counsels and just works; grant unto us Thy servants that peace which the world cannot give, that our hearts may be devoted to Thy commands, and that, being delivered from the fear of our enemies, we may pass our time in peace under Thy protection. Through Christ our Lord. Amen.

154. TIMES OF CALAMITY.

The following prayers and ejaculations are suggested to the faithful, that they may thereby have recourse to God to vouchsafe to free them, through the Passion of Jesus Christ, and through the intercessions of most holy Mary, from any scourge which they have too justly deserved for their sins; and to all who say them with a contrite heart and with devotion, Pope Gregory XIV., of holy memory, by a Rescript of the S. Congr. of Indulgences, Aug. 21, 1837, granted -

An indulgence of forty days, once a day.

PRAYERS AND EJACULATIONS.

Mercy of our God, encompass us, and deliver us from every plague.
Gloria Patri, &c.
Eternal Father, sign us with the Blood of the Immaculate Lamb, its Thou didst sign the dwellings of Thy people.
Gloria Patri, &c.
Most precious Blood of Jesus our Love, cry for mercy for us from Thy Divine Father, and deliver us.
Gloria Patri, &c.
Wounds of my Jesus, mouths of love and mercy, speak for us, in pity, to the Eternal Father; hide us within yourselves, and deliver us.
Gloria Patri, &c.
Eternal Father, Jesus is ours; ours His Blood, ours His infinite Merits; to Thee we offer ourselves wholly: then if Thou lovest Him, and holdest precious this gift we make Thee, Thou oughtest to deliver us; and for this we hope with fullest confidence.
Gloria Patri, &c.
Eternal Father, Thou desirest not the death of a sinner, but rather that he should be converted and live: in Thy mercy grant that we may live before Thee and be ever Thine.
Gloria Patri, &c.
Salva nos, Christe Salvator, per virtutem sanctae crucis; qui salvasti Petrum in mari, miserere nobis.
Save us, Christ our Saviour, by the virtue of Thy holy cross; Thou who didst save Peter in the sea, have mercy upon us.
Mary, Mother of mercy, pray for us, and we shall be delivered; Mary, our advocate, speak for us, and we shall be saved.
The Lord justly scourgeth us for our sins; but do thou, Mary, plead for us, for

thou art our most tender Mother.

Mary, in thy Jesus, and in thee, have we put our hope; O, let us never be confounded.

Salve Regina, &c.

---

155. FOR TROUBLED TIMES.

His Holiness Pope Pius IX., by an Autograph Rescript, kept in the *Segretaria* of the S. Congr. of Indulgences, of April 6, 1848, grants -

i. The indulgence of seven years and seven quarantines, to all the faithful every time they say the following prayers with devotion, or make the accompanying pious intention and offering, especially in times of trouble and of the merited chastisement of Christ.

ii. The plenary indulgence, once a month, to those who shall have said them once a day for a month together; to be gained on that day when, after having Confessed and Communicated, they shall pray according to the mind of his Holiness.

PRAYERS.

Respice, Domine, sancte Pater, de sanctuario tuo et de excelso coelorum habitaculum, et vide hanc sacrosanctam Hostiam, quam tibi offert Magnus Pontifex noster sanctus, innocens, dilectus Filus tuus Dominus noster Jesus Christus pro peccatis fratrum suorum, et esto placabilis super multitudinem malitiae mundi. Ecce vox sanguinis fratris nostri Primogeniti Jesu clamat ad te de cruce. Exaudi Domine, placare Domine, attende, et fac; ne moreris propter temetipsum, Deus noster, quia nomen tuum invocatum est super domum et civitatem istam, et super universum populum tuum, et fac nobiscum secundum infinitam misericordiam tuam. Per eundem Christum Dominum nostrum. Amen.

V. Ut ad veram poenitentiam nos perducere digneris.

R. Te rogamus audi nos.

V. Ut domum, civitatem istam, et universum populum tuum, Domine, defendere, pacificare, custodire, conservare, et piissima misericordia tua respicere digeris,

R. Te rogamus audi nos.

V. Per sacrosancta humanae redemptionis Mysteria,

R. Cito anticipent nos, Domine, misericordiae tuae, et parce populo tuo.

V. Per merita, et intercessionem Beatissimae Genitricis tuae, et omnium Angelorum atque Sanctorum,

R. Cito anticipent nos, Domine, misericordiae tuae, et parce populo tuo.

V. Sancta Maria sine labe originali concepta, et omnes Angeli et Sancti, intercedite pro nobis ad Dominum,

R. Ut cito anticipent nos misericordiae Dornini, et parcat populo suo; ut omnes cum ipso gaudere possimus in saecula saeculorum. Amen.

Oremus.

Omnipotens et misericors Deus, fiat semper et in omnibus sanctissima voluntas tua secundum infinitam et aeternam misericordiam tuam. Per Christum Dominum nostrum. Amen.

TRANSLATION. *

Look down, O Lord, from Thy sanctuary, and from Heaven Thy dwelling-place on high, and behold this sacred Victim which our great High-Priest, Thy holy Child, our Lord Jesus, offers up to Thee for the sins of This brethren; and be appeased for the multitude of our transgressions. Behold the voice of the Blood of Jesus, our Brother, cries to Thee from the Cross. Give ear, O Lord! be appeased, O Lord! hearken, and do not tarry for Thine own sake, O my God, for Thy Name is invoked upon this city and upon Thy people; and deal with us according to Thy mercy. Amen.

V. That Thou wouldst vouchsafe to bring us to true penance,
R. We beseech Thee, hear us.
V. That Thou wouldst vouchsafe to defend this house and city, and all Thy people, to keep them in peace, to guard, preserve, and look down on them with Thy most tender pity,
R. We beseech Thee, hear us.
V. Through the holy Mysteries of the redemption of man.
R. Let Thy mercies come quickly to aid us, O Lord, and spare Thy people.
V. Through the merit and intercession of Thy most blessed Mother, and all the angels and saints.
R. Let Thy mercies come quickly to aid us, O Lord, and spare Thy people.
V. Holy Mary, conceived without original sin, and all ye Angels and Saints, intercede for us to our Lord.
R. That the mercies of our Lord may come quickly to aid us, and that He may spare His people; that so we all may rejoice with Him for ever and ever. Amen.

Let us pray.

Almighty and merciful God, may Thy most holy will be done, at all times and in all things, according to Thine infinite and eternal mercy. Through Christ our Lord. Amen.

* See also above, the same prayer with Notice of the Indulgence annexed to it.

DEVOUT INTENTION AND OFFERING.

Eternal Father, in union with all the heavenly host, and with the Hearts of Jesus and of Mary, I desire that from all eternity, and for eternity, the most Precious Blood of Jesus Christ, his infinite merits, and the merits of His Church be offered to Thee, in discharge of our debt of sin, of the sin of the whole world, for the deliverance of the holy souls in purgatory, and in thanksgiving, first, that Thou hast granted to us, and to all who are at present in this world, and wilt grant to all who shall hereafter be born, such gifts, graces, and mercies as redound to Thine own greater glory and the greater sanctification of all souls in these present tribulations, justly deserved as Thy chastisements; and, secondly, that Thou hast formed of the whole world one Fold and one Shepherd, that all who on earth live in the faith, hope, and charity of our Lord Jesus Christ may meet together in heaven, to sing Thy divine mercies for ever and ever. Amen.

156. ANOTHER PRAYER IN ANY PLAGUE OR TROUBLE.

In order that the faithful may with the greater fervour address their humble supplications to God, and by the invocation of His holy Name may mercifully be delivered from the scourge of His divine wrath, as well as from every other trouble, our holy Father Pope Pius IX., by a decree of Nov. 8, 1849, dated from Portici in the kingdom of Naples, granted -
The indulgence of 100 days every time the following prayer is said with contrite heart and devotion.

THE PRAYER.

Adjuva nos, Deus salutaris nostri, et propter gloriam nominis tui libera nos; et propitius esto peccatis nostris propter nomen tuum.

Ps. 53.

Deus, in nomine tuo salvum me fac: * et in virtute tua judica me
Deus, exaudi orationem meam: * auribus percipe verba oris mei.
Quoniam alieni insurrexerunt adversum me, et fortes quaesierunt animam meam: * et non proposuerunt Deum ante conspectum suum.
Ecce enim Deus adjuvat me: * et Dominus susceptor est animae meae.
Averte mala inimicis meis: * et in veritate tua disperde illos.
Voluntarie sacrificabo tibi: et confitebor nomini tuo, Domine, quoniam bonum est.
Quoniam ex omni tribulatione eripuisti me: * et super inimicos meos despexit oculus meus.
Gloria Patri, et Filio: * et Spiritui Sancto.
Sicut erat in principio, et nunc, et semper: * et in saecula saeculorum. Amen.

V. Propter gloriam nominis tui libera nos.
P. Et propitius esto peceatis nostris propter nomen tuum.

Oremus.
Preces populi tui, quaesumus, Domine, clementer exaudi: ut qui juste pro peecatis nostris affligimur, pro gloria nominis tui misericorditer liberemur. Per Christum Dominum nostrum. R. Amen.

To ergo quaesumus tuis famulis subveni, quos Pretioso Sanguine redemisti.

TRANSLATION.

Help us, O God of our salvation, and for the glory of Thy Name deliver us: be merciful to our sins for Thy Name's sake.

Ps. 53.

Save me, O Lord, in Thy Name; and judge me in Thy strength.
O God, hear my prayer; give ear to the words of my mouth
For strangers have risen up against me, and the mighty have sought after my soul, and they have not set God before their eyes.
For behold, God is my helper, and the Lord is the protector of my soul.
Turn away evil from me upon my enemies, and scatter them in Thy truth.
I will freely sacrifice to Thee; and will give praise, O God, to Thy Name, because it is good.
For Thou hast delivered me out of all my trouble, and mine eye hath looked down upon mine enemies.
Glory be to the Father, &c.

V. For the glory of Thy Name, deliver us.
R. And deal mercifully with our sins for Thy Name's sake.

Let us pray.
Lord, we beseech Thee, in Thy pity hear the prayers of Thy people; that we who suffer justly for our sins, may for the glory of Thy Name mercifully be delivered. Through Christ our Lord. R. Amen.

We beseech Thee, therefore, help Thy servants, whom Thou hast redeemed with Thy Precious Blood.

157. PRAYER TO OBTAIN A GRACE AND THE MERCY OF GOD IN EVERY NECESSITY, PLAGUE, AND TROUBLE.

The Sovereign Pontiff Pius IX., by a Rescript of his Reverence the Cardinal-Vicar of August 5, 1854, kept in the Archivium of the Venerable Congregation of Missionaries of the Most Precious Blood in Rome, granted to the faithful -

The indulgence of 100 days every time that, with contrite hearts and devotion, they say the following prayer so efficaciously worded by the Venerable Benedict Joseph Labrè.

THE PRAYER.

Jesus Christus, Rex gloriae, venit in pace.
Deus homo factus est.
Verbum caro factum est.
Christus de Maria Virgine natus est.
Christus per medium illorum ibat in pace.
Christus crucifixus est.
Christus mortuus est.
Christus sepultus est.
Christus resurrexit.
Christus ascendit in coelum.
Christus vincit.
Christus regnat.
Christus imperat.
Christus ab omni malo nos defendat.
Jesus nobiscum est.

Pater, Ave, *and* Gloria.

TRANSLATION.

Jesus Christ, the King of Glory, hath come in peace.
God was made man.
The Word was made flesh.
Christ was born of Mary the Virgin.
Christ went through the midst of them in peace.
Christ was crucified.
Christ died.
Christ was buried.
Christ rose from the dead.
Christ ascended into heaven.
Christ is victorious.
Christ reigns.
Christ is Lord of all.
May Christ defend us from all evil.
Jesus is with us.

Pater, Ave, *and* Gloria.

Eternal Father, by the Blood of Jesus have mercy; sign us with the Blood of the Immaculate Lamb Jesus Christ, as Thou didst sign the people of Israel, in order

to deliver them from death: and do thou, Mary, Mother of mercy, pray to God and appease him for us, and obtain for us the grace we ask.
Gloria Patri, &c.

Eternal Father, by the Blood of Jesus have mercy; save us from the shipwreck of the world, as Thou didst save Noe from the universal deluge: and do thou, Mary, Ark of salvation, pray to God and appease Him for us, and obtain for us the grace we ask.
Gloria Patri, &c.

Eternal Father, by the Blood of Jesus have mercy; deliver us from the plagues which we have deserved for our sins, as Thou didst deliver Lot from the flames of Sodom: and do thou, Mary, our Advocate, pray to God and appease Him for us, and obtain for us the grace we ask.
Gloria Patri, &c.

Eternal Father, by the Blood of Jesus have mercy; comfort us under our present necessities and troubles, as Thou didst comfort Job, Anna, and Tobias in their afflictions: and do thou, Mary, Comforter of the afflicted, pray to God and appease Him for us, and obtain for us the grace we ask.
Gloria Patri, &c.

Eternal Father, by the Blood of Jesus have mercy; Thou who wouldest not the death of a sinner, but rather that he should be converted and live, grant us through Thy mercy time for penance; that, filled with contrition and penance for our sins, which are the cause of all our evils, we may live in the holy faith, hope, charity, and peace of our Lord Jesus Christ: and do thou, Mary, Refuge of sinners, pray to God and appease Him for us, and obtain for us the grace we ask.
Gloria Patri, &c.

Precious Blood of Jesus, our Love, cry unto the Diviue Father for mercy, pardon, grace, and peace for , sfor N., and for all the world.
Gloria Patri, &c.

Mary, our Mother and our Hope, pray to God for us, for N., and for all, and obtain for us the grace we ask.
Gloria Patri, &c.

Eternal Father, I offer Thee the Blood of Jesus Christ in discharge of all my debt of sin, for the wants of Holy Church, and for the conversion of sinners.
Gloria Patri, &c.

Mary Immaculate, Mother of God, pray to Jesus for us, for N., and for all. Jesu, Mary, mercy!
St. Michael Archangel, St. Joseph, SS. Peter and Paul, protectors of all the

faithful in the Church of God, and all ye Angels and Saints of Paradise, men and women, pray to God, and by your intercession obtain grace and mercy for us, for N., and for all. Amen.

158. TO IMPLORE PEACE.

The same Sovereign Pontiff Pius IX., by a decree of the S. Congr. of Indulgences of May 18 and Sept. 18,1848, grants -
i. The indulgence of 100 days, to all the faithful, every time that with contrite hearts they say the following Antiphon and Prayer to implore peace from God.
ii. The plenary indulgence to those who shall have said it once a day for a whole month; to be gained on the day when, having Confessed and Communicated, they shall visit a public church, and pray there for a time according to the mind of his Holiness.

Ant. Da pacem, Domine, in diebus nostris: quia non est alius qui pugnet pro nobis, nisi tu Deus noster.

V. Fiat pax in virtute tua,
R. Et abundantia in turribus tuis.

Oremus.
Deus, a quo sancta desideria, recta consilia, et justa sunt opera: da servis tuis illam, quam mundus dare non potest, pacem: ut et corda nostra mandatis tuis dedita, et hostium sublata formidine, tempora sint tua protectione tranquilla. Per Christum Dominum nostrum. Amen.

TRANSLATION.

Ant. Give peace, O Lord, in our days; for there is none other to fight for us, but only Thou, our God.

V. Let peace be in Thy strength, O Lord,
R. And plenty in Thy strong places.

Let us pray.
O God, from whom proceed all holy desires, all right counsels and just works; grant unto us Thy servants that peace which the world cannot give, that our hearts may be devoted to Thy commands, and that, being delivered from the fear of our enemies, we may pass our time in peace under Thy protection. Through Christ our Lord. Amen.

159. SPIRITUAL CANTICLES.

At the prayer of the priests of the Union of St. Paul, and in order to hinder as far as possible he singing of corrupting profane songs, introduced by the profligacy of many at the present time, Pius VII., by a Rescript of Jan. 10, 1817, through the *Segretaria* of the Memorials, the original of which is kept in the *Segretaria* of the court of his Eminence the Cardinal- Vicar, granted -
i. An indulgence of one year, to all the faithful, every time they promote the singing of the spiritual Canticles, revised, approved, and collected together in the new Roman edition of 1817, published by Bourliè for the said Pious Union. Also -
ii. An indulgence of 100 days every time any one, with contrition of heart, practises this devotion.
iii. A plenary indulgence, once a month, to all who promote or frequent this exercise; to be gained in the course of the said month on any one day when, after Confession and Communion, they shall pray according to the intention of the Sovereign Pontiff.

BLESSED CROSSES, CRUCIFIXES, ROSARIES, MEDALS, ETC.

160. BLESSED CROSSES, CRUCIFIXES, ROSARIES, MEDALS, ETC.

However ancient may have been the custom of the Sovereign Pontiff to bless and distribute to the faithful sacred articles of gold, silver, or other metal (whence originated the Pontifical blessing and distribution of crosses, crucifixes, rosaries, medals, &c.), yet is it certain that, previous to the sixteenth century, no Indulgences were annexed to such articles. It was Pope Sixtus V. who, when, on the rebuilding of the Lateran Arch-Basilica, many medals of gold were found in various places by the falling of the walls of the former building on which were impressed the Holy Cross and other figures hearing the cross, caused a distribution to be made of them, and granted many Indulgences to those who had any one of these medals in their possession, provided they fulfilled certain works enjoined them: this we learn from the Constitution *Laudemus viros*, of Dec. 1, 1587. From that time the Popes, his successors, annexed the Indulgences to other objects besides medals blessed by Him - such as chaplets, rosaries, crosses, crucifixes, &c., - persuaded that the usage of these sacred objects excites in the minds of the faithful faith and acts of adoration towards God, and reverence for the Blessed Virgin, and the Saints. Having given this short historical sketch upon this matter, we will now transcribe

THE SUMMARY OF INDULGENCES

granted by his Holiness Pope Pius IX. to the faithful who shall do the pious works mentioned in this summary, and possess one of the chaplets, rosaries, crosses, crucifixes, statues, or medals blessed by his Holiness, or by some one who has faculties for the purpose. This grant is renewed by every fresh Sovereign Pontiff elect, being published in Latin and the vulgar tongue and it has been reformed and augmented by the above-named Sovereign Pontiff Pius IX. through the S. Congr. of Indulgences, May 14, 1853.
All the faithful of both sexes are instructed:- In the first place, that in order to gain the Indulgences with which his Holiness the Pope by his apostolic blessing enriches chaplets, rosaries, crosses, crucifixes, images, and medals, it is necessary to *wear* or to keep in their possessions some one of the aforesaid chaplets, &c.
And, in the second place, that they must say the devout prayers prescribed below as the conditions required in order to gain the Indulgences, *at that time that they are wearing* some one of the aforesaid chaplets, crucifixes, &c.; or, if not wearing them, they must keep them in their own room, or in some other fitting place in their abode, and recite their prayers before them.
Furthermore, his Holiness does not allow for this purpose *prints* or *pictures*, nor yet crosses, crucifixes, statues, and medals of tin, lead, or of any material that can be easily broken or destroyed. He does, however, allow them to be made of iron, although that material has been hitherto forbidden.
He also desires that the images of Saints engraved upon them should be of those who are already canonised, or of others mentioned in the Roman Martyrology.
All this is premised in order to make his Holiness's intention as clear as possible. The Indulgences which can be gained by those who possess one of the aforesaid objects when blessed, and the pious works to be performed, are as follows:
i. A plenary indulgence, on the undermentioned days, to all who shall say at

least once a week the Chaplet of our Lord, or of the Blessed Virgin Mary, or the Rosary, or a third part thereof, or the Divine Office, or the Office of the Blessed Virgin, and of the Dead, or the Seven Penitential or the Gradual Psalms; or whose custom it is to teach the Catechism, or visit prisoners, or the sick in a hospital, or help the poor, or hear Mass, or say Mass if they be priests, provided that they be truly penitent, and have Confessed to a confessor approved by the ordinary, and shall go to Communion on any of the following days, viz. Christmas Day, the Epiphany, Easter Day, Ascension Day, Pentecost, the Feast of the Most Holy Trinity, of Corpus Christi, the Purification, Annunciation, Assumption, and Nativity of the Blessed Virgin Mary, the Nativity of St. John Baptist, the Holy Apostles Peter and Paul, Andrew, James, John, Thomas, Philip and James, Bartholomew, Matthew, Simon and Jude, Matthias, St. Joseph the espoused husband of the Blessed Virgin, and All Saints; at the same time praying to God for the extirpation of heresies and schisms, for the propagation of the Catholic faith, for peace and concord amongst Christian princes, and for the other necessities of Holy Church.

ii. An indulgence of seven years and seven quarantines, on the other Feasts of our Lord and of the Blessed Virgin Mary, to all who shall perform the aforesaid good works on these feasts; and the indulgence of five years and five quarantines to those who shall do them on any Sunday or feast in the year; and lastly, an indulgence of 100 days to those who shall perform them on any other day in the year.

iii. An indulgence of 100 days to those who are accustomed to say at least once a week the Chaplet, or the Rosary, or the Office of the Blessed Virgin Mary, or of the Dead, or the Vespers, or at least one Nocturn of it, together with Lauds; or who shall say the Seven Penitential Psalms with the litanies and Prayers; to be gained on the day on which they shall say the same.

iv. A plenary indulgence to all who, at the point of death, shall devoutly recommend their souls to God; and who, according to the instruction of Benedict XIV. of happy memory, expressed in his Constitution of the 5th of April 1747, which begins *Pia Mater,* shall be ready to receive death with resignation from the hands of God; provided they be truly penitent and have gone to Confession and Communion, or, if unable to comply with this duty, shall at least have invoked with contrition the most Holy Name of Jesus with the heart, if not able to do so with the lips.

v. An indulgence of fifty days to those who shall use any kind of prayer as a preparation before saying Mass, or before the Holy Communion, or before saying the Divine Office, or the Office of the Blessed Virgin.

vi. An indulgence of 200 days to the faithful every time they shall visit prisoners, or the sick in hospitals, assisting them by some pious action, or shall teach the Catechism in church, or at home to their own children, relations, and servants.

vii. An indulgence of 100 days every time, to all who at the sound of the bell of some church in the morning, midday, or evening, shall say the usual prayers *Angelus Domini, &*c. or not knowing them, one *Pater noster* and one *Ave Maria:* or who, in like manner, when the signal-bell for the dead is rung at one hour after nightfall, shall say the Psalm *De profundis, &*c.; or, not knowing it, one *Pater noster* and one *Ave Maria.*

viii. An indulgence of 100 days to those who, on Friday, shall devoutly meditate on the Passion and Death of our Lord Jesus Christ, and say three *Pater noster's* and three *Ave Maria's.*

ix. An indulgence of 100 days to all those who, being truly sorry for their sins, shall, with a firm purpose of amendment, examine their conscience and say with devotion three times the *Pater noster* and *Ave Maria* in honour of the Most Holy Trinity, or the *Pater noster* and *Ave Maria* five times in memory of the Five Wounds of Jesus Christ.

x. An indulgence of fifty days to those who shall pray devoutly for the faithful who are near their departure out of this life, or at least shall say for them one *Pater noster* and one *Ave Maria.*

All and each of the Indulgences above named, his Holiness permits every one to gain for himself, or to apply by way of suffrage to the souls in purgatory.

His Holiness further declares, that by the grant of the aforesaid Indulgences he in no way intends to derogate from the Indulgences already granted by different Popes, his predecessors, in favour of certain pious works named above; but desires that they should all remain in their full force.

His Holiness also commands that in the distribution and use of the chaplets, rosaries, &c. blessed as above, the decree of Pope Alexander VII., of holy memory, issued the 6th of February 1657, shall be observed, viz. that the Indulgences annexed to the said objects shall not go beyond the person of him to whom these blessed objects shall be confided, or at least of those to whom who shall distribute them for the first time; and that when one of them is lost, another shall not be substituted for it at pleasure, all grants or privileges to the contrary notwithstanding; and that they shall not be lent or given to others for a time for the purpose of communicating the Indulgences, in which case they would lose the Indulgences: as also that the said objects, when they have received the papal blessing, shall not be sold, according to the decree of the S. Congr. of Indulgences and Holy Relics published the 5th of June 1721.

His Holiness also confirms the decree of Benedict XIV. of holy memory, issued the 19th of August 1752, by which he expressly declares that Mass said at an altar where such crucifixes, medals, &c. may be placed, or which is celebrated by a priest who wears them, does not become privileged in virtue of crucifixes, medals, &c. blessed as above.

Moreover it is forbidden to all persons who assist the dying to give them the blessing, with the Plenary Indulgence *in articulo mortis,* by means of these crucifixes or medals, without a special faculty obtained in writing, as the said Sovereign Pontiff Benedict XIV. had already sufficiently provided for that blessing in his Constitution *Pia Mater* already quoted.

Finally, his Holiness desires and enjoins that this present list of Indulgences, now revised and corrected for the greater convenience of the faithful, be printed in Latin and Italian, and in any other language, provided that each such version have the approbation of the Holy See, or of the S. Congr. of Indulgences; but it is not to be printed out of Rome in any language *before* this approbation has been obtained; all other decrees, constitutions, or impositions to the contrary, however minutely specified, notwithstanding.

161. CROSSES, CHAPLETS, AND ROSARIES OF THE HOLY LAND.

All the Indulgences mentioned in the aforesaid summary may be obtained by any of the faithful who possess any of the crosses, chaplets, or rosaries which have touched the Holy Places and Sacred Relics of the Holy Land, by the concession of the Venerable Pope Innocent XI., as appears by his brief *Unigeniti Dei Filii,* of January 28th, 1688, confirmed by Pope Innocent XIII., in a decree of the S. Congr. of Indulgences of June 5, 1721, prohibiting the selling of these crosses, &c. after they have touched these Sacred Relics, or the exchange of them for other wares, or the lending of them for the purpose of communicating the Indulgences to others. See also decrees of the same Sacred Congregation, March 11, 1721, and Feb. 11, 1722.

APPENDIX OF INDULGENCES FOR RELIGIOUS PERSONS OF BOTH SEXES.

Religious of both sexes of every order and institute may, on fulfilling the works enjoined, gain the above Indulgences, since all, a very few excepted, are granted to persons in every state of life.

Moreover Pope Paul V., by his universal Brief, May 23, 1606, commencing *Romanus Pontifex*, after revoking (with the exception of the Indulgences annexed to churches, as the S. Congr. of Indulgences declared,

Sept. 7, 1607, and the S. Congr. of Bishops and Regulars, Aug. 21, 1615) all and every Indulgence previously granted to the regular orders of both sexes being religious of any denomination whatsoever, and having taken the three solemn vows, according to the declaration of the S. Congr. of Indulgences of May 8, 1713, and April 23, 1714, - granted anew for ever the following Indulgences to the religious of every order, whether monastic or mendicant, and to the nuns of every approved rule living under the three solemn vows in perpetual cloister, viz.:

i. A plenary indulgence to all the faithful of both sexes who, in accordance with the Apostolical Constitutions, wear the religious habit for the purpose of professing that Regular Institute which they have chosen; to be gained on the first day of their entrance into religion, or on the day of their clothing, on condition of their being truly penitent for their sins, and having gone to Confession, and Communion.

ii. A plenary indulgence to every novice, male and female, on the day of their making their religious profession, after having finished the year of their clothing, on condition of their being truly penitent, and having gone to Confession and Communion.

(With regard to nuns, Pope Benedict XIII., by a Brief, universal and perpetual, *In supremo,* of April 11, 1728, granted the plenary indulgence afresh, on the same conditions as above, on the day of their veiling, benediction, or consecration, as in the case of their religious profession.)

iii. The plenary indulgence to every religious of both sexes, as above, who, having Confessed, shall go to Communion on the principal Feast of his or her order; or who, being a priest, shall celebrate the Holy Mass and pray to God for the Holy Church, &c.

iv. A plenary indulgence *in articulo mortis*, to all religious of both sexes, as above, who, being penitent, have gone to Confession and Communion; or who, being unable to do so, shall be at least contrite for their sins, and invoke devoutly with their lips or heart the most holy Name of Jesus.

v. A plenary indulgence to every religious man on the day that, after having been canonically promoted to the priesthood, he shall, after Confession, celebrate for the first time Holy Mass; and also the plenary indulgence to his fellow- religious who shall be present at his first Mass, provided that they have Confessed and Communicated on that day, or who, being priests, have celebrated Holy Mass.

vi. A plenary indulgence and remission of all sins to all religious of both sexes, as often as they shall, with the leave of their respective superiors, make for ten days the spiritual exercises, applying themselves during that time to meditation on the four last things, on the Passion of our Lord Jesus Christ, on the blessings of God, &c., and passing at least two hours each day in mental prayer, and exercising themselves in other practices of virtue, mortification, vocal prayer, or ejaculatory prayer, or the like; and provided also that, having made either a general, or annual, or ordinary Confession, they shall go to Communion, or, if priests, celebrate Holy Mass.

vii. The indulgences of the Stations to all religious of both sexes, as above, who, on the days of the Stations described in the Roman Missal, shall visit devoutly their own church, and pray there as if they were making the visit personally to the churches of the Stations in Rome on the days prescribed.

viii. An indulgence of five years and five quarantines to all religious of both sexes, an above, who shall say five *Pater noster's* and five *Ave Maria's* before the altar of their church. The same Indulgence to those religious who, being for a legitimate reason away from home on a journey, or dwelling out side the walls of their monastery in the capacity of lecturers, preachers, &c., with leave of their superiors, shall say the said five *Pater noster's* and *Ave Maria's* before any altar whatever.

ix. An indulgence of sixty years and sixty quarantines on the last Sunday in the month, after Confession and Communion, or, if priests, after having celebrated holy Mass, to all religious of both sexes, as above, who for an entire month shall make daily half an hour's mental prayer.

x. A indulgence of three years and three quarantines to all religious of both sexes, as above, who, being contrite in heart and penitent, shall at Chapter, or whenever they shall hold spiritual conference together, say *Meâ culpâ*, accusing themselves of their sins, defects, and imperfections.

xi. A plenary indulgence to every religious each time that, in obedience to the Sovereign Pontiff and with leave of superiors, he goes into the countries of the infidels or heretics to preach the faith of Jesus Christ and instruct them, &c., after Confession and Communion, or, if a priest, after having celebrated Holy Mass, as well on setting out for his journey, as on entering the aforesaid provinces or kingdoms.

xii. Finally, plenary indulgence to all religious of both sexes, when, on a General Visitation, the Superior sets up the Quarant' Ore in the convents and monasteries of his order for the happy event of the same, as often as they make two hours' prayer at intervals before the Blessed Sacrament for peace amongst Christian princes, &c., for the better observance of rule and regular discipline; to be gained after Confession and Communion, or, in the case of priests, celebration of Holy Mass.

These are the Indulgences which regard all the aforesaid religious of both sexes in general; and according to the tenor of the said Brief of Paul V., they are also conceded generally to other congregations and colleges of religious men, as well as to monasteries, congregations, and communities of nuns who live without cloister, and with simple vows alone. In particular, however, every regular order, every convent, monastery, college, and congregation if religious persons of both sexes, enjoy many other Plenary and Partial Indulgences, of which we do not here undertake to make mention, inasmuch as our object ins this *Raccolta* is to restrict ourselves to the mention of those prayers and pious works enriched with holy Indulgences, which are for the most part universal, and common to every condition of person.

DECRETUM

Romani Pontifices, quibus praecipua demandata est cura de Christi gregis aeterna procuranda salute, apertis Ecclesiae thesauris, pene innumeris Indulgentias concesserunt ad spiritualem Christianorum utilitatem, cum *"Indulgentiarum usum Christiano populo maxime salutarem esse,"* Sacra Tridentina Synodus doceat. (Sess. xxv. *in Decret. in Indulg.*) Accidit tamen, et persaepe evenire solet, ut a fidelibus praefatae Indulgentiae non acquirantur ex eo quod vel earum concessiones, aut injunctae conditiones adinrplendae omnino ignorantur, vel ex eo quod in nonnullis praesertim opusculis, aut impressis foliis, quae per orbem absque hujus Sacrae Congregationis approbatione circumferuntur, ne quid de illis Indulgentiis dicatur, quae apocryphae quoque sunt et falsae, nec singulae nec integrae conditiones declarentur. Quamobrem opportunum et necessarium jamdudum S. eidem Congregationi videbatur, ut preces ac pia opera illa praecipue quibus ex generalibus Summorum Pontificum elargitionibus Indulgentiae sunt annexae ex suis germanis fontibus fideliter hausta et simul collecta, atque ordine digesta in vulgus ederentur. Quod quidem ad annum usque millesimum octogesimum quadragesimum quartum perfecit clar. me. Canonicus Telesphorus Galli hujus S. Congregationis consultor. Ne autem posteriores Indulgentiarum concessiones tum a felic. rec. Gregorio Papa XVI. a Pio IX. Pontifice Optimo Maximo, peractae in praefata collectione deessent, ipsas Aloisius Prinzivalli Archipresbyter insignia Basilicae S. Mariae in Cosmedin de urbe, Secretariae ejusdem Sacrae Congregationis substitutus, in decima secunda editione collectas, in hac urbe evulgavit, atque iterum ab eo ex Typographia Salvioniana novis generalibus quo concessionibus locupletata in lucem emmittitur.

Itaque Sacra haec Congregatio Indulgentiis Sacrisque Reliquiis praeposita non solum praedictum opus omnibus Christi fidelibus vivis atque defunctis maxime peutile fore probavit et ut authenticum recognovit, verum etiam monuit, ut si in quacunque ejusdem operis editione seu versione cujuscunque idiomatis tam intra quam extra urbem jam exarata, vol in posterum exaranda, dubium aliquod subinde emerserit, sive quoad Indulgentiarum concessiones, sive quoad praescriptas conditiones adimplendas ad praesentem decimam tertiam Romanam editionem in Actis ipsius S. Congregationis relatam recursus habeatur; ac propterea ut hoc Decretum omnibus omnino pateat, typis similter tum Latino tum Italico idiomate impres sum, ad calcem praefatae Editionis apponi mandavit.

Datum Romam ex Segretaria ejusdem S. Congregationis Indulgentiarum, die 15 Decembris 1854.

F. CARD. ASQUINIUS, *Praefectus.* Loco + signi.

Aloisius Colombo, *Segretarius.*

TRANSLATION

The Sovereign Pontiffs of Rome, to whom especially has been committed the care of advancing the eternal salvation of the flock of Christ, have granted an almost countless number of Indulgences for the spiritual benefit of Christians, the holy Council of Trent teaching that "the use of Indulgences is most wholesome to Christian people." (Sess. xxv. in *the Decree of Indulgences.*) Cases, however, occur, and that not unfrequently, when the said Indulgences are not gained by the faithful, either because the grants of the Indulgences, or the conditions enjoined to be fulfilled, are altogether unknown, or because, in certain little tracts or printed pipers hawked about without the approbation of the Holy Congregation (not to speak of those Indulgences which are apocryphal and false), the conditions are not singly and integrally specified. For this reason it has long seemed to the said Sacred Congregation fitting and necessary that the prayers and good works, and especially those to which, from the *general* grant of Sovereign Pontiffs, Indulgences have been annexed, should be faithfully extracted from their genuine sources, collected together, and published in order under their proper headings. Accordingly those Indulgences, up to the year 1844, were collected and published by Canon Telesphorus Galli, Consultor of this Holy Congregation. In order, however, that the later grants of Indulgences, made both by Pope Gregory XVI. of happy memory, and by our present Sovereign Pontiff Pius IX., might not be omitted from the said collection, Aloysius Prinzivalli, Archpresbyter of the illustrious basilica of St. Mary in Cosmedin, in this holy city, Sub-Secretary of the Office of the said Holy Congregation, has published them together with the rest in this thirteenth edition, this being now the second time that this collection has been published by him from the Salvionian Press, enriched with the new general grants.

Wherefore this Holy Congregation presiding over Indulgences and Sacred Relics hath not only approved of this work of his, as most useful to the living and dead, and recognised it as authentic, but has also issued an admonition that in future, if in any edition of this work, or version in any language, any doubt hereafter arise, either as regards the grants of Indulgences themselves or the conditions prescribed, recourse is to he had to this thirteenth Roman edition, referred to in the Acts of the said Holy Congregation; and accordingly, that all men may everywhere have access to this Decree, the said Holy Congregation hath commanded it to be printed in Latin and the vulgar tongue, and annexed to the end of the said thirteenth edition.

Given at Rome, from the Secretary's Office of the said Holy Congregation of Indulgences, this 15th of December 1854.

F. CARD. ASQUINIUS, *Prefect.* In the place + of the seal.

Aloysius Colombo, *Secretary.*

www.ingramcontent.com/pod-product-compliance
Lightning Source LLC
Chambersburg PA
CBHW020342180626
46812CB00001B/310